# MORE
# FILTHY
# DIRTY
# JOKES

# Contents

# MORE FILTHY DIRTY JOKES

*Edited by Platinum Press, LLC*

POCKET BOOKS
New York   London   Toronto   Sydney

Pocket Books
A Division of Simon & Schuster, Inc.
1230 Avenue of the Americas
New York, NY 10020

Copyright © 2007 by Platinum Press LLC
Originally published by Platinum Press LLC.

First Pocket Books paperback edition October 2008

POCKET and colophon are registered trademarks of Simon & Schuster, Inc.

For information about special discounts for bulk purchases, please contact Simon & Schuster Special Sales at 1-800-456-6798 or business@simonandschuster.com.

Cover design by Mary Ann Smith.

Manufactured in the United States of America

10  9  8  7  6  5  4  3  2  1

ISBN-13: 978-1-4165-9000-2
ISBN-10:    1-4165-9000-5

# MORE
# FILTHY
# DIRTY
# JOKES

# Business

Last week, we took some friends out to a new restaurant, and noticed that the waiter who took our order carried a spoon in his shirt pocket.

It seemed a little strange. When the busboy brought our water and utensils, I noticed he also had a spoon in his shirt pocket.

Then I looked around and saw that all the staff had a spoon in their pockets. When the waiter came back to serve our soup, I asked, "Why the spoon?"

"Well," he explained, "the restaurant's owners hired a management consultant to revamp all our processes. After several months of analysis, they concluded that the spoon was the most frequently dropped utensil. It represents a drop frequency of approximately three spoons per table per hour. If our personnel are better prepared, we can reduce the number of trips back to the kitchen and save fifteen man-hours per shift."

As luck would have it, I dropped my spoon and the waiter was able to replace it with his spare. "I'll get another spoon next time I go to the kitchen instead of making an extra trip to get it right now."

I was impressed. I also noticed that there was a string hanging out of the waiter's fly. Looking around, I noticed that all the waiters had the same string hanging from their flies. So before he walked off, I asked the waiter, "Excuse me, but can you tell me why you have that string right there?"

"Oh, certainly!" Then he lowered his voice. "Not everyone is so observant. That consulting firm I mentioned also found out that we can save time in the restroom. By tying this string to the tip of you-know-what, we can pull it out without touching it and eliminate the need to wash our hands, shortening the time spent in the restroom by 76.39 percent."

I asked, "After you get it out, how do you put it back?"

"Well," he whispered, "I don't know about the others, but I use the spoon."

•

A fellow checked into a hotel on a business trip recently and was a bit lonely, so he thought he'd get one of those girls you see advertised in the phone books under "Escorts and Massages."

He opened the phone book to an ad for a lovely girl calling herself Erotique, bending over in the photo. She had all the right curves in all the right places, beautiful long wavy hair, long graceful legs all the way up. So he was in his room and figured, what the hell, and gave her a call.

"Hello?" the woman said. God, she sounded sexy!

"Hi, I hear you give a great massage and I'd like you to come to my room and give me one. No, wait, I should be straight with you. I'm in town all alone and what I really want is sex. I want it hard, I want it hot, and I want it now. I'm talking kinky the whole night long. You name it, we'll do it. Bring implements, toys, everything you've got in your bag of tricks. We'll go hot and heavy all night; tie me up, cover me in chocolate syrup and whipped cream, anything you want, baby. Now, how does that sound?"

She said, "That sounds fantastic . . . but for an outside line you need to press 9."

•

A hooker was visiting her doctor for a regular checkup.

"Any specific problems you should tell me about?" the doctor asked.

"Well, I have noticed lately that if I get even the tiniest cut, it seems to bleed for hours," she replied. "Do you think I might be a hemophiliac?"

"Well," the doctor answered, "hemophilia is a genetic disorder and it is more often found in men, but it is possible for a woman to be a hemophiliac. Tell me, how much do you lose when you have your period?"

After calculating for a moment, the hooker replied, "Oh, about seven or eight hundred dollars, I guess."

•

A woman walks into her accountant's office and tells him that she needs to file her taxes. The accountant says, "Before we begin, I'll need to ask you a few questions." He gets her name, address, Social Security number, etc., and then asks, "What is your occupation?"

"I'm a whore," she says.

The accountant balks and says, "No, no, no, that won't work; too gross. Let's try to rephrase that."

The woman says, "Okay, I'm a high-end call girl."

"Sorry, that is still too crude. Try again."

They both think for a minute, then the woman says, "How about 'elite chicken farmer'?"

Stunned, the accountant asks, "What does chicken farming have to do with being a high-end call girl?"

"Well, I raised over a thousand little peckers last year."

•

A dedicated shop steward was at a convention in Las Vegas and decided to check out the local brothels. When he got to the first one, he asked the madam, "Is this a union house?"

"No, I'm sorry, it isn't."

"Well, if I pay you a hundred dollars, what cut do the girls get?"

"The house gets eighty dollars and the girls get twenty dollars."

Mighty offended at such unfair dealings, the man stomped off down the street in search of a more equitable shop. His search continued, until finally he reached a brothel where the madam said, "Why yes, this is a union house."

"And if I pay you a hundred dollars, what cut do the girls get?"

"The girls get eighty dollars and the house gets twenty dollars."

"That's more like it!" the man said. He looked around the room and pointed to a stunningly attractive redhead. "I'd like her for the night."

"I'm sure you would, sir," said the madam, gesturing to a fat fifty-year-old woman in the corner, "but Ethel here has seniority."

•

A little old lady answered a knock on the door one day, only to be confronted by a well-dressed young man carrying a vacuum cleaner.

"Good morning," said the young man. "If I could take a couple minutes of your time, I would like to demonstrate the very latest in high-powered vacuum cleaners."

"Go away!" said the old lady. "I haven't got any money." She tried to close the door. Quick as a flash, the young man wedged his foot in the door and pushed it wide open.

"Don't be too hasty!" he said. "Not until you have at least seen my demonstration." And with that, he emptied a bucket of horse shit all over her hallway carpet. "If this vacuum cleaner does not remove all traces of this horse shit from your carpet, Madam, I will personally eat the remainder."

"Well," she said, "I hope you've got a good appetite, because the electricity was cut off this morning."

•

A guy walks into a bank and says to the teller at the window, "I want to open a f***in' checking account."

To which the lady replied, "I beg your pardon, what did you say?"

"Listen up, dammit, I said I want to open a f***in' checking account right now."

"Sir, I'm sorry, but we do not tolerate that kind of language in this bank!"

The teller left the window and went over to the bank manager and told him about her situation. They both returned and the manager asked, "What seems to be the problem here?"

"There's no damn problem," the man said. "I just won $50 million in the lottery and I want to open a f***in' checking account in this damn bank!"

"I see, sir," the manager said, "and this bitch is giving you a hard time?"

•

There is a factory in East Texas that makes the Tickle Me Elmo toys. The toy laughs when you squeeze it.

Loretta is hired at the Tickle Me Elmo factory, and she reports for her first day promptly at 8 A.M.

The next day at 8:45 A.M., there is a knock at the personnel manager's door. The foreman throws open the door and begins to rant about Loretta. He complains that she is incredibly slow and the whole line is backing up, putting the entire production line behind schedule.

The personnel manager decides he should see this for himself, so the two men march down to the factory floor.

When they get there, the line is so backed up that there are Tickle Me Elmos all over the factory floor and they're really beginning to pile up. At the end of the line stands Loretta, surrounded by mountains of Tickle Me Elmos.

She has a roll of plush red fabric and a huge bag of small marbles. The two men watch in amazement as she cuts a little piece of fabric, wraps it around two marbles, and begins to carefully sew the little package between Elmo's legs.

The personnel manager bursts out laughing. After several minutes of hysterics, he pulls himself together and approaches Loretta. "I'm sorry," he says to her, barely able to keep a straight face, "but I think you misunderstood the instructions I gave you yesterday. Your job is to give Elmo two *test tickles.*"

•

*What happens when I'm at work and I have to poop?*

We've all been there, but don't like to admit it. We've all kicked back in our cubicles and suddenly felt something abrew down below. As much as we try to convince ourselves, the work poop is inevitable.

For those of you who hate pooping at work as much as we do, we give you

THE SURVIVAL GUIDE FOR TAKING A DUMP AT WORK

Memorize these definitions and pooping at work will become a pure pleasure:

*ESCAPEE:* A fart that slips out while taking a leak at the urinal or forcing poop in a stall. This is usually accompanied by a sudden wave of panic/embarrassment. This is similar to the hot flash you receive when passing a police car while speeding. If you release an escapee, do not acknowledge it. Pretend it did not happen. If you are standing next to the farter at the urinal, pretend that you did not hear it. No one likes an escapee, it is uncomfortable for all involved. Making a joke or laughing makes both parties feel uneasy.

*JAILBREAK* (used in conjunction with ESCAPEE): When forcing a poop, several farts slip out at a machine gun's pace. This is usually a side effect of diarrhea or a hangover. If this should happen, do not panic; remain in the stall until everyone has left the bathroom so as to spare everyone the awkwardness of what just occurred.

*COURTESY FLUSH:* The act of flushing the toilet the instant the nose cone of the poop log hits the water and the poop is whisked away to an undisclosed location. This reduces the amount of air time the poop has to stink up the bathroom. This can help you avoid being caught doing the WALK OF SHAME.

*WALK OF SHAME:* Walking from the stall to the sink or the door after you have just stunk up the shitter. This can be a very uncomfortable moment if someone walks in and busts you. As with all farts, it is best to pretend that the smell does not exist. Can be avoided with the use of a courtesy flush.

*OUT OF THE CLOSET POOPER:* A colleague who poops at work and is damn proud of it. You will often see an Out of the Closet Pooper enter the bathroom with a newspaper or magazine under their arm. Always look around the office for the Out of the Closet Pooper before entering the bathroom.

*THE POOPING FRIENDS NETWORK (PFN):* This is a group of coworkers who band together to ensure emergency pooping goes off without incident. This group can help you to monitor the whereabouts of Out of the Closet Poopers and identify SAFE HAVENS.

*SAFE HAVEN:* A seldom-used bathroom somewhere in the building where you can least expect visitors. Try floors that are predominantly of the opposite sex. This will reduce the odds of a pooper of your sex entering the bathroom.

*TURD BURGLAR:* A pooper who does not realize that you're in the stall and tries to force the door open. This is one of the most shocking and vulnerable moments that occur when taking a dump at work. If this occurs, remain in the stall until the Turd Burglar leaves. This way you will avoid all uncomfortable eye contact. Turd Burglars have been known to cause premature pinchage, which inevitably means you pinch one off in the middle.

*CAMO-COUGH:* A phony cough that alerts all new entrants into the bathroom that you are in a stall. This can be used to cover up a WATERMELON or to alert potential Turd Burglars. Very effective when used in conjunction with an ASTAIRE.

*ASTAIRE:* This is a subtle toe-tap that is used to alert all potential Turd Burglars that you are occupying a stall. This will remove all doubt that the stall is occupied. If you hear an Astaire, leave the bathroom immediately, so the pooper can poop in peace.

*WATERMELON:* A turd that creates a loud splash when hitting the toilet water. This is also an embarrassing incident. If you feel a Watermelon coming on, create a diversion. See CAMO-COUGH.

*HAVANA OMELET:* A load of diarrhea that creates a series of loud splashes in the toilet water. Often accompanied by an Escapee. Try using a Camo-Cough with an Astaire.

*UNCLE TED:* A bathroom user who seems to linger around forever. Could spend extended lengths of time in front of the mirror or sitting on the pot. An Uncle Ted makes it difficult to relax while on the crapper, as you should always wait until the bathroom is empty to drop your load. This benefits you as well as the other bathroom attendees.

*FLYBY:* The act of scouting out a bathroom before pooping. Walk in, check for other poopers. If there are others in the bathroom, leave and come back later. Be careful not to become a FREQUENT FLYER. People may become suspicious if they catch you constantly going into the bathroom.

•

Two car salesmen were sitting at the bar. One complained to the other, "Boy, business sucks. If I don't sell more cars this month, I'm going to lose my ass."

Then he noticed a beautiful blonde sitting two stools away. Immediately, he apologized for his bad language.

"That's okay," she said. "If I don't sell more ass this month, I'm going to lose my car."

•

Dave walks into a house of ill repute in Nevada and says, "I'll give twenty thousand dollars to any woman here who'll come into the desert with me and f*** my way."

One of the ladies agrees, and off they go driving into the desert. After about an hour of hot sex, she gets curious and asks him, "Just what is your way?"

"On credit."

•

A bill collector came knocking at the door of a woman who had fallen behind on her bills. "All right, lady," said the bill collector. "How about the next installment on that couch?"

The lady shrugged. "I guess that's better than having to give you money."

•

The boss came in early one morning and found his manager kissing and fondling his secretary. He shouted at him, "Is this what I pay you for?"

The manager replied, "No, sir, this I do free of charge."

•

Goldstein, in his late eighties and still gainfully employed as a ribbon salesman, had been trying unsuccessfully for many years to sell ribbon to Macy's.

Last week, he was making another attempt and was speaking to the hard-nosed son-of a-bitch buyer.

"Goldstein," the buyer said, "you've been trying to sell ribbon to me for at least twenty-five years. Now is your chance. Send me some yellow ribbon, enough to reach from the tip of your nose to the tip of your penis."

Three days later, four tractor trailers full of yellow ribbon drove up to the receiving dock at Macy's. The ribbon buyer went ballistic. He called Goldstein and said, "I ordered yellow ribbon, enough to reach from the tip of your nose to the tip of your penis, and you send four tractor trailers full of ribbon."

Goldstein replied, "Yes, but the tip of my penis is in Poland."

•

Upon arriving home, a husband was met at the door by his sobbing wife. Tearfully she explained, "It's the pharmacist. He insulted me terribly this morning on the phone."

The husband immediately drove downtown to confront the druggist and demand an apology.

Before he could say more than a word or two, the druggist told him, "Now, just a minute, listen to my side of the story . . .

"This morning my alarm failed to go off, so I was late getting up. I went without breakfast and hurried out to the car, only to realize that I locked the house with both house and car keys inside.

"I had to break a window to get my keys. Then, driving a little too fast, I got a speeding ticket. When I was about three blocks from the store, I got a flat tire. When I finally got here, there was a bunch of people waiting for me to open up. I got the store open and started waiting on these people and, all the time, the damn phone was ringing off the hook.

"Then I had to break a roll of nickels against the cash register drawer to make change, and they spilled all over the floor. I got down on my hands and knees to pick up the nickels. The phone was still ringing. When I came up, I cracked my head on the open cash drawer which made me stagger back against a showcase with a bunch of perfume bottles on it . . . all of them hit the floor and broke.

"Meanwhile, the phone is still ringing with no letup, and I finally got to answer it. It was your wife. She wanted to know how to use a rectal thermometer. And believe me, mister, as God is my witness, all I did was tell her."

•

The Perfect CALLING IN SICK

Employee: "I'm sorry but I can't come in today . . . my doctor says I suffer from Anal Glaucoma."

Boss: "Anal Glaucoma? What's that?"

Employee: "I just can't see my ass coming to work!"

•

Seeking a loan from a bank, an inventor told his banker that he'd discovered a remarkable substance that, brushed lightly over a lady's pussy, would give it an orange flavor.

"No good," the banker responded, after some thought. "But if you can invent something to put into an orange that will make it taste like pussy, you can have your loan and we'll both be rich!"

•

An old lady was in the carpet store. Bending over, she touched a swatch of carpet and farted. When she got up, she noticed a salesman standing behind her.

She then asked the salesman, "How much is this carpet?"

The salesman replied, "Well, lady . . . if you farted just touching it, you're gonna crap when you hear the price."

# Medical

"Doctor, Doctor, please kiss me," says the patient.

"No, I'm sorry, that would be against the code of ethics," says the doctor.

Ten minutes later, the patient says: "Doctor, please, kiss me just once."

"No, I'm sorry, I just can't," he says.

Five minutes later, she asks again: "Please, please kiss me!"

"Look," says the doctor, "it's out of the question. In fact, I probably shouldn't even be f***ing you."

•

A woman fell for her handsome new dentist like a ton of bricks and pretty soon talked him into a series of passionate rendezvous in the dental clinic after hours.

But one day he said sadly, "Honey, we have to stop seeing each other. Your husband's bound to get suspicious."

"No way, sweetie, he's dumb as a post," she assured him. "Besides, we've been meeting here for six months now and he doesn't suspect a thing."

"True," agreed the dentist, "but you're down to one tooth!"

•

Charlie's wife, Lucy, had been after him for several weeks to paint the seat on their commode. He finally got around to doing it while Lucy was out. He left to take care of another matter before she returned. She came in and undressed to take a shower. Before getting in the shower, she sat on the commode. As she tried to stand up, she realized that the not-quite-dry epoxy paint had glued her to the commode seat. About that time, Charlie got home and realized her predicament.

They both pushed and pulled without any success whatsoever. Finally, in desperation, Charlie undid the commode seat bolts. Lucy wrapped a sheet around herself and Charlie drove her to the hospital emergency room. The ER doctor got her into a position where he could study how to free her. Lucy tried to lighten the embarrassment of it all by saying, "Well, Doctor, I'll bet you've never seen anything like this before."

The doctor replied "Actually, I've seen a lot of them. I just never saw one *framed* before."

•

A guy goes to his eye doctor for an examination. They start talking as the doctor is examining him. In the middle of their conversation, the doctor casually says, "You need to stop masturbating."

The guy replies, "Why, Doc? Am I going blind?"

The doctor says, "No, but you're upsetting the other patients in the waiting room."

•

A guy walks into a psychiatrist's office covered only in Saran Wrap. He says to the doctor, "I've felt so weird lately, Doc, can you tell me what's wrong?"

The doctor replied, "Well, I can clearly see your nuts!"

•

This guy goes to a doctor and says he has a problem with sex. "Doc, I think my dick is just too damn small."

The doctor asks him which drink he prefers. "Well, American beer," the guy replies, quite bemused.

"Aaaahhh. There's your problem. It shrinks things, those silly American beers . . . you should try drinking Guinness. That makes things grow."

Two months later, the man returns to the doctor with a big smile on his face. He shakes the doctor's hand and thanks him.

"I take it you now drink Guinness?" asked the doctor.

"Oh no, Doc," replies the man, "but I've got the wife on American beer!"

•

A woman went to her doctor for a follow-up visit after he had prescribed testosterone for her. She was a little worried about some of the side effects she was experiencing.

"Doctor, the hormones you've been giving me have really helped, but I'm afraid that you're giving me too much. I've started growing hair in places that I've never grown hair before."

The doctor reassured her, "A little hair growth is a perfectly normal side effect of testosterone. Just where has this hair appeared?"

"On my balls."

•

A man goes to the doctor, because every time he walks, he farts. He arrives at the doctor's office and *Parp! Fumph! Toot! Poop!* go his bowels.

The doctor tells him to walk across the room to show him the problem. He walks across the room and again his ass explodes with each stride: *Parp! Fumph! Toot! Poop!* He walks back to sit down: *Toot! Fumph! Parp! Poop!*

The doctor says, "I know what I'm going to do!" He goes to his cupboard and brings out a giant pole with a great big hook on the end of it.

The fellow looks in horror and says, "Jeez, Doc, what the hell are you gonna do with that?"

The doctor replies, "I'm going to open the window, of course. This place stinks!"

•

John's divorce left him lonely and horny, but after so many years away from the dating scene, he was a little awkward about how to proceed. Still, with his doctor's encouragement, he started to go out on a regular basis.

One Saturday night, the doctor's phone rang. "I'm sorry to bother you at home," blurted John, obviously rather agitated, "but I just had to have your advice right away. See, I've met this terrific woman, we get along great, I really think she could be the one for me, everything's going great—"

"So?" interrupted the doctor, trying to conceal his irritation at having been summoned away from the dinner table.

"There's one little problem," John explained. "I really want to take her home with me, but I can't remember from our first date whether she said she had VD or TB. What should I do?"

The doctor thought for a moment, then advised, "If she coughs, f*** her."

•

At her annual checkup, an attractive young woman was informed that it was necessary to have her temperature taken rectally. She agreed, but a few moments later cried indignantly, "Doctor, that's not my rectum!"

"And it's not my thermometer either," admitted the doctor with a grin.

Just then the woman's husband, who had come to pick her up, walked into the examination room. "What the hell's going on here?" he demanded.

"Just taking your wife's temperature," the doctor explained coolly.

"Okay, Doc," grumbled the fellow, "but that thing better have numbers on it."

•

The doctor went into his patient's room and said, "I've got some good news and some bad news. Which do you want to hear first?"

"The bad news," said the frightened patient.

"Well, during your hernia operation, the surgeon's knife slipped and cut off your penis."

"My God!" the patient said. "Then what is the good news?"

"It wasn't malignant."

•

A businessman returns from the Far East. After a few days, he notices a growth on his penis.

He sees several doctors. They all say: "You've been screwing around in the Far East, very common there, no cure. We'll have to cut it off."

The man panics, but figures if it is common in the Far East, they must know how to cure it. So he goes back and sees a doctor in Thailand.

The doctor examines him and says, "You've been fooling around in my country. This is a very common problem here. Did you see any other doctors?"

The man replies, "Yes, a few in the USA."

The doctor says, "I bet they told you it had to be cut off."

The man answers, "Yes!"

The doctor smiles and nods. "That is not correct. It will fall off by itself."

•

A guy went out hunting. He had all the gear—the jacket, the boots, and the double-barreled shotgun. As he was climbing over a fence, he dropped the gun and it went off, shooting him right in the penis.

When he woke up from surgery, he found that the doctor had done a marvelous job repairing it. As he got ready to go home, the doctor gave him a business card. "This is my brother's card. I'll make an appointment for you to see him."

The guy says, "Is your brother a doctor?"

"No," the doctor replies, "he plays the flute. He'll show you where to put your fingers so you don't piss in your eye."

•

A man goes into the doctor's office feeling really bad. After a thorough examination, the doctor calls him into his office and says, "I have some bad news. You have HAGS."

"What is HAGS?" the man asks.

"It's herpes, AIDS, gonorrhea, and syphilis," says the doctor.

"Oh my God," says the man. "What am I going to do?"

"We are going to put you in an isolated room and feed you pancakes and pizza."

"Is that going to help me?" says the man.

"No," says the doctor. "But it's the only food we can think of that we can slide under the door."

•

There's nothing worse than a snotty doctor's receptionist who insists you tell her what is wrong in a room full of other patients. Here's the way one guy handled it.

An eighty-six-year-old man walked into a crowded doctor's office. As he approached the desk, the receptionist said, "Yes sir, what are you seeing the doctor for today?"

"There's something wrong with my dick," he replied.

The receptionist became irritated and said, "You shouldn't come into a crowded office and say things like that."

"Why not? You asked me what was wrong and I told you," he said.

The receptionist replied, "You've obviously caused some embarrassment in this room full of people. You should have said there is something wrong with your ear or something, and then discussed the problem further with the doctor in private."

The man walked out, waited several minutes, and then re-entered.

The receptionist smiled smugly and asked, "Yes?"

"There's something wrong with my ear," he stated.

The receptionist nodded approvingly, knowing he had taken her advice. "And what is wrong with your ear, sir?"

"I can't piss out of it," the man replied.

•

A cardiologist died and was given an elaborate funeral. A huge heart covered in flowers stood behind the casket during the service.

Following the eulogy, the heart opened, and the casket was rolled inside.

The heart then closed, sealing the doctor in the beautiful heart forever.

At that point, one of the mourners burst into laughter. When all eyes stared at him, he said, "I'm sorry, I was just thinking of my own funeral . . . I'm a gynecologist."

And at that point, the proctologist fainted.

•

A man walks into a psychiatrist's office and lies down on the couch.

The shrink says, "What makes you think you need the services of a psychiatrist?"

The man replies that he wakes up every night in the kitchen after some pretty crazy sleepwalking.

The shrink says, "So, would you like me to try to cure you of sleepwalking?"

The man explains that the sleepwalking isn't really the problem. Every time he wakes up he is in the same place, doing the same thing—he has his pajamas around his ankles and his dick in a jar of peanuts.

The psychiatrist says, "I think I know what your problem is. You're f***ing nuts."

•

A woman and a baby were in the doctor's examination room, waiting for the doctor to come in for the baby's first exam.

The doctor arrived, examined the baby, and checked his weight. Being a little concerned, he asked if the baby was breast-fed or bottle-fed.

"Breast-fed," the woman replied.

"Well, strip down to your waist," the doctor ordered.

She did. He pinched her nipples, then pressed, kneaded, and rubbed both breasts for a while in a detailed examination. Motioning to her to get dressed, he said, "No wonder this baby is underweight. You don't have any milk."

"I know," she said, "I'm his grandma, but I'm glad I came."

•

The seventy-year-old man sat down in the orthopedic surgeon's office. "You know, Doc," he said, "I've made love in more exotic cars than anyone I know. Must be at least a thousand."

"And now, I suppose, you want me to treat you for the arthritis you got from scrunching up in all those uncomfortable positions," the medic said.

"Heck no," the old fellow replied. "I want to borrow your Lamborghini!"

•

A woman in her forties went to a plastic surgeon for a face-lift.

The surgeon told her about a new procedure called "The Knob": a small knob is placed on top of a person's head and can be turned to tighten up the skin, producing the effect of a face-lift.

Of course, the woman wanted The Knob.

Over the course of the years, the woman tightened the knob, and the effects were wonderful—she remained young-looking and vibrant.

After fifteen years, the woman returned to the surgeon with two problems.

"I've had to turn The Knob many times and I've always loved the results. But now I've developed two annoying problems: First, I have these terrible bags under my eyes and The Knob won't get rid of them."

The doctor looked at her closely and said, "Those aren't bags, those are your breasts."

She said, "Well, I guess there's no point in asking about the goatee."

•

Joe went to see the doctor the other day for that pain in his back.

"So what happened?" I asked.

"Well, he ran a bunch of tests, gave me some pills, and sent me home. Told me to stay in bed for a week. He also told me to sit down whenever I had to pee. Can you imagine that? A grown man having to sit to pee?"

"Why would he want you to sit to pee?" I asked.

"Well," said Joe, "with my bad back, he doesn't want me picking up anything too heavy."

•

Two women had been having a friendly lunch when the subject turned to sex. "You know, John and I have been having some sexual problems," Linda told her friend.

"That's amazing!" Mary replied, "So have Tom and I."

"We're thinking of going to a sex therapist," said Linda.

"Oh, we could never do that! We'd be too embarrassed!" responded Mary. "But after you go, will you please tell me how it went?"

Several weeks passed, and the two friends met for lunch again. "So how did the sex therapy work out, Linda?" Mary asked.

"Things couldn't be better!" Linda exclaimed. "We began with a physical exam, and afterward the doctor said he was certain he could help us. He told us to stop at the grocery store on the way home and buy a bunch of grapes and a dozen doughnuts. He told us to sit on the floor nude, and toss the grapes and doughnuts at each other. Every grape that went into my vagina, John had to get it out with his tongue. Every doughnut that I ringed his penis with, I had to eat. Our sex life is wonderful . . . in fact, it's better than it's ever been!"

With that endorsement Mary talked her husband into an appointment with the same sex therapist. After the physical exams were completed, the doctor called Mary and Tom into his office. "I'm afraid there is nothing I can do for you," he said.

"But Doctor," Mary complained, "you did such good for Linda and John, surely you must have a suggestion for us! Please, please, can't you give us some help? Any help at all?"

"Well, okay," the doctor answered. "On your way home, I want you to stop at the grocery store and buy a sack of apples and a box of Cheerios . . ."

•

In the days before birth control pills, a young bride-to-be asked her gynecologist to recommend some sort of contraceptive. He suggested she try withdrawal, douches, or condoms.

Several years later, the woman was walking down the

street with three children when she happened to run across her old doctor.

"I see you decided not to take my advice," he said, eyeing the young children.

"On the contrary, Doc!" she exclaimed. "Davey here was a pullout, Darcy was a washout, and Delores was a blowout!"

•

When Ralph first noticed that his penis was growing larger and staying erect longer, he was delighted, as was his wife. But after several weeks, his penis had grown to nearly twenty inches. Ralph became quite concerned, so he and his wife went to see a prominent urologist.

After an initial examination, the physician explained to the couple that, though rare, Ralph's condition could be cured through corrective surgery.

"How long will Ralph be on crutches?" the wife asked anxiously.

"Crutches? Why would he need crutches?" responded the surprised doctor.

"Well," said the wife, "you are planning to lengthen Ralph's legs, aren't you?"

•

A new bride went to her doctor for a check-up. Lacking knowledge of the male anatomy, she asked the doctor, "What's that thing hanging between my husband's legs?"

The doctor replied, "We call that the penis."

The new bride then asked, "What's that reddish-purple thing on the end of the penis?"

The doctor replied, "We call that the head of the penis."

The bride then asked, "What are those two round things about fifteen inches from the head of the penis?"

The doctor replied, "Lady, on him I don't know, but on me they're the cheeks of my ass!"

•

This woman goes to the dentist. After he is through examining her, he says, "I am sorry to tell you this, but I am going to have to drill a tooth."

The woman then says, "Ooooohhhh, the pain is so awful I'd rather have a baby!"

To which the dentist replies, "Make up your mind, I have to adjust the chair."

•

A pert and pretty nurse took her troubles to a psychiatrist in the hospital where she worked.

"Doctor, you must help me," she pleaded. "It's gotten so that every time I date one of the young doctors here, I end up in bed with him. And then afterward, I feel guilty and depressed for a week."

"I see." The psychiatrist nodded. "And you want me to strengthen your willpower and resolve in this matter?"

"For God's sake, no!" exclaimed the nurse. "I want you to fix it so I won't feel guilty and depressed afterward."

•

Patient: "Doc, you gotta help me. I'm under a lot of stress. I keep losing my temper with people."

Doctor: "Tell me about your problem."

Patient: "I just did, you f***ing jackass!"

•

A man and woman are at a bar having a few beers. They start talking and soon realize they're both doctors. After an hour, the man says, "Hey, how about if we sleep together tonight? No strings attached." The woman doctor agrees to it. They go back to her place and he goes in the bedroom. She goes into the bathroom and starts scrubbing up like she's about to go into the operating room. She scrubs for a good ten minutes. At last, she goes into the bedroom and they have sex. Afterward, the man says, "You're a surgeon, aren't you?"

"Yes," says the woman, "how did you know?"

"I could tell by the way you scrubbed up before we started," he says.

"That makes sense," says the woman. "You're an anesthesiologist, aren't you?"

"Yeah, how did you know?" asks the man.

The woman replies, "Because I didn't feel a thing."

•

Mr. Jones gets a call from the hospital. They tell him his wife's been in a terrible car accident. He rushes to the hospital and runs into the ER. He's told that Dr. Smith is handling the case and the doctor is paged. He comes out to the waiting room.

"Mr. Jones?" the doctor asks.

"Yes sir, what's happened? How is my wife?"

The doctor sits next to him and says, "Not good news. Your wife's accident resulted in two fractures of her spine."

"Oh, my God," says Mr. Jones, "what is her prognosis?"

Dr. Smith says, "Well, Mr. Jones, her vital signs are stable. However, her spine is inoperable. She'll have no motor skills or capability. This means you will have to feed her." Mr. Jones begins to sob. "And you'll have to turn her in her bed every two hours to prevent pneumonia."

Mr. Jones begins to wail and cry loudly. "Then, of course," the doctor continues, "you'll have to diaper her as she'll have no control over her bladder and of course these diapers must be changed at least five times a day."

Mr. Jones begins to shake as he cries, sobs, wails. The doctor concludes, "And you'll have to clean up her feces on a regular basis as she'll have no control over her sphincter. Her bowel will disgorge whenever, and quite often, I'm afraid. Of course, you must clean her immediately to avoid accumulation of the putrid effluent she'll be emitting regularly."

Now Mr. Jones is convulsing, sobbing uncontrollably and beginning to slump off the bench into a pitiful mass. Just then Dr. Smith reaches out his hand and pats Mr. Jones on the shoulder. "Hey, I'm just f***ing with you. She's dead."

A nurse from England was on duty in the emergency department, when a punk rocker entered. The patient had purple hair, a variety of tattoos, and strange clothing. It was quickly determined that the patient had acute appendicitis, so she scheduled her for immediate surgery.

When the patient was completely disrobed on the operating table, the surgeons noticed that her pubic hair had been dyed green, and just above it there was a tattoo that read, "Keep off the grass."

After the surgical procedure was completed, the surgeon added a small note to the dressing that said, "Sorry, had to mow the lawn."

•

A man with a terrible sore throat walks into a pharmacy and asks the pharmacist if he can give him something to relieve it. The pharmacist says, "Well, I could give you any number of things but they won't really do you much good. However, I can tell you what I do when I have a bad sore throat like you have."

"Really? What?" asks the man.

"I go straight home and have my wife give me a good blow job. I suggest you try that."

"Sounds great!" says the man. "Is your wife home now?"

•

The tired doctor was awakened by a telephone call in the middle of the night. "Please come right over," pleaded the distraught young mother. "My child has swallowed a contraceptive."

The physician dressed quickly but before he could get out the door, the phone rang again. "You don't have to come after all," the woman said with a sigh of relief. "My husband just found another one."

•

During her annual checkup, the well-constructed woman was asked to disrobe and climb onto the examining table. "Doctor," she replied shyly, "I just can't undress in front of you."

"All right," said the physician, "I'll flick off the lights. You undress and tell me when you're through."

In a few moments, her voice rang out in the darkness: "Doctor, I've undressed. What shall I do with my clothes?"

"Put them on the chair, on top of mine."

•

This lady goes to the gynecologist, but won't tell the receptionist what's wrong with her . . . just that she must see a doctor.

After hours of waiting, the doctor sees her in. "Okay, my good woman, what is your problem?" the doctor asks.

"Well," she says, "my husband is a very compulsive gambler, every nickel he can get his hands on. So, I had five hundred dollars and I stuffed it in my vagina, but now I can't get it out."

The doctor says, "Don't be nervous, I see this happen all the time."

He asks her to pull down her underwear, sits her down with her legs wide open, puts on his gloves, and says: "I only have one question. What am I looking for? Bills or loose change?"

•

Having determined that the husband was infertile, a childless couple decided to try artificial insemination. When the woman showed up at the clinic, she was told to undress, get up on the table, and place her feet in the stirrups. She was feeling very uncomfortable about the whole situation, and when the doctor started dropping his pants, she freaked. "Wait a second! What the hell is going on here?" she yelled.

"Don't you want to get pregnant?" asked the doctor.

"Well, yes, but . . ." stammered the woman.

"Well, lie back and spread 'em," replied the doctor. "We're out of the bottled stuff, so you'll just have to settle for what's on tap."

•

A salesman in a strange city was feeling horny and wanted release. He inquired for the address of a good house of ill repute. He was told to go to 225 West 42nd Street. By mistake, he went to 255 West 42nd Street, the office of a podiatrist. Being met by a beautiful woman in a white uniform surprised but intrigued him. She directed him to an examination room and told him to uncover and someone would be with him soon. He loved the thought of the table and the reclining chair, and was really getting aroused because of the strange and different approach this house offered.

Finally the doctor's assistant, a really gorgeous redhead, entered and found the salesman sitting in the chair with his generous member in his hand. "My goodness," she exclaimed, "I was expecting to see a foot."

"Well," he said, "if you're going to complain about an inch, then I'll take my business elsewhere."

•

The phone rings and the lady of the house answers: "Hello."

"Mrs. Ward, please."

"Speaking."

"Mrs. Ward, this is Dr. Jones at the Medical Testing Laboratory. When your doctor sent your husband's biopsy to the lab yesterday, a biopsy from another Mr. Ward arrived as well, and we are now uncertain which one is your husband's. Frankly the results are either bad or terrible."

"What do you mean?" Mrs. Ward asks nervously.

"Well, one of the specimens tested positive for Alzheimer's and the other one tested positive for AIDS. We can't tell which is your husband's."

"That's dreadful! Can't you do the test again?" questioned Mrs. Ward.

"Normally we can, but Medicare will only pay for these expensive tests one time."

"Well, what am I supposed to do now?"

"The people at Medicare recommend that you drop your husband off somewhere in the middle of town. If he finds his way home, don't sleep with him."

# Husband/Wife

A man and woman were having marital problems, so they went to see a marriage counselor. The counselor, in an attempt to find some common ground from which to begin his analysis, said, "Tell me about anything the two of you have in common."

The husband spoke up. "Well, neither one of us sucks dicks."

•

A circus owner runs an ad for a lion tamer and two people show up. One is a good-looking older man in his mid-sixties and the other is a gorgeous blonde in her mid-twenties.

The circus owner tells them, "I'm not going to sugarcoat it. This is one ferocious lion. He ate my last tamer, so you guys better be good or you're history. Here's your equipment—a chair, a whip, and a gun. Who wants to try out first?"

The girl says, "I'll go first." She walks past the chair, the whip, and the gun, and steps right into the lion's cage. The lion starts to snarl and pant and begins to charge her.

When the lion is about halfway there, she throws open her coat, revealing her beautiful naked body. The lion stops dead in his tracks, sheepishly crawls up to her, and starts licking her feet and ankles. He continues to lick and kiss her entire body for several minutes and then rests his head at her feet.

The circus owner's mouth is on the floor. He says, "I've never seen a display like that in my life." He then turns to the older man and asks, "Can you top that?"

The older man replies, "No problem, just get that damn lion out of the way."

•

A woman is in the kitchen preparing to boil eggs for breakfast.

Her husband walks in. She turns to him and says, "You've got to make love to me—this very moment."

His eyes light up and he thinks, *This is my lucky day.* Not wanting to lose the moment, he embraces her and then gives it his all on the kitchen table.

Afterward she says, "Thanks," and returns to the stove.

More than a little puzzled, he asks, "What was that all about?"

"The egg timer's broken."

•

A man goes to a tattoo artist and says, "I'd like you to tattoo a one-hundred-dollar bill onto my dick."

The tattoo artist is surprised. "Well, that could hurt a lot! Why would you want a hundred-dollar bill on your dick?"

The man answers, "Three reasons: One, I like to watch my money grow; two, I like to play with my money; and three, next time my wife wants to blow a hundred bucks, she won't have to leave the house!"

•

"You and your husband don't seem to have an awful lot in common," said the new tenant's neighbor. "Why on earth did you get married?"

"I suppose it was the old business of opposites attract," was the reply. "He wasn't pregnant and I was."

•

A man came down with the flu and was forced to stay home from work. He was glad for the interlude because it taught him how much his wife loved him. She was so thrilled to have him around that when a deliveryman or the mailman arrived, she ran out and yelled, "My husband's home! My husband's home!"

•

A sex researcher phones one of the participants in a recent survey to check on a discrepancy. He asks the man, "In response to the question on frequency of intercourse, you answered 'twice weekly.' Your wife, on the other hand, answered 'several times a night.' "

"That's right," replies the man, "and that's how it's going to stay until our second mortgage is paid off."

•

A man was going door-to-door doing a sexual survey in Don's neighborhood. "How often a week do you sleep with your wife?" asked the inquirer.

"Three times," Don said without hesitation.

"That is once more often than your neighbor," the inquirer said, writing.

"That makes sense," Don said, "after all, she's my wife."

•

A couple was going to a costume party. The husband was unsure of what costume to wear. His wife was telling him to hurry or they would be late for the party.

Suddenly she was walking down the stairs from the bedroom, completely naked, except for a big old floppy pair of boots.

"Where is your costume?" the husband asked.

"This is it," replied his wife.

"What the heck kind of costume is that?"

"Why, I am going as Puss in Boots," explains the wife. "Now hurry and get your costume on."

The husband went upstairs and was back in about two

minutes. He also was completely naked, except for a vase slid over his penis.

"What the heck kind of costume is that?" asked the wife.

"I am a fire alarm," he replied. "In case of fire break the glass, pull twice, and I come."

•

A man was in prison for seven years. The day he got out, his wife and son were there to pick him up. He came through the gates and got into the car.

The only thing he said was, "F. F."

His wife turned to him and answered, "E. F."

Out on the highway, he said, "F. F."

She responded simply, "E. F."

He repeated, "F. F."

She again replied, "E. F."

"Mom! Dad!" their son yelled. "What's going on?"

The man answered, "Your mother wants to eat first!"

•

A fellow was talking to his buddy: "I don't know what to get my wife for her birthday. She has everything, and besides, she can afford to buy anything she wants. So, I'm stumped."

His buddy said, "I have an idea. Why don't you make up a certificate that says she can have two hours of great sex, any way she wants it. She'll be thrilled!" So the fellow did just that.

The next day, his buddy asked, "Well, did you take my suggestion? How did it turn out?"

"She loved it. She jumped up, thanked me, kissed me on the mouth, and ran out the door yelling, 'I'll see you in two hours.' "

•

A woman decided to have her own portrait painted by a very famous artist. She told the artist, "Paint me with three-carat diamond earrings, a large diamond necklace, glimmering emerald bracelets, and a beautiful red ruby pendant."

"But ma'am, you are not wearing any of those things."

"I know," she said. "My health is not good and my husband is having an affair with his secretary. When I die I'm sure he will marry her, and I want the bitch to go nuts looking for the jewelry."

•

After a few years of married life, this guy finds that he is unable to get it up anymore. He goes to his doctor, who tries a few things, but nothing works. Finally the doctor says to him, "This is all in your mind," and refers him to a psychiatrist.

After a few visits, the shrink confesses, "I am at a loss as to how you could possibly be cured." Finally the psychiatrist refers him to a witch doctor.

The witch doctor tells him, "I can cure this," and throws some powder on a flame. There is a flash with billowing blue smoke.

The witch doctor says, "This is powerful healing, but you can only use it once a year! All you have to do is say 'one, two, three' and it shall rise for as long as you wish!"

The guy then asks the witch doctor, "What happens after it's over?"

The witch doctor says, "All you have to say is 'one, two, three, four' and it will go down. But be warned—it will not work again for a year!"

The guy goes home and that night is ready to surprise his wife with the good news. So he is lying in bed with her and says, "One, two, three," and suddenly he gets a hard-on.

His wife turns over and says, "What did you say 'one, two, three' for?"

•

Harry and Shirley have been married for forty-three years. They began seeing each other around the age of sixteen.

Shortly after Harry and Shirley began dating, they started having sex.

There were two problems at that time. One, the only place they could do it was Harry's bedroom. Two, Harry was messy and Shirley was obsessed with cleanliness. Shirley would not have sex with Harry until he cleaned his room.

To this day, Harry gets an erection every time he hears a vacuum cleaner.

•

Jacob, Benny, Max, and Hyman are out fishing early one Sunday morning. After an hour of fishing, Jacob suddenly breaks the silence and says, "You three have no idea what I had to do before I could come out fishing today. I had to promise my Rivkah that I would decorate our bedroom next Sunday."

"That's nothing," says Benny, "I had to promise my Leah that I would build her a new terrace by the swimming pool."

"Well," says Max, "you both had it easy. I had to promise my Sharon that I would completely refit our kitchen with new mahogany cupboards and the latest state-of-the-art equipment."

But Hyman has not said a word, so they ask him what he did to come out fishing. Hyman replies, "I just set my alarm for 5:30 A.M. When it went off, I gave my Faye a firm nudge and said, 'Fishing or sex?' She replied, 'Don't forget your sweater.'"

•

A husband, returning home unexpectedly, found his wife on her hands and knees scrubbing the kitchen floor. The movement of her buttocks excited him so much that he lifted her gown, unzipped himself, and proceeded to mount her.

After they had sighed in mutual satisfaction, the wife resumed her task. This time he booted her in the behind.

"Is that nice, Sam, kicking me after I gave you so much pleasure?"

"That," he said, "is for not looking to see who it was!"

•

A newly married sailor was informed by the navy that he was going to be stationed away from home for a year on a remote island in the Pacific. A few weeks after he arrived there, he began to miss his new wife, so he wrote her a letter.

"My love," he wrote, "we are going to be apart for a very long time. Already I'm missing you and there's really not much to do here in the evenings. Besides that, I'm constantly surrounded by young, attractive native girls. Do you think if I had a hobby of some kind, I would not be tempted?"

So his wife sent him back a harmonica saying, "Why don't you learn to play this?"

Eventually his tour of duty came to an end and he rushed back to his wife. "Darling," he said, "I can't wait to get you into bed so that we can make passionate love."

She kissed him and said, "First let's see you play that harmonica."

•

One night after work, a man was greeted at the door by his wife clad in a flimsy negligee. Before he has a chance to remove his coat, she falls to her knees, yanks his fly down, pulls his dick out, and proceeds to give him a wonderful blow job.

"All right!" he says. "So what happened to the car?"

•

Mr. Jones went to see a sex therapist as a last resort, and confided that his sex life was terrible.

The therapist leaned back in his big leather chair. "I advise having a few martinis first, to loosen things up; then let your mind roam over the whole business of how exciting sex with your wife used to be."

The two men glanced out the window, where two dogs happened to be banging away with great abandon in the courtyard. "Now look at the energy and vitality of those two animals," observed the doctor. "Go home, fix a couple of drinks, and think about those spontaneous creatures. Then come back and see me in two weeks."

Two weeks later, the therapist asked, "Well, how did it go?"

"Terrible," moaned Jones. "It took seven martinis just to get her out in the yard."

•

Husband: "Honey, if I died, would you get married again?"

Wife: "Probably."

Husband: "Would you kiss this other guy? Would you cook for the guy?"

Wife: "Probably, honey."

Husband: "Would you sleep with him?"

Wife: "Most likely. He would be my husband, you know."

Husband: "Would he have blond hair like me?"

Wife: "No, he has black hair."

•

### Five Kinds of Sex

The first kind of sex is Smurf Sex. This kind of sex happens when you first meet someone and you both have sex until you are blue in the face.

The second kind of sex is Kitchen Sex. This is when you have been with your partner for a short time and you are so horny that you will have sex anywhere, even in the kitchen.

The third kind of sex is Bedroom Sex. This is when you have been with your partner for a long time. Your sex has gotten routine and you usually have sex in your bedroom.

The fourth kind of sex is Hallway Sex. This is when you

have been with your partner for too long. When you pass each other in the hallway you both say, "F*** you."

The fifth kind of sex is Courtroom Sex. This is when you cannot stand each other anymore. She takes you to court and screws you in front of everyone.

●

A very repressed married couple could never bring themselves to talk about "sex," so they always referred to it as "doing the laundry."

One evening, the husband was feeling romantic, so he suggested his wife come upstairs with him, so they could "do the laundry." She declined, saying she had a headache.

Later that night, the wife slid into bed next to her husband, and told him she was willing to help him do the laundry now. He replied, "That's all right, dear. It was a small load, so I did it by hand."

●

A huge guy marries a tiny girl. At the wedding, one of his friends says to him: "How the hell do the two of you have sex?"

The big guy says, "I just sit there, naked, on a chair, she sits on top, and I bob her up and down."

His friend says, "You know, that doesn't sound too bad."

The big guy says, "Yeah, well, it's kind of like jerking off, only I got somebody to talk to."

●

A newly married man was discussing his honeymoon. He says to his buddy at lunch, "Last night, I rolled over, tapped my beautiful young wife on the shoulder, gave her a wink, and we had ourselves a performance! Later that night, about two o'clock, I rolled over, gave my sweetie a nudge, and we had ourselves another performance. Well, being so newly married and not yet tired of the task, I waited quietly in bed while my beauty slept until I couldn't wait any longer. It was four o'clock when I gave her a little nudge. She opened her blue eyes and smiled sweetly. We immediately had ourselves a rehearsal."

"A rehearsal?" his buddy asks. "Don't you mean a performance?"

"No, because a rehearsal is when nobody comes."

•

A husband suspects his wife is having an affair. He needs to go on a business trip for several days, so he decides to set a trap for her. He puts a bowl of milk under the bed. From the bed springs, he suspends a spoon. He has it calibrated so that her weight on the bed will not drop the spoon into the milk. But, if there is any more weight than that, the spoon will drop into the milk and he will detect it upon his return home.

He comes home several days later. The first thing he does is reach under the bed and retrieve the bowl.

The bowl is full of butter.

•

A fireman came home from work one day and told his wife, "You know, we have a wonderful system at the fire station: Bell 1 rings and we all put on our jackets, Bell 2 rings and we all slide down the pole, Bell 3 rings and we're on the fire truck ready to go.

"From now on when I say Bell 1, I want you to strip naked. When I say Bell 2, I want you to jump in bed. And when I say Bell 3, we are going to make love all night."

The next night he came home from work and yelled, "Bell 1!" The wife promptly took all her clothes off.

When he yelled "Bell 2!" the wife jumped into bed. When he yelled "Bell 3!" they began making love.

After a few minutes the wife yelled, "Bell 4!"

"What the hell is Bell 4?" asked the husband.

"Roll out more hose," she replied. "You're nowhere near the fire."

•

Three men were waiting to go to heaven. Saint Peter was at the gate and said, "However good you were to your wife, that is the vehicle you will get in heaven."

The first guy comes up to the gate and says, "I never, ever cheated on my wife and I love her." So Saint Peter gives him a Rolls-Royce.

The next man comes up and says, "I cheated on my wife a little, but I still love her." He gets a Mustang and drives off into heaven.

The next guy came up and said, "I cheated on my wife a lot." He gets a scooter.

The next day, the guy who got the scooter was riding along and he saw the guy who owned the Rolls-Royce crying.

He asked, "Why are you crying? You have such a nice car!"

The man sobbed, "My wife just went by on roller skates."

•

### FIVE RULES FOR MEN
### TO FOLLOW FOR A HAPPY LIFE:

1. It's important to have a woman who helps at home, who cooks from time to time, cleans up, and has a job.
2. It's important to have a woman who can make you laugh.
3. It's important to have a woman you can trust and who doesn't lie to you.
4. It's important to have a woman who is good in bed and who likes to be with you.

5. It's very, very important that these four women don't
   know each other.

•

Jane was a first-time contestant on the $65,000 quiz show,
where you have to answer questions to win the cash prize.

Lady Luck had smiled in her favor, as Jane had gained a
substantial lead over her opponents. She even managed to
win the game but, unfortunately, time had run out before the
show's host could ask her the big question. Needless to say,
Jane agreed to return the following day.

Jane was nervous and fidgety as her husband drove them
home. "I've just gotta win tomorrow. I wish I knew what the
answers are. You know I'm not going to sleep at all tonight. I
will probably look like garbage tomorrow."

"Relax, honey," her husband, Roger, reassured her. "It will
all be okay."

Ten minutes after they arrived home, Roger grabbed the
car keys and started heading out the door.

"Where are you going?" Jane asked.

"I have a little errand to run. I should be back soon," he
replied.

Jane waited impatiently for Roger's return. After an ago-
nizing three-hour absence, Roger returned, sporting a very
wide and wicked grin. "Honey, I managed to get tomorrow's
question and answer!"

"What is it?" she cried excitedly.

"Okay. The question is: 'What are the three main parts of
the male anatomy?' And the answer is: 'The head, the heart,
and the penis.' "

Shortly after that, the couple went to sleep with Jane, now
feeling confident and at ease, plummeting into a deep and
restful slumber.

At 3:30 in the morning, however, Jane was shaken awake by Roger, who was asking her the quiz show question.

"The head, the heart, and the penis," Jane replied groggily before returning to sleep.

Roger asked her again in the morning, this time as Jane was brushing her teeth. Once again, she replied correctly.

Jane was once again on the set of the quiz show. Even though she knew the question and answer, she could feel the butterflies conquering her stomach and nervousness running through her veins.

The cameras began running and the host, after reminding the audience of the previous day's events, faced Jane and asked the big question.

"Jane, for $65,000, what are the main parts of the male anatomy? You have ten seconds."

"Hmm, uhm, the head?" she said nervously.

"Very good. Six seconds."

"Eh, uh, the heart?"

"Very good! Four seconds."

"I, uhh, oooooohh, darn! My husband drilled it into me last night and I had it on the tip of my tongue this morning . . ."

"That's close enough," said the game show host. "CON-GRATULATIONS!!!"

•

A man wanted to determine if both his wife and mistress were faithful to him. So he decided to send them on the same cruise, then later question each one on the other's behavior. When his wife returned, he asked her about the people on the trip in general, then casually asked her about the specific behavior of the passenger he knew to be his mistress. "She slept with nearly every man on the ship," his wife reported. The disheartened man then rendezvoused with his cheating mistress to ask her the same questions about his wife. "She was a real lady," his mistress said. "How so?" the encouraged man asked.

"She came on board with her husband and never left his side."

•

A guy is walking around in a supermarket yelling, "Cris-co? Cris-co?"

A store clerk says to him, "Sir, the Crisco is in Aisle Five."

He says, "I'm not looking for cooking Crisco, I'm calling my wife."

The clerk says, "Your wife is named Crisco?"

He says, "No, I only call her that in public."

The clerk says, "What do you call her when you're home?"

He says, "Lard ass."

•

A husband emerged from the bathroom naked and was climbing into bed when his wife complained, as usual, "I have a headache."

"Perfect," her husband said. "I was just in the bathroom powdering my penis with aspirin. You can take it orally or as a suppository, it's up to you!"

•

The couple had been married for twenty years. It was a happy, wonderful marriage, except that the wife was very unfaithful. The husband finally got so tired of her unfaithfulness that he made her promise to never again be untrue to him.

One day he came home and found her in bed with a midget. He cried out, "My wife, my love, after you made all those promises, I find you in bed with another man, and a midget at that!"

She replied, "My dearest husband, the love of my life, do

you not believe me, do you not see, do you not understand? I am tapering off."

•

Saturday morning I got up early, put on my long johns, dressed quietly, made my lunch, grabbed the dog, slipped quietly into the garage to hook the boat up to the truck, and proceeded to back out into a torrential downpour.

There was snow mixed with the rain and the wind was blowing 50 mph. I pulled back into the garage, turned on the radio, and discovered that the weather would be bad throughout the day.

I went back into the house, quietly undressed, and slipped back into bed. There I cuddled up to my wife's back, now with a different anticipation, and whispered, "The weather out there is terrible."

She sleepily replied, "Can you believe my stupid husband is out fishing in that shit?"

•

A husband walks into the bedroom holding two aspirin and a glass of water. His wife asks, "What's that for?"

"It's for your headache."

"I don't have a headache."

He replies, "Gotcha!"

•

The couple has been married only two weeks. The husband, although very much in love, can't wait to go out on the town and party with his old buddies. "Honey," he says to his new bride, "I'll be right back."

"Where are you going, Coochy Coo?" asks the wife.

"I'm going to the bar, Pretty Face. I'm going to have a beer."

"You want a beer, my love?" She opens the refrigerator door and shows him 25 different brands of beer from 12 different countries: Germany, Holland, Japan, India, plus places he's never even heard of.

The husband is nonplussed, and all he can think to say is, "Yes, Honey Pie, but the bar, you know . . . the frozen glass . . ."

He hasn't finished the sentence before wifey interrupts him by saying, "You want a frozen glass, Puppy Face?" She hands him a mug out of the freezer that is so cold that it burns his fingers.

"Yes, Tootsie Roll," hubby says a bit desperately, "but at the bar they have those hors d'oeuvres that are really delicious . . . I won't be long. I'll be right back. I promise. Okay?"

"You want hors d'oeuvres, Pookie Pooh?" She opens the oven and removes 15 different hors d'oeuvres: chicken wings, pigs in a blanket, mushroom caps, etc.

"But, Sweetie, Honey . . . at the bar . . . you know . . . the swearing, the dirty words and all that . . ."

"You want dirty words, Cutie Pie? Here . . . DRINK YOUR F***ING BEER IN YOUR FROZEN F***ING MUG AND EAT YOUR F***ING SNACKS, BECAUSE YOU AREN'T GOING ANYWHERE! GOT IT, ASSHOLE?!!"

•

Bob says to Lester, "You know, I reckon I'm about ready for a vacation, only this year I'm gonna do it a little different. The last few years, I took your advice as to where to go. Two years ago you said to go to Hawaii, I went to Hawaii, and Marie got pregnant. Then last year, you told me to go to the Bahamas, I went to the Bahamas, and Marie got pregnant again."

Lester says, "So what you gonna do different this year?"

Bob says, "This year, I'm takin' Marie with me."

•

After hearing a couple's complaints that their intimate life wasn't what it used to be, the sex counselor suggested they vary their position.

"For example," he suggested, "you might try the wheelbarrow. Lift her legs from behind and off you go."

The eager husband was all for trying this new idea as soon as they got home. "Well, okay," the hesitant wife agreed, "but on two conditions. First, if it hurts you have to stop right away, and second . . . you have to promise we won't go past my parents' house."

●

An old man woke up in the middle of the night and found, to his utter astonishment, that his pecker was as hard as a rock for the first time in two years. He shook his wife by the shoulder until she woke up and showed her his enormous boner.

"Check this out!" he happily exclaimed. "What do you think we should do with it?"

With one eye open, his wife replied, "Well, now that you've got all the wrinkles out, this would be a good time to wash it."

●

Wife: "I dreamt they were auctioning off dicks. The big ones went for ten dollars and the thick ones went for twenty dollars."

Husband: "How about the ones like mine?"

Wife: "Those they gave away."

Husband: "I had a dream, too . . . I dreamt they were auctioning off cunts. The pretty ones went for a thousand dollars, and the little tight ones went for two thousand."

Wife: "And how much for the ones like mine?"

Husband: "That's where they held the auction."

●

A woman goes to her doctor, complaining that her husband is 300 percent impotent. The doctor says, "I'm not sure I understand what you mean."

She says, "Well, the first one hundred percent you can

imagine. In addition, he burned his tongue and broke his finger!"

•

A man walked into a therapist's office looking very depressed. "Doc, you've got to help me. I can't go on like this."

"What's the problem?" the doctor inquired.

"Well, I'm thirty-five years old and I still have no luck with the ladies. No matter how hard I try, I just seem to scare them away."

"My friend, this is not a serious problem. You just need to work on your self-esteem. Each morning, I want you to get up and run to the bathroom mirror. Tell yourself that you are a good person, a fun person, and an attractive person. But, say it with real conviction. Within a week you'll have women buzzing all around you."

The man seemed content with this advice and walked out of the office a bit excited. Three weeks later he returned with the same downtrodden expression on his face.

"Did my advice not work?" asked the doctor.

"Oh, it worked, all right. For the past several weeks I've enjoyed some of the best moments in my life with the most fabulous-looking women."

"So, what's your problem?"

"I don't have a problem," the man replied. "My wife does."

•

Two women were picking potatoes one autumn day. The first woman had two potatoes in her hands. She looked at the other woman and said, "These potatoes remind me of my husband's testicles."

The other woman said, "Are his testicles that big?"

"No. They're that dirty."

•

The mortician calls Mrs. Banley, and says, "Excuse me, Mrs. Banley, but I can't seem to close the lid to your husband's coffin because he has a huge erection."

To which she replies, "Why don't you cut it off and stick it up his ass? That's the only hole in town it hasn't been in."

•

A woman accompanied her husband to the doctor's office. After his checkup, the doctor called the wife into his office alone. He said, "Your husband is suffering from a very severe stress disorder. If you don't do the following, your husband will surely die. Each morning, fix him a healthy breakfast. Be pleasant at all times. For lunch make him a nutritious meal. For dinner prepare an especially nice meal for him. Don't burden him with chores. Don't discuss your problems with him, it will only make his stress worse. No nagging. And most important, make love with your husband several times a week. If you can do this for the next ten months to a year, I think your husband will regain his health completely."

On the way home, the husband asked his wife, "What did the doctor say?"

"He said you're going to die."

•

A businessman and his secretary, overcome by passion, retire to his house for what is popularly termed a "nooner."

"Don't worry," he purrs. "My wife is out of town on a business trip, there's no risk."

As one thing leads to another, the woman reaches into her purse and suddenly gasps, "We have to stop, I forgot to bring birth control!"

"No problem," her lover replies. "I'll get my wife's diaphragm."

After a few minutes of searching, he returns to the bedroom in a fury. "That bitch!" he exclaims. "She took it with her! I always knew she didn't trust me!"

•

A young couple, on the brink of divorce, visits a marriage counselor. The counselor asks the wife, "What's the problem?"

She responds, "My husband suffers from premature ejaculation."

The counselor turns to her husband and inquires, "Is that true?"

The husband replies, "Well, not exactly, she's the one who suffers, not me."

•

John woke up one morning with an enormous erection so he turned over to his wife's side of the bed. Mary had already awakened, though, and was downstairs preparing breakfast in the kitchen. Afraid that he might spoil things by getting up, John called his little boy into the room, wrote a note, and asked him to bring it to his wife. The note read:

> *The Tent Pole Is Up,*
> *The Canvas Is Spread,*
> *The Hell with Breakfast,*
> *Come Back to Bed.*

Mary answered the note and then asked her son to bring it to her husband. The note read:

> *Take the Tent Pole Down,*
> *Put the Canvas Away,*
> *The Monkey Had a Hemorrhage,*
> *No Circus Today.*

John read the note and quickly scribbled a reply. Then, he asked his son to bring it to his wife. The note read:

*The Tent Pole's Still Up,*
*And the Canvas Is Still Spread,*
*So Drop What You're Doing,*
*And Come Give Me Some Head.*

She answered the note and then asked her son to bring it to her husband. The note read:

*I'm Sure That Your Pole's*
*The Best in the Land.*
*But I'm Busy Right Now,*
*So Do It by Hand!*

•

The wife comes home early and finds her husband in their master bedroom making love to a beautiful, sexy young lady.

"You unfaithful, disrespectful pig! What are you doing? How dare you do this to me, the faithful wife, the mother of your children! I'm leaving this house, I want a divorce!"

The husband replies, "Wait, wait a minute! Before you leave, at least listen to what happened."

"Hummmmm, I don't know. Well, it'll be the last thing I will hear from you. But make it fast, you unfaithful pig."

The husband begins to tell his story. "While I was driving home, this young lady stopped me and asked for a ride. She seemed so defenseless that I went ahead and allowed her in my car. I noticed that she was very thin, not well dressed, and very dirty.

"She mentioned that she had not eaten for three days. With great compassion, I brought her home and warmed up the enchiladas that I made for you last night that you wouldn't eat because you're afraid you'll gain weight; the poor thing practically devoured them.

"Since she was very dirty, I asked her to take a shower.

"While she was showering, I noticed her clothes were dirty and full of holes so I threw her clothes away.

"Since she needed clothes, I gave her the pair of jeans that you have had for a few years, that you can no longer wear because they are too tight on you. I also gave her the blouse that I gave you on our anniversary and you don't wear because I don't have good taste. I gave her the pullover that my sister gave you for Christmas that you will not wear just to bother my sister, and I also gave her the boots that you bought at the expensive boutique that you never wore again after you saw your coworker wearing the same pair.

"The young woman was very grateful to me and I walked her to the door. When we got to the door, she turned around and, with tears coming from her eyes, she asks me:

" 'Sir, do you have anything else that your wife does not use?' "

•

There is a new study just released by the American Psychiatric Association about how women feel about their asses. The results are pretty interesting:

1. Eighty-five percent of women surveyed feel their ass is too big.
2. Ten percent of women surveyed feel their ass is too small.
3. The remaining 5% say they don't care, they love him, he's a good man, and they would have married him anyway.

•

This is a story about a couple who had been happily married for years. The only friction in their marriage was the husband's habit of farting loudly every morning when he awoke. The noise would wake his wife and the smell would make her eyes water and make her gasp for air.

Every morning she would plead with him to stop ripping them off because it was making her sick. He told her he couldn't stop, and that it was perfectly natural. She told her to see a doctor. She was concerned that one day he would blow his guts out.

The years went by and he continued to rip them out! Then one Thanksgiving morning as she was preparing the turkey for dinner and he was upstairs sound asleep, she looked at the bowl where she had put the turkey's spare parts, and a malicious thought came to her.

She took the bowl and went upstairs where her husband was sound asleep and, gently pulling back the bedcovers, she pulled back the elastic waistband of his underpants and emptied the bowl of turkey guts into his shorts.

Some time later, she heard her husband waken with his usual trumpeting—which was followed by a blood-curdling scream and the sound of frantic footsteps as he ran into the bathroom.

The wife could hardly control herself as she rolled on the floor laughing, tears in her eyes. After years of torture, she reckoned she had got him back pretty good.

About twenty minutes later, her husband came downstairs in his stained underpants with a look of horror on his face.

She bit her lip as she asked him what was the matter. He said, "Honey, you were right. All these years you have warned me and I didn't listen to you."

"What do you mean?" asked his wife.

"Well, you always told me that one day I would end up farting my guts out, and today it finally happened. But by the grace of God, some Vaseline, and these two fingers, I think I got most of them back in."

•

The husband had just finished reading the book, *Man of the House*. He stormed into the kitchen and walked directly up to his wife. Pointing a finger in her face, he said, "From now on, I want you to know that I am the man of this house, and my word is law! I want you to prepare me a gourmet meal tonight, and when I'm finished eating my meal, I expect a sumptuous dessert afterward. Then, after dinner, you're going to draw me my bath so I can relax. And when I'm finished with my bath, guess who's going to dress me and comb my hair?"

His wife replied, "The f***ing funeral director."

•

The young immigrant couple had just left the courthouse after being sworn in as American citizens.

"It is wonderful," the husband exclaimed. "We are American citizens at last! Do you know what this means to us, my dear wife?"

"Yes, you male chauvinist pig," his wife replied. "Tonight, you cook dinner and I get on top!"

•

Husband and wife had a bitter quarrel on the day of their fortieth wedding anniversary. The husband yells, "When you die, I'm getting you a headstone that reads, 'Here Lies My Wife—Cold as Ever.' "

"Yeah?" she replies. "When you die, I'm getting you a headstone that reads, 'Here Lies My Husband, Stiff at Last.' "

•

Husband (a doctor) and his wife are having a fight at the breakfast table.

Husband gets up in a rage and says, "And you are no good in bed either," and storms out of the house. After some time, he realizes he was nasty and decides to make amends and rings her up. She comes to the phone after many rings and the irritated husband says, "What took you so long to answer the phone?"

She says, "I was in bed."

"In bed this early, doing what?"

"Getting a second opinion!"

•

A man has six children and is very proud of his achievement. He is so proud of himself that he starts calling his wife "Mother of Six" in spite of her objections. One night, they go to a party. The man decides that it's time to go home and wants to find out if his wife is ready to leave as well. He shouts at the top of his voice, "Shall we go home, Mother of Six?"

His wife, irritated by her husband's lack of discretion, shouts right back, "Anytime you're ready, Father of Four."

•

A woman's husband had been slipping in and out of a coma for several months, yet she had stayed by his bedside every single day.

One day, when he came to, he motioned for her to come nearer.

As she sat by him, he whispered, eyes full of tears, "You know what? You have been with me all through the bad times. When I got fired, you were there to support me. When my business failed, you were there. When I got shot, you were by my side. When we lost the house, you stayed right here. When my health started failing, you were still by my side . . . you know what?"

"What, dear?" she gently asked, smiling as her heart began to fill with warmth.

"I think you're bad luck, get the f*** away from me."

•

A black man and his wife were going to a Halloween party in a couple of days.

So the husband tells his wife to go to the store and get costumes for them to wear.

When he comes home that night, he goes into the bedroom and there, laid out on the bed, is a Superman costume.

The husband yells at his wife, "What are you doing? Have you ever heard of a black Superman? Take this back and get me something else I can wear."

The next day the wife, not too happy, returns the costume and gets a replacement.

The husband comes home from work, goes to the bedroom, and there, laid out on the bed, is a Batman costume.

He again yells at his wife, "What are you doing? Have you ever heard of a black Batman? Take this back and get me something I can wear to the costume party!"

The next morning his irate wife goes shopping. When the husband comes home again from work, there, laid out on the bed, are three items: one is a set of three white buttons, the second is a thick white belt, and the third item is a 2 x 4.

The husband yells at the wife, "What the hell are these for?"

The wife yells back, "Take your clothes off. You can put the three white buttons on the front of you and go as a domino. If you don't like that one, you can put the white belt on and go as an Oreo. And if you don't like THAT one, you can stick the two-by-four up your ass and go as a Fudgesicle."

•

On the first night of their honeymoon, the couple wash up and start to get ready for bed. When they get into bed, they start exploring each other's bodies. Things are going fine until the bride discovers her husband's penis.

"Oh my," she says, "what is that?"

"Well, darlin'," the cowboy says, "that's ma rope."

She slides her hands farther down and gasps.

"Oh my goodness. What's them?" she asks.

"Honey, them's my knots," he answers.

Finally, the couple begins to make love.

After several minutes, the bride says, "Stop, honey. Wait a minute."

Her husband, panting a little, asks, "What's the matter, honey? Am I hurting you?"

"No," the bride replies. "Just undo them darn knots. I need more rope!"

•

What's the difference between "guts" and "balls"?

Guts is arriving home late after a night out with the guys, being assaulted by your wife with a broom, and having the guts to ask: "Are you still cleaning, or are you flying somewhere?"

Balls is coming home late after a night out with the guys, smelling of perfume and beer, wearing lipstick on your collar, slapping your wife on the ass, and having the balls to say, "You're next."

•

An old married couple no sooner hit the pillows than the old man passes gas and says, "Seven points."

His wife rolls over and says, "What in the world was that?"

The old man replies, "It's fart football."

A few minutes later his wife lets one go and says, "Touchdown, tie score."

After about five minutes, the old man lets another one go and says, "Aha. I'm ahead 14 to 7."

Not to be outdone, the wife rips out another one and says, "Touchdown, tie score."

Five seconds go by and she lets out a little squeaker and says, "Field goal, I lead 17 to 14." Now the pressure is on the old man.

He refuses to get beaten by a woman, so he strains real

hard. Since defeat is totally unacceptable, he gives it every-thing he's got, and accidentally poops in the bed.

The wife says, "What the hell was that?"

The old man says, "Halftime, switch sides."

•

A married man was having an affair with his secretary.

One day they went to her place and made love all after-noon. Exhausted, they fell asleep and woke up at 8 P.M. The man hurriedly dressed and told his lover to take his shoes outside and rub them in the grass and dirt. He put on his shoes and drove home.

"Where have you been?" his wife demanded.

"I can't lie to you," he replied, "I'm having an affair with my secretary. We had sex all afternoon."

She looked down at his shoes and said: "You lying bastard! You've been playing golf!"

•

A middle-aged couple had two beautiful daughters, but al-ways talked about having a son. They decided to try one last time for the son they'd always wanted. The wife got pregnant and delivered a healthy baby boy. The joyful father rushed to the nursery to see his new son.

He was horrified at the ugliest child he had ever seen.

He told his wife, "There's no way I can be the father of this baby. Look at the two beautiful daughters I fathered! Have you been fooling around behind my back?"

The wife smiled sweetly and replied: "Not this time!"

•

Jake was dying. His wife sat at the bedside. He looked up and said weakly, "I have something I must confess."

"There's no need to," his wife replied.

"No," he insisted, "I want to die in peace. I slept with your sister, your best friend, her best friend, and your mother!"

"I know," she replied, "now just rest and let the poison work."

•

On the evening of their fiftieth anniversary, a reminiscing wife found the negligee she'd worn on her wedding night and put it on. She went to her husband, a retired marine pilot, and said, "Honey, do you remember this?"

He looked up from his newspaper and said, "Yes, dear, I do. You wore that same negligee the night we were married."

She said, "Yes, that's right. Do you remember what you said to me that night?"

He nodded and said, "Yes, dear, I still remember."

"Well, what was it?" she asked.

He was not much in the mood for this, but he sighed and responded, "Well, honey, as I remember, I said: 'Oh baby, I'm going to suck the life out of those boobs and screw your brains out.' "

She giggled and said, "Yes dear, that's it. That's exactly what you said. So now it's fifty years later, and I'm in the same negligee. What do you have to say tonight?"

He looked her up and down and replied, "Mission accomplished."

•

A woman awakes during the night, and her husband isn't in bed with her. She goes downstairs to look for him. She finds him sitting at the kitchen table with a cup of coffee in front of him. He appears to be in deep thought, just staring at the wall. She watches as he wipes a tear from his eye and takes a sip of his coffee. "What's the matter, dear?" she asks. "Why are you down here at this time of night?"

The husband looks up from his coffee. "Do you remember twenty years ago when we were dating, and you were only sixteen?" he asks solemnly.

"Yes, I do," she replies.

"Do you remember when your father caught us in the backseat of my car making love?"

"Yes, I remember," says the wife, lowering herself into a chair beside him.

The husband continues, "Do you remember when he shoved the shotgun in my face and said, 'Either you marry my daughter, or I'll send you to jail for twenty years?' "

"I remember that, too," she replies softly.

He wipes another tear from his cheek and says, "I would have gotten out today."

•

A woman recently lost her husband. She had him cremated and brought his ashes home. Picking up the urn that he was in, she poured him out on the counter.

Then, while tracing her fingers in the ashes, she started talking to him. "Irving, you know that fur coat you promised me? I bought it with the insurance money! Remember that new car you promised me? Well, I also bought it with the insurance money!"

Still tracing her finger in the ashes, she said, "Irving, remember that blow job I promised you? Here it comes."

•

A funeral service is being held for a woman who has just passed away. At the end of the service, the pallbearers are carrying the casket out when they accidentally bump into a wall, jarring the casket. They hear a faint moan. They open the casket and find that the woman is actually alive. She lives for ten more years, and then dies. A ceremony is again held at the same place, and at the end of the ceremony the pallbearers are again carrying out the casket. As they are walking, the husband cries out, "Watch out for the f***ing wall!"

•

She left him on the sofa when the phone rang, and was back in a few seconds.

"Who was it?" he asked.

"My husband," she replied.

"I better get going," he said. "Where was he?"

"Relax. He's downtown playing poker with you."

•

A husband is trying to fly a kite in his backyard. He throws the kite up in the air, the wind catches it for a few seconds, then it comes crashing back down to earth. He tries this a few more times with no success.

All the while, his wife is watching from the kitchen window, muttering to herself how men need to be told how to do everything.

She opens the window and yells to her husband, "You need more tail."

The man turns with a confused look on his face and says, "Make up your mind. Last night, you told me to go fly a kite!"

•

A wife went in to see a therapist and said, "I've got a big problem, Doctor. Every time we're in bed and my husband climaxes, he lets out this earsplitting yell."

"My dear," the shrink said, "that's completely natural. I don't see what the problem is."

"The problem," she complained, "is that it wakes me up."

•

A married couple was in a terrible accident where the woman's face was severely burned. The doctor told the husband that they couldn't graft any skin from her body because she was too skinny. So the husband offered to donate some of his own skin.

However, the only skin on his body that the doctor felt was

suitable would have to come from his buttocks. The husband and wife agreed that they would tell no one about where the skin had come from, and requested that the doctor also honor their secret. After all, this was a very delicate matter.

After the surgery was completed, everyone was astounded at the woman's new beauty. She looked more beautiful than she ever had before! All her friends and relatives just went on and on about her youthful beauty! One day, she was alone with her husband, and she was overcome with emotion at his sacrifice. She said, "Dear, I just want to thank you for everything you did for me. There is no way I could ever repay you."

"My darling," he replied, "think nothing of it. I get all the thanks I need every time I see your mother kiss you on the cheek."

•

Jon left for a two-day business trip to Chicago. He was only a few blocks away from his house when he realized he'd left his plane ticket on top of his dresser. He turned around and headed back to the house. He quietly entered the door and walked into the kitchen. He saw his wife washing the break-fast dishes, wearing her skimpiest negligee.

She looked so good that he tiptoed up behind her, reached out, and squeezed her left tit. "Leave only one quart of milk," she said. "Jon won't be here for breakfast tomorrow."

•

A newlywed couple checked into a quiet, out-of-the way lakeside hotel. The clerk and the bellhop winked broadly at each other, smiling in anticipation of the honeymoon antics to come. But lo and behold, in the middle of the newlyweds' first night, who but the groom tromped down the stairs fully laden with his fishing gear! The manager couldn't believe it. This happened again on the second night and again on the

third night. The manager could contain his curiosity no longer. "You're fishing in the middle of the night on your honeymoon? Why aren't you making love to your new wife?"

The groom looked bewildered when he first heard the
question from the motel manager. "Make love to her? Oh no,
I couldn't do that. She's got gonorrhea."

Embarassed silence. "Oh. Well, what about anal sex?" the
manager asked.

"Oh no, I couldn't do that. She's got diarrhea!"

"I see," the manager said. "Well, there is always oral sex."

"Oh no. She's got pyorrhea as well!"

"Gonorrhea, diarrhea, and pyorrhea! Why, may I ask, did
you marry her?"

"Because she also has worms, and I just love to fish!"

•

On their wedding night, the young bride approached her new
husband and asked for $20 for their first lovemaking encoun-
ter. In his highly aroused state, her husband readily agreed.

This scenario was repeated each time they made love, for
more than thirty years, with him thinking that it was a cute
way for her to afford new clothes and other incidentals that
she needed.

One day around noon, he surprised his wife by coming
home early in a very drunken state. During the next few minutes, he explained that his employer was going through a process of corporate downsizing, and he had been let go. It was
unlikely that, at the age of 59, he'd be able to find another
position that paid anywhere near what he'd been earning and
therefore, they were financially ruined.

Calmly, his wife handed him a bankbook that showed
more than thirty years of steady deposits and interest totaling
nearly $1 million. Then she showed him certificates of depos-
its issued by the bank worth over $2 million, and informed

him that they were one of the largest depositors in the bank.

She explained that for the more than three decades she had "charged" him for sex, these holdings had multiplied and these were the results of her savings and investments.

Faced with this evidence of cash and investments worth almost $3 million, her husband was so astounded he could barely speak. Finally he found his voice and blurted out, "If I'd had any idea what you were doing, I would have given you all my business!"

•

A man, returning home a day early from a business trip, got into a taxi at the airport. It was after midnight. While en route to his home, he asked the cabby if he would be a witness. The man suspected his wife was having an affair and he intended to catch her in the act. For $100, the cabby agreed.

Quietly arriving at the house, the husband and cabby tip-toed into the bedroom.

The husband switched on the lights, yanked the blanket back, and there was his wife in bed with another man. The husband put a gun to the naked man's head.

The wife shouted, "Don't do it! This man has been very generous! I lied when I told you I inherited money. He paid for the Corvette I bought for you . . . he paid for our new cabin cruiser . . . he paid for your season football tickets . . . he paid for our house at the lake. He paid for our country club membership, and he even pays the monthly dues!" Shaking his head from side to side, the husband slowly lowered the gun. He looked at the cabdriver and said, "What would *you* do?" The cabby said, "I'd cover his ass up with that blanket before he catches a cold."

•

A husband and wife are watching *Who Wants to Be a Millionaire* while they're in bed.

The husband turns to the wife and asks, "Do you want to have sex?"

"No," she answers.

The husband then asks, "Is that your final answer?"

"Yes," she replies.

He says, "Then I'd like to phone a friend."

•

A man walking home late at night sees a woman in the shadows.

"Twenty dollars . . ." she whispers.

He's never been with a hooker before, but he decides, what the hell, it's only twenty bucks. So they hide in the bushes.

They're going at it for a minute when all of a sudden a light flashes on them . . . it's a police officer.

"What's going on here, people?" asks the officer.

"I'm making passionate love to my wife!" the man answers indignantly.

"Oh, I'm sorry," says the cop. "I didn't know."

"Well," says the man, "neither did I, until you shined that light in her face!"

•

*To My Dearest Wife,*

*During the past year, I have attempted to make love to you 365 times. I have succeeded 36 times, which is an average of only once every 10 days. The following is a list of why I didn't succeed more often:*

*We will wake the kids—54 times*
*It's too late—15 times*
*I'm too tired—42 times*
*It's too early—12 times*
*It's too hot—18 times*
*Pretending to be asleep—31 times*
*The neighbors will hear—9 times*

*Headache or backache—26 times*
*Sunburn—10 times*
*Your mother will hear us—9 times*
*Not in the mood—21 times*
*Watching the late show—17 times*
*Too sore—26 times*
*New hairdo—6 times*
*Wrong time of the month—14 times*
*Had to go to the bathroom—19 times*

*Of the 36 times that I DID succeed, the result was not always satisfying because 10 times you just lay there, 8 times you reminded me that there was a crack in the ceiling, 4 times you told me to hurry up and get it over with, 7 times I had to wake you up to tell you I was finished, and once I was afraid that I had hurt you when you started thrashing around and breathing heavily. Let's try to improve this, shall we??*
*Love, Your Hubby*

To My Dearest Husband,
I think things are a little confused. Here are the REAL reasons you didn't get laid more than you did this past year:

*Came home drunk and tried to screw the cat—23 times*
*Did not come home at all—36 times*
*Did not come—21 times*
*Came too soon—38 times*
*Went soft before you got it in—19 times*
*Cramps in your leg—16 times*
*Working too late—33 times*
*You had a rash, probably from a toilet seat—29 times*
*Caught yourself in your zipper—15 times*
*You had a cold and your nose kept running—21 times*
*You had burned your tongue on hot coffee—9 times*
*You had a splinter in your finger—11 times*

> *You lost the notion after thinking about it—42 times*
> *Came in your pajamas after reading a dirty book—*
>    *16 times*
>
> *The reason I lay still was because you had missed me and were screwing the pillow. You seemed to be having a good time and I didn't want to move and spoil it. I wasn't talking about the crack in the ceiling. What I said was, "Would you like me on my back or kneeling?" The time I was thrashing around and gasping was when you farted and I was fighting for air. Maybe you can work on your "shortcomings."*
>
>    *Love, Your Wife*

•

A married man keeps telling his wife, "Honey, you have such a beautiful butt." Every person in the town agrees that she does have a very beautiful butt. The man's birthday is coming up so she decides to take a trip to the tattoo parlor and get the words "Beautiful butt" tattooed on her ass.

She walks in and tells the tattoo artist her husband thinks she has a beautiful butt. He looks and says, "You do have a beautiful butt." She then tells the man she wants "Beautiful butt" tattooed on her ass. The man tells her, "I can't fit that on your ass, it takes up too much space. But I tell you what, I will tattoo the letter B on each cheek and that can stand for Beautiful Butt." She agrees and gets it done.

On the man's birthday she hears him come home and is only wearing a robe. She then stands at the top of the stairs. He opens the door and she says, "Look, honey." She then takes off the robe she is wearing and bends over, and the man yells, "WHO THE HELL IS BOB?"

•

The quarterback was petitioning the court to have his recent marriage annulled. "On what grounds?" questioned the judge. "This court does not take annulments lightly."

"Non-virginity," replied the quarterback. "When I married her, I thought I was getting a tight end, but instead, I found that I had married a wide receiver."

•

One night, a happily married man asked his wife to have sex "doggy style."

"No!" she said, aghast.

Throughout their long relationship, he would periodically ask her to have sex "doggy style."

She always emphatically said, "No!"

Finally, on the man's deathbed, he asked his wife why she had refused his simple request to have sex on her hands and knees.

"Hands and knees?" she said. "I thought you meant in the front yard!"

•

A Russian is strolling down the street in Moscow and kicks a bottle lying in the street. Suddenly, out of the bottle comes a genie. The Russian is stunned and the genie says, "Hello, Master. I will grant you one wish, anything you want."

The Russian begins thinking, "Well, I really like drinking vodka." Finally the Russian says, "I wish to drink vodka whenever I want, so make me piss vodka."

The genie grants him his wish. When the Russian gets home he gets a glass out of the cupboard and pisses in it. He looks in the glass and it's clear. Looks like vodka. Then he smells the liquid. Smells like vodka. So he takes a taste and it is the best vodka he has ever tasted.

The Russian yells to his wife, "Natasha, Natasha, come quickly!" She comes running down the hall and the Russian takes another glass out of the cupboard and pisses into it. He tells her to drink, it is vodka. Natasha is reluctant but goes ahead and takes a sip. It is the best vodka she has ever tasted.

The two drink and party all night. The next night the Russian comes home from work and tells his wife to get two glasses out of the cupboard. He proceeds to piss in the two glasses. The result is the same, the vodka is excellent and the couple drink until the sun comes up.

Finally Friday night comes and the Russian comes home and tells his wife, "Natasha, grab one glass from the cupboard and we will drink vodka." His wife gets the glass from the cupboard and sets it on the table.

The Russian begins to piss in the glass, and when he fills it, his wife asks him, "But Boris, why do we need only one glass?" Boris raises the glass and says, "Because tonight, my love, you drink from the bottle."

•

A young wife who was becoming frustrated with her young husband's constant demands for sex decides to make a schedule for him, to cut down on the amount of times that they will have to make love for the rest of their marriage.

While getting ready for work, she writes on a piece of paper:

*"Honey, you know I love you, but your neverending requests for sex are leaving me drained and really tired. So I propose that we only have sex on days that start with the letter T, to minimize the frequency of our lovemaking sessions. Don't be mad at me, honey, just understand where I am coming from, and let me know if my request is too demanding of you."*

On her way out the door, she uses a magnet and sticks the note to the fridge door, hoping that her sex-crazed husband will be understanding and accepting of her proposal when he reads it.

Upon returning home, she glances at the refrigerator and

notices that her note has been replaced with one from her husband.

> *"Baby, I didn't realize that I was putting you under so much pressure and I'm sorry. I accept your proposal and have even taken the extra step of listing at the bottom of this letter those days starting with the letter T to make sure that we are on the same page.*
>
> *1. TUESDAY*
>
> *2. THURSDAY*
>
> *3. TODAY*
>
> *4. TOMORROW*
>
> *P.S. I love you, too; and remember, it's still TODAY. I am waiting for you upstairs."*

•

John O'Reilly hoisted his beer and said, "Here's to spending the rest of me life, between the legs of me wife!"

That won him the top prize at the pub for the best toast of the night!

He went home and told his wife, Mary, "I won the prize for the best toast of the night."

She said, "Aye, did ye now. And what was your toast?"

John said, "Here's to spending the rest of me life, sitting in church beside me wife."

"Oh, that is very nice indeed, John!" Mary said.

The next day, Mary ran into one of John's drinking buddies on the street corner. The man chuckled leeringly and said, "John won the prize the other night at the pub with a toast about you, Mary."

She said, "Aye, he told me, and I was a bit surprised myself. You know, he's only been there twice in the last four years. Once he fell asleep, and the other time I had to pull him by the ears to make him come."

•

A man and a woman were having dinner in a fine restaurant. Their waitress, taking another order at a table a few paces away, noticed that the man was slowly sliding down his chair and under the table, with the woman acting unconcerned.

The waitress watched as the man slid all the way down his chair and out of sight under the table.

Still, the woman dining across from him appeared calm and unruffled, apparently unaware that her dining companion had disappeared.

After the waitress finished taking the order, she came over to the table and said to the woman, "Pardon me, ma'am, but I think your husband just slid under the table."

The woman calmly looked up at her and replied firmly, "No, he didn't. He just walked in the door."

•

A man and his wife are returning from holiday. While on holiday, they decided to buy themselves some pets. He bought a snake, while the woman got a skunk.

As they are passing through airport control, they notice a sign that says:

"NO ANIMALS WILL BE ALLOWED THROUGH QUARANTINE"

Slightly distressed, the woman turns to her husband and asks what they should do. After thinking hard for five minutes, the man comes up with a plan.

"What I'll do is tie the snake around my waist and try to pretend that it's a snakeskin belt."

"Yes," the woman replies, "but what about the skunk?"

"I don't know, you'll just have to hide it up your skirt."

"But what about the smell?" the woman asks.

To which the man replies, "Look, if it dies, it dies!"

•

Two young lovers go up to the mountains for a romantic winter vacation. When they get there, the guy goes out to chop some wood. When he gets back, he says, "Honey, my hands are freezing!"

She says, "Well, put them here between my thighs and that will warm them up."

After lunch, he goes back out to chop some more wood and comes back and says again, "Man! My hands are really freezing!"

She says again, "Well, put them here between my thighs and warm them up." He does, and again that warms him up.

After dinner, he goes out one more time to chop some wood to get them through the night. When he returns, he says again, "Honey, my hands are really, really freezing!"

She looks at him and says, "For crying out loud, don't your ears ever get cold?"

•

A husband walks into Frederick's of Hollywood to purchase some sheer lingerie for his wife. He is shown several possibilities that range from $250 to $500 in price, the more sheer, the higher the price.

He opts for the sheerest item, pays the $500, and takes the lingerie home. He presents it to his wife and asks her to go upstairs, put it on, and model it for him.

Upstairs, the wife thinks, "I have an idea. It's so sheer that it might as well be nothing. I won't put it on, I'll do the modeling naked, return it tomorrow, and keep the $500 refund for myself."

So she appears naked on the balcony and strikes a pose.

The husband says, "Good Lord! You'd think that for $500, they'd at least iron it!"

•

A fifteen-year-old boy came home with a Porsche and his parents began to scream, "Where did you get that car?"

He calmly told them, "I bought it today."

"With what money?" demanded his parents. "We know what a Porsche costs."

"Well," said the boy, "this one cost me fifteen dollars."

So the parents began to yell even louder, "Who would sell a car like that for fifteen dollars?"

"It was the lady up the street," said the boy. "I don't know her name—they just moved in. She saw me ride past on my bike and asked me if I wanted to buy a Porsche for fifteen dollars."

"Dear God," moaned the mother, "she must be a child abuser. Who knows what she will do next? John, you go right up there and see what's going on."

So the boy's father walked up the street to the house where the lady lived and found her out in the yard calmly planting petunias. He introduced himself as the father of the boy to whom she had sold a Porsche for fifteen dollars and demanded to know why she did it.

"Well," she said, "this morning I got a phone call from my husband. I thought he was on a business trip, but it seems he has run off to Hawaii with his secretary and doesn't intend to come back. He asked me to sell his new Porsche and send him the money. So I did."

# Gay

A man dies and unfortunately is sent to hell. Fearing the worst, he approaches the entry gate where he is met by a laughing, joking devil. The man asks why is he so happy to be in such a bad place.

"Oh, we have fun down here. Today is Monday, and it's booze night. We get all the best drinks sent in and we all get blind drunk."

The man is impressed and is starting to like what he sees.

"And Tuesday," says the devil, "is sex night. We bring in women and men and have an orgy all night.

"Wednesday is drugs night—you name it, we have it. We get as high as a kite.

"By the way," says the devil, "are you gay?"

"No," says the man.

"Then you are going to hate Thursdays."

•

Four gay guys walk into a bar and start arguing over whose penis is longer.

Well, the bartender finally got sick of hearing them arguing, so told them he had a way to solve this problem.

He told them to stick their penises on the bar and he'd tell them whose was bigger.

Well, just as they put them up there, another gay guy walks in and yells, "I'll have the buffet!"

•

Some retired deputy sheriffs went to a retreat in the mountains. To save money, they decided to sleep two to a room. No one wanted to room with Daryl, because he snored so badly. They decided it wasn't fair to make one of them stay with him the whole time, so they voted to take turns.

The first deputy slept with Daryl and came to breakfast the next morning with his hair a mess and his eyes all bloodshot. The other guys said, "Man, what happened to you?"

He said, "Daryl snored so loudly, I just sat up and watched him all night."

The next night it was a different deputy's turn. In the morning, same thing—hair all standing up, eyes all bloodshot. They said, "Man, what happened to you? You look awful!"

He said, "That Daryl shakes the roof. I sat and watched him all night."

The third night was Frank's turn. Frank was a big, burly ex–football player; a man's man. The next morning, he came to breakfast bright-eyed and bushy-tailed, with a cheerful, "Good morning!"

They couldn't believe it! They said, "Man, what happened?"

He said, "Well, we got ready for bed. I went and tucked Daryl into bed and kissed him good night. He sat up and watched me all night."

•

Two firefighters are buttf***ing in a smoke-filled room.

The fire chief walks in and says, "What the hell is going on in here?!"

The firefighter says, "Well sir, this man has got smoke inhalation."

The chief says, "Why didn't you give him mouth-to-mouth?"

The firefighter says, "How do you think this shit got started?"

•

It was 5:00 in the morning at the U.S. Marine boot camp, well below freezing, and the soldiers were asleep in their barracks.

The drill sergeant walks in and bellows, "This is an inspection! I wanna see youse all formed up outside butt-naked NOW!"

So, the soldiers quickly jumped out of bed, naked and shivering, and ran outside to form up in their three ranks.

The sarge walked out and yells, "Close up the ranks, conserve your body heat!" So they close in slightly.

The captain comes along with his swagger stick.

He goes to the first soldier and whacks him right across the chest with it. "DID THAT HURT?" he yells.

"No, sir!" came the reply.

"Why not?"

"Because I'm a U.S. Marine, sir!"

The captain is impressed, and walks on to the next man.

He takes the stick and whacks the soldier right across the rear.

"Did THAT hurt?"

"No, sir!"

"Why not?"

"Because I'm a U.S. Marine, sir!"

Still extremely impressed, the captain walks to the third guy, and sees he has an enormous erection. Naturally, he gave his target a huge *whack* with the swagger stick.

"Did THAT hurt?"

"No, sir!"

"Why not?"

"Because it belongs to the guy behind me, sir!"

•

A gay man walks into the roughest truck stop on the highway with a parakeet on his shoulder. He looks around the restaurant at all the burly truckers and announces loudly, "Whichever one of you big bruisers can guess the weight of this darling parakeet gets to go home with me."

Silence falls over the truck stop. Then one of the toughest-looking guys speaks up. "That's an easy one—five hundred pounds."

The man shrieks delightedly, "We have a winner! We have a winner!"

•

"In the center ring," cries the ringmaster, "we have Harvey, the boldest and bravest animal trainer in the world. Watch, ladies and gentlemen, as he puts his head between the jaws of our man-eating lion!" The crowd roars as Harvey pulls out his head unscathed.

"Now, folks, watch this!" shouts the announcer, as Harvey unzips his pants and puts his prick between the giant teeth. "Don't do it!" shrieks the audience as the lion's jaws clamp shut. But without flinching Harvey pulls them open and removes his unharmed penis. Wild cheers fill the arena.

When the noise dies down, the ringmaster steps forward and announces, "Ladies and gentlemen, a prize of five thousand, yes, five thousand dollars, to the man in our audience who'll try that trick." His jaw drops as a small, effeminate man steps right up to the ringside. "You're going to repeat that trick in front of all these people?" he asks incredulously.

"Certainly," says the man, "but I must tell you something first. I don't think I can open my mouth as wide as the lion did."

•

Don was completely smitten by a handsome man who passed him on the sidewalk, so he trailed him into a building and up to his office. What luck—the fellow happened to be a proctologist! Don instantly called for an appointment. But as the examination progressed, his patient's sighs of evident pleasure infuriated the doctor. His job was to cure, not to titillate. Making that perfectly clear, he tossed the patient out of his office.

But Don had fallen in love. Unable to keep away from the object of his desire, he soon telephoned for another appointment, assuring the doctor of a legitimate medical reason. Reluctantly the doctor agreed to see him again. Beginning his examination, he was astonished to find a long green stem protruding from the gay guy's ass, then another, and another.

"My God!" exclaimed the proctologist angrily. "You've got a dozen red roses stuck up your ass. I warned you not to try any funny business—"

"Read the card," gasped Don, "read the card!"

•

A fellow was having a few beers at his local pub on a Saturday afternoon when he was approached by a man dressed all in green. "Know what?" the man in green asked confidingly. "I'm a leprechaun, and I'm feeling extremely generous. So generous, in fact, that I'm willing to grant you any three wishes you'd like."

"No kidding! Gee, that's great," blurted the lucky fellow. "I could sure use some extra cash."

"No problem," said the leprechaun with a gracious wave. "The trunk of your car is now crammed with hundred-dollar bills. What's next?"

"Well, I wouldn't mind moving to a nicer house."

"Consider it done," announced the leprechaun grandly. "Four bedrooms, three-and-a-half baths. And your third wish?"

"Well, uh, how about a gorgeous blonde?" suggested the fellow, blushing a bit.

"She's in your new house, waiting for you in a flimsy negligee."

"This is really great," said the lucky guy, getting down from his stool and starting for the door. "I wish there were some way to thank you."

"Oh, but there is," spoke up the man in green. "I'd like a blow job."

"A blow job?" The man wasn't sure he'd heard right.

"Yup. And after all I've given you, it doesn't seem like much to ask, now does it?"

The lucky fellow had to admit this was true, so in a dark alley behind the bar he obliged his benefactor. As he pulled on his jacket and turned away, the man in green stopped him. "Just one question," he asked. "How old are you?"

"Thirty-four."

"Isn't that a little old to believe in leprechauns?"

•

John had been at the university for more than two years, and his grades had gradually become worse. His father called the dean to find out why.

"Well," the dean replied, "I have good news and I have bad news. Your son is in such poor shape with his schoolwork because he does nothing but chase the boys on the football and basketball teams."

"My God, that's awful!" replied the father. "Tell me quickly, what is the good news?"

The dean replied, "He's been voted Queen of the May."

•

A rancher died and left everything to his devoted wife. She was a very good-looking woman and determined to keep the ranch, but knew very little about ranching, so she decided to place an ad in the newspaper for a ranch hand.

Two cowboys applied for the job. One was gay and the

other a drunk. She thought long and hard about it, and when no one else applied she decided to hire the gay man, figuring it would be safer to have him around the house than the drunk.

He proved to be a hard worker who put in long hours every day and knew a lot about ranching.

For weeks the two of them worked and the ranch was doing very well. Then one day the rancher's widow said to the hired hand, "You have done a really good job, and the ranch looks great. You should go into town and kick up your heels."

The hired hand readily agreed and went into town one Saturday night.

One o'clock came, however, and he didn't return. Two o'clock, and no hired hand. He returned around two-thirty, and upon entering the room, he found the rancher's widow sitting by the fireplace with a glass of wine, waiting for him.

She quietly called him over to her. "Unbutton my blouse and take it off," she said. Trembling, he did as she directed. "Now take off my boots." He did as she asked, ever so slowly. "Now take off my socks." He removed each gently and placed them neatly by her boots.

"Now take off my skirt." He slowly unbuttoned it, constantly watching her eyes in the firelight.

"Now take off my bra." Again, with trembling hands, he did as he was told and dropped it to the floor.

"Now," she said, "take off my panties." By the light of the fire, he slowly pulled them down and off.

Then she looked at him and said, "If you ever wear my clothes into town again, you're fired."

•

An airline's passenger cabin was being served by a gay flight attendant, who seemed to put everyone in a good mood as he served them food and drinks.

As the plane prepared to descend, he came down the aisle and said to the passengers, "Captain Marvey has asked me to announce that he'll be landing the big scary plane shortly, so lovely people, if you could just put your trays up, that would be super."

On his trip back up the aisle, he noticed a well-dressed, rather exotic-looking woman hadn't moved a muscle. "Perhaps you didn't hear me over those big brute engines. I asked you to raise your trazy-poo, so the main man can pitty-pat us on the ground."

She calmly turned her head and said, "In my country, I am called a princess. I take orders from no one."

To which the flight attendant replied, without missing a beat, "Well, sweet cheeks, in my country I'm called a queen, so I outrank you. Tray up, bitch."

•

Twelve priests were about to be ordained. The final test was for them to line up in a straight row in a garden, totally nude, while a sexy and beautiful big-breasted nude model danced before them.

Each priest had a small bell attached to his weenie and they were told that anyone whose bell rang when she danced in front of them would not be ordained because he had not reached a state of spiritual purity.

The beautiful model danced before the first candidate, with no reaction. She proceeded down the line with the same response from all the priests until she got to the final priest, Carlos.

As she danced, his bell began to ring so loudly that it flew off and fell clattering to the ground.

Embarrassed, Carlos took a few steps forward and bent over to pick it up. Then all the other bells began to ring.

•

A gay man walks into the doctor's office. He takes off his clothes before his examination. When he takes his clothes off, the doctor sees a Nicoderm patch at the end of his penis. The doctor says, "Hmmm, that's interesting. Does it work?"

The man answers, "Sure does. I haven't had a butt in three weeks!"

•

A truck driver pulled over to the side of the road and picked up two homosexuals who were hitchhiking. They climbed into the cab and the truck driver pulled the rig back onto the highway. A few minutes later, the first man said, "Excuse me, but I have to fart." He held his breath, then the truck driver heard a low *hsssssss*. A few miles down the road, the second man announced, "Excuse me, but I have to fart." The announcement was followed by another low *hsssssss*. "Jesus F***in' Christ!" the trucker exclaimed. "Listen to this." A moment later he emitted a deafening staccato machine-gun burst from his ass. "Ohhh!" one man exclaimed, turning to the other. "You know what we have here, Bruce? A real virgin!"

•

Two men were walking down the road when one looked at the other and said, "You see that guy across the road?" "Wow, he's cute!!!" the other said. "Well, I had sex with that guy a couple of years back." "No shit?" the other asked. "Not much," replied the first.

•

There were three gay men whose partners all died at around the same time. The guy who worked at the morgue asked them where they wanted to spread their partners' ashes. The first man says, "I want to spread his ashes over the ocean because he loved to swim!" The second man says, "I want to spread his ashes on a mountain because he loved to climb." And then the third man says, "I want to spread him all over my chili." The guy who worked at the morgue asks, *"Why?"* and he says, "So he can tear my ass up one more time."

•

Two gay men decide that they want to have a baby, but they don't want to adopt because they want the baby to be as close to their own as possible. So they both masturbate into a cup and have a doctor use their sperm to impregnate a female friend of theirs. Nine months later, the two men are looking at their baby in the hospital nursery. All of the babies are crying and screaming except for theirs. "Wow," one of the men says, "our baby is the most well-behaved one in here." A nurse who happens to be walking by says, "Now he's quiet, but wait till we take the pacifier out of his ass."

# Kids

A small boy was lost at a large shopping mall. He approached a uniformed policeman and said, "I've lost my grandpa!"

The cop asked, "What's he like?"

The little boy replied, "Crown Royal whiskey and women with big tits."

•

A kid is in his bedroom, near ecstasy as he masturbates ever more vigorously. In walks his father. "You'd better stop that, son," says the dad. "Otherwise, you're liable to go blind." The boy dutifully affirms that he will stop immediately.

A week later, the dad once again walks in on the boy as he is masturbating. "I thought we had an agreement," Dad sputters angrily.

"Well," says the kid, "I figured I'd just quit when I need glasses."

•

Jack comes home from school with a great big smile on his face.

His mom asks him, "Why are you so happy?"

Jack replies, "I just had sex today!"

Well, this does not sit well with Mom, and she immediately begins shouting at Jack, telling him at fourteen he has no business having sex! She tells him to go to his room and to wait for his dad to come home. When Dad finally arrives, Mom fills him in. She asks him to go upstairs and to have a chat with Jack. He knocks on the door and proceeds to go in.

"Hey Jack, your mom tells me you had sex today?"

"Yes," replies Jack sadly.

Dad looks around the room and whispers to him, "Hey, way to go, son! Your dad is very, very proud. But if your mom asks what we talked about, just tell her it was guy stuff."

The next day, Dad shares the news with all his coworkers, bragging that at the age of fourteen his son is a man!

When Dad goes home that night, he kisses his wife and runs straight upstairs to see Jack. "Hey Jack! Did you have sex again today, son?"

Jack replies, "No, Dad, my ass still hurts from yesterday."

•

One day, a priest went into a public bathroom to use the stall. While he was on the toilet, he heard moaning coming from the stall next to him. He stood up to look over, and there was little Jimmy, sitting on the toilet masturbating.

The priest was shocked. He told Jimmy that he knew what he was doing in there and that he should save it for marriage.

Little Jimmy agreed to this only because it was coming from a priest.

About a week later the priest ran into Jimmy at the mall and asked him how he was doing with his problem.

Jimmy replied, "Great, Father. I've saved a whole quart!"

•

A little black boy and girl go trick-or-treating. They knock on the door of this house and the man who answers it says, "Well, you two are awful cute. Who are you supposed to be?"

"We're Jack and Jill," she replies.

The man says, "You can't be Jack and Jill, you're black!"

So, they go off and a while later they come back dressed differently. They ring the doorbell and once again the man opens the door.

"Well now, that is just darn cute. Who are you this time?"

"We're Hansel and Gretel," says the little boy.

"Well, I hate to disappoint you, son, but you can't be Hansel and Gretel because you're black!"

Heads hung low, they leave. Not too much later the man hears the bell ring again. This time when he opens the door, there stand the two children, but this time they are buck naked.

"Oh my! And just who are you supposed to be now?!" he asks.

"Chocolate M and M's," said the little girl. "I'm plain. He's got nuts."

•

Little Jason came up to his father at the breakfast table one morning and declared, "Daddy, when I grow up, I want to be just like you."

"Aw, son, that makes me feel great," said his dad, patting him on the head. "I'd love to have an engineer for a son."

"That's not what I mean, Daddy," said Jason. "I mean I want to f*** Mommy."

•

The kids filed back into class Monday morning. They were very excited. Their weekend assignment was to sell something, then give a talk on productive salesmanship.

Little Mary led off. "I sold Girl Scout cookies and I made thirty dollars," she said proudly. "And my sales approach was to appeal to the customers' civic spirit and I credit that approach for my obvious success."

"Very good," said the teacher.

Little Sally was next. "I sold magazines," she said. "I made forty-five dollars and I explained to everyone that magazines would keep them abreast of current events."

"Very good, Sally," said the teacher.

Eventually, it was Little Johnny's turn. The teacher held her breath. Little Johnny walked to the front of the classroom and dumped a box full of cash on the teacher's desk.

"$2,467," he said.

"$2,467!" cried the teacher. "What in the world were you selling?"

"Toothbrushes," said Little Johnny.

"Toothbrushes?" echoed the teacher. "How could you possibly sell enough toothbrushes to make that much money?"

"I found the busiest corner in town," said Little Johnny. "I set up a dip and chip stand. I gave everybody who walked by a sample. They all said the same thing: 'Hey, this tastes like shit.' Then I would say, 'It is, wanna buy a toothbrush?' "

•

Brooklyn Tony was sitting on a park bench munching on one candy bar after another. After the sixth one, a man on the bench across from him said, "Son, you know eating all that candy isn't good for you. It will give you acne, rot your teeth, and make you fat."

Brooklyn Tony replied, "You know, my grandfather lived to be one hundred and seven years old."

The man asked, "Did your grandfather eat six candy bars at a time?"

Brooklyn Tony answered, "No, he minded his own f***ing business."

•

Every day, Little Johnny walks home from school past a fourth-grade girl's house. One day, he is carrying a football and he stops to taunt the little girl. He holds up the football and says, "Hey Mary! See this football? Football is a boy's game and girls can't have one!"

Little Mary runs into the house crying and tells her mother

about the encounter. Her mother immediately runs out and buys the girl a football.

The next day, Johnny is riding home on his bike and Little Mary shows him the football and yells, "Nyah nyah nyah nyah nyah!"

Little Johnny gets mad and points to his bike. "See this bike? This is a boy's bike and girls can't have 'em!"

The next day, Johnny comes by and Little Mary is riding a new boy's bike. Now he is really mad. So he immediately drops his pants, points at his penis, and says, "You see *this*? Only *boys* have these and not even *your* mother can go out and buy you one!"

The next day as Johnny passes the house, he asks Mary, "Well, what do you have to say *now*?"

She pulls up her dress and replies, "My mother told me that as long as I have one of these, I can have as many of *those* as I want!"

•

A kindergarten class had a homework assignment to find out something exciting and relate it to the class the next day. When the time came to present what they'd found, the first little boy the teacher called on walked up to the front of the class and, with a piece of chalk, made a small white dot on the blackboard, then sat back down.

Very puzzled, the teacher asked him what it was.

"It's a period," he replied.

"I can see that," said the teacher, "but what is so exciting about a period?"

"Darned if I know," he said, "but this morning my oldest sister was missing one. Mommy fainted, Daddy almost had a heart attack, and the boy next door joined the navy."

•

Due to a power outage, only one paramedic responded to the call about a woman giving birth. The house was very, very dark, so the paramedic asked Kathleen, a three-year-old girl, to hold a flashlight high over her mommy so he could see while he helped deliver the baby. Very diligently, Kathleen did as she was asked. The mom pushed and pushed, and after a little while the baby was born. The paramedic lifted him by his little feet and spanked him on his bottom. The baby began to cry.

The paramedic then thanked Kathleen for her help, and asked the wide-eyed three-year-old what she thought about what she had just witnessed. Kathleen quickly responded, "He shouldn't have crawled in there in the first place . . . smack his ass again!"

•

It was the first day of school and a new student named Pedro Martinez, the son of a Mexican restaurant owner, entered the fourth grade. The teacher said, "Let's begin by reviewing some American history. Who said, 'Give me Liberty, or give me Death'?"

She saw a sea of blank faces, except for Pedro, who had his hand up. "Patrick Henry, 1775."

"Very good!" praised the teacher. "Now, who said, 'Government of the people, by the people, for the people, shall not perish from the earth'?"

Again, no response except from Pedro: "Abraham Lincoln, 1863."

The teacher snapped, "Class, you should note that Pedro, who is new to our country, knows more about its history than you do!"

She heard a loud whisper from the back of the room: "Screw the Mexicans!"

"Who said that?" she demanded. Pedro put his hand up. "Jim Bowie, 1836."

At that point, a student in the back said, "I'm gonna puke."

The teacher glared and asked, "All right! Now, who said that?"

Again, Pedro answered. "George Bush to the Japanese prime minister, 1991."

Now furious, another student yelled, "Oh yeah? Suck this!"

Pedro jumped out of his chair, waving his hand and shouting to the teacher, "Bill Clinton to Monica Lewinsky, 1997!"

Now, with almost a mob hysteria, the teacher said, "You little shit. If you say anything else, I'll kill you!"

Pedro frantically yelled at the top of his voice, "Gary Condit to Chandra Levy, 2001."

The teacher fainted. As the class gathered around her on the floor, someone said, "Oh, shit, we're in *big* trouble now!"

Pedro whispered, "Saddam Hussein, 2003."

When someone threw an eraser at Pedro, a friend shouted, "Duck!"

The teacher, just waking, looked around and asked, "Who said that?"

Pedro: "Dick Cheney, 2006."

•

A teacher noticed that a little boy at the back of the class was squirming around, scratching his crotch, and not paying attention. She went back to find out what was going on. He was quite embarrassed and whispered that he had just recently been circumcised and he was quite itchy.

The teacher told him to go down to the principal's office. He was to telephone his mother and ask her what he should do about it. He did it and returned to his class. Suddenly, there was a commotion at the back of the room. She went back to investigate only to find him sitting at his desk with his penis hanging out.

"I thought I told you to call your mom!" she said.

"I did," he said, "and she told me that if I could stick it out till noon, she'd come and pick me up from school."

•

Little Johnny's kindergarten class was on a field trip to their local police station where they saw pictures tacked to a bulletin board of the 10 most-wanted criminals. One of the youngsters pointed to a picture and asked if it really was the photo of a wanted person.

"Yes," said the policeman. "The detectives want very badly to capture him."

Little Johnny asked, "Why didn't you keep him when you took his picture?"

•

Little Johnny attended a horse auction with his father. He watched as his father moved from horse to horse, running his hands up and down the horse's legs and rump and chest.

After a few minutes, Johnny asked, "Dad, why are you doing that?"

His father replied, "Because when I'm buying horses, I have to make sure that they are healthy and in good shape before I buy."

Johnny, looking worried, said, "Dad, I think the UPS guy wants to buy Mom."

•

A first-grade teacher, Mrs. Brooks, was having trouble with one of her students.

The teacher asked, "Johnny, what is your problem?"

Johnny answered, "I am too smart for the first grade. My sister is in the third grade and I am smarter than she is! I think I should be in third grade, too."

Mrs. Brooks had had enough. She took Johnny to the principal's office.

While Johnny waited in the outer office, the teacher explained to the principal what the situation was.

The principal told Mrs. Brooks he would give the boy a test, and if he failed to answer any of his questions, he was to go back to the first grade and behave. She agreed.

Johnny was brought in and the conditions explained to him and he agreed to take the test.

Principal: "What is three times three?"

Johnny: "Nine."

Principal: "What is six times six?"

Johnny: "Thirty-six."

And so it went with every question the principal thought a third-grader should know. The principal looked at Mrs. Brooks and told her, "I think Johnny can go to the third grade."

Mrs. Brooks said to the principal, "Let me ask him some questions."

The principal and Johnny both agreed.

Mrs. Brooks: "What does a cow have four of that I have only two of?"

Johnny, after a moment: "Legs."

Mrs. Brooks: "What is in your pants that you have but I do not have?"

Johnny: "Pockets."

Mrs. Brooks: "What starts with C and ends with T; is hairy, oval, and delicious; and contains a whitish liquid?"

Johnny: "Coconut."

Mrs. Brooks: "What goes in hard and pink and comes out soft and sticky?"

The principal's eyes opened really wide and before he could stop the answer, Johnny took charge: "Bubble gum."

Mrs. Brooks: "What does a man do standing up, a woman do sitting down, and a dog do on three legs?"

The principal's eyes opened really wide but before he could stop the answer, Johnny spoke: "Shake hands."

Mrs. Brooks said, "Now I will ask some 'Who am I' questions, okay? You stick your poles inside me. You tie me down to get me up. I get wet before you do."

Johnny: "Tent."

Mrs. Brooks: "A finger goes inside me. You fiddle with me when you're bored. The best man always has me first."

The principal was looking restless and a bit tense.

Johnny: "Wedding ring."

Mrs. Brooks: "I have a stiff shaft. My tip penetrates. I come with a quiver."

Johnny: "Arrow."

Mrs. Brooks: "What word starts with F and ends in K and means a lot of heat and excitement?"

Johnny: "Fire truck."

The principal breathed a sigh of relief and said to the teacher, "Send Johnny to university. I got the last ten questions wrong myself!"

•

A woman takes a lover home during the day, while her husband is at work. Unbeknownst to her, her nine-year-old son is hiding in the closet. Her husband comes home unexpectedly, so she puts the lover in the closet with the little boy.

The little boy says, "Dark in here."

The man says, "Yes, it is."

Boy: "I have a baseball."

Man: "That's nice."

Boy: "Want to buy it?"

Man: "No, thanks."

Boy: "My dad's outside."

Man: "OK, how much?"

Boy: "Two hundred fifty dollars."

In the next few weeks, it happens again that the boy and the mom's lover are in the closet together.

Boy: "Dark in here."

Man: "Yes, it is."

Boy: "I have a baseball glove."

The lover, remembering the last time, asks the boy, "How much?"

Boy: "Seven hundred fifty dollars."

Man: "Fine."

A few days later, the father says to the boy, "Grab your glove. Let's go outside and toss the baseball back and forth."

The boy says, "I can't. I sold them."

The father asks, "How much did you sell them for?"

The son says, "One thousand dollars."

The father says, "That's terrible to overcharge your friends like that. That is much more than those two things cost. I'm going to take you to church and make you confess."

They go to church and the father makes the little boy sit in the confession booth, then he closes the door.

The boy says, "Dark in here."

The priest says, "Don't start that shit again."

•

"Daddy, what are those dogs doing?" asked the little girl, catching sight of two dogs across the street stuck together in the act of intercourse.

"Uh . . . one dog's hurt and the other one's helping him out, honey," explained her red-faced father hastily.

"What a f***in' world, huh, Dad?" she said, looking up at him sweetly. "Just when you're down and out, somebody gives it to you up the ass."

•

One day a teacher had a taste test with her students.

She picked a little boy to do the first test. She blindfolded him, put a Hershey's Kiss in his mouth, and asked, "Do you know what it is?"

"No, I don't," said the little boy.

"Okay, I'll give you a clue. It's the thing your daddy wants from your mom before he goes to work."

Suddenly, a little girl at the back of the room yells: "Spit it out! It's a piece of ass!"

•

Once there was a little boy who lived in the country. They had to use an outhouse, and the little boy hated it because it was hot in the summer and cold in the winter and stank all the time. The outhouse was sitting on the bank of a creek, and the boy determined that one day he would push that outhouse into it.

One day, after a spring rain, the creek was swollen so the little boy decided today was the day to push the outhouse into it. So, he got a large stick and started pushing. Finally, the outhouse toppled into the creek and floated away.

That night his dad told him they were going to the wood-shed after supper. Knowing that meant a spanking, the little boy asked why.

The dad replied, "Someone pushed the outhouse into the creek today. It was you, wasn't it, son?"

The boy answered yes. Then he thought a moment and said, "Dad, I read in school today that George Washington chopped down a cherry tree and didn't get into trouble because he told the truth."

The dad replied, "Well, son, George Washington's father wasn't in the cherry tree."

•

A three-year-old boy was examining his testicles while taking a bath.

"Mom," he asked, "are these my brains?"

"Not yet," replied his mother.

•

Little Tony was staying with his grandmother for a few days. He'd been playing outside with the other kids for a while when he came into the house and asked her, "Grandma, what is that called when two people are sleeping in the same room and one is on top of the other?"

She was a little taken aback, but decided to tell him the truth. "It's called sexual intercourse, darling."

Little Tony just said, "Oh, OK," and went back outside to talk and play with the other kids.

A few minutes later he came back in and said angrily, "Grandma, it is not called sexual intercourse! It's called bunk beds! And Jimmy's mom wants to talk to you!!"

•

A little boy and his dad are walking down the street when they see two dogs having sex. The little boy asks his father, "Daddy, what are they doing?" The father says, "Making a puppy." So they walk on and go home.

A few days later, the little boy walks in on his parents having sex.

The little boy says, "Daddy, what are you doing?"

The father replies, "Making a baby."

The little boy says, "Well, flip her around! I'd rather have a puppy instead!"

•

A few days after Christmas, a mother was working in the kitchen listening to her young son playing with his new electric train in the living room. She heard the train stop and her son said, "All of you sons of bitches who want off, get the hell off now, 'cause this is the last stop! And all of you sons of bitches who are getting on, get your asses in the train, 'cause we're going down the tracks."

The mother went nuts and told her son, "We don't use that kind of language in this house. Now I want you to go to your room and you are to stay there for *two hours*. When you come out, you may play with your train, but I want you to use nice language."

Two hours later, the son came out of the bedroom and resumed playing with his train. Soon the train stopped and the mother heard her son say, "All passengers who are disembarking from the train, please remember to take all of your belongings with you. We thank you for riding with us today and hope your trip was a pleasant one. We hope you will ride with us again soon." She heard the little boy continue, "For those of you just boarding, we ask you to stow all of your hand luggage under your seat. Remember, there is no smoking on the train. We hope you will have a pleasant and relaxing journey with us today."

As the mother began to smile, the child added, "For those of you who are pissed off about the *two-hour* delay, please see the bitch in the kitchen."

•

A little girl goes to her mother after school and says, "Mommy, Mommy, I just saw Johnny's willy. It was like a peanut."

The mother giggles, and replies, "Why? Was it small?"

The little girl says, "No! It was salty."

•

The kindergartners were now in the first grade. Their teacher wanted them to be more grown-up since they were no longer in kindergarten. She told them to use grown-up words instead of baby words. She then asked them to tell her what they did during the summer.

The first little one said he went to see his Nana. The

teacher said, "No, you went to see your grandmother. Use the grown-up word."

The next little one said she went for a trip on a choo-choo. The teacher said, "No, no, you went on a trip on a train. That's the grown-up word."

Then the teacher asked the third little one what he did during the summer. He proudly stated that he had read a book. The teacher asked what book he had read. He puffed out his chest and in a very adult way replied, "Winnie the Shit."

•

A kid comes home from school and says to his mom, "Mom, I've got a problem."

She says, "Tell me." He tells her that the boys at school are using two words he doesn't understand.

She asks him what they are.

He says, "Well, pussy and bitch."

She says, "Oh, that's no big deal. Pussy is a cat like our little Mittens, and bitch is a female dog like our Sandy."

He thanks her, and goes to visit Dad in the workshop in the basement. He says to his dad, "Dad, the boys at school are using words I don't know, and I asked Mom and I don't think she told me the exact meaning."

Dad says, "Son, I told you never to go to Mom with these matters, she can't handle them. What are the words?"

He tells him pussy and bitch.

Dad says, "OK," and pulls a *Playboy* down from the shelf, takes a marker, circles the pubic area of the centerfold, and says, "Son, everything inside this circle is pussy."

"OK, Dad, so what's a bitch?"

"Son," he says, "everything outside that circle."

•

A grade school teacher asked her students to use the word "fascinate" in a sentence.

Molly put up her hand and said, "My family went to my granddad's farm, in Lakefield and we all saw his pet sheep. It was fascinating."

The teacher said, "That was good, but I wanted you to use the word fascinate, not fascinating."

Sally raised her hand. She said, "My family went to see *Charlie and the Chocolate Factory* and I was fascinated."

The teacher said, "Well, that was good, Sally, but I wanted you to use the word fascinate."

Little Johnny raised his hand. The teacher hesitated because she had been burned by Little Johnny before.

She finally decided there was no way he could damage the word fascinate, so she called on him. Johnny said, "My aunt Gina has a sweater with ten buttons, but her tits are so big she can only fasten eight."

The teacher cried.

•

A kindergarten pupil told his teacher he'd found a cat, but it was dead.

"How do you know that the cat was dead?" she asked her pupil.

"Because I pissed in its ear and it didn't move," answered the child innocently.

"You did WHAT?!" the teacher exclaimed in surprise.

"You know," explained the boy, "I leaned over and went 'Pssst!' and it didn't move."

•

A little boy was doing his math homework. He said to himself, "Two plus five, that son of a bitch is seven. Three plus six, that son of a bitch is nine. . . ."

His mother heard what he was saying and gasped, "What are you doing?"

The little boy answered, "I'm doing my math homework, Mom."

"And this is how your teacher taught you to do it?" the mother asked.

"Yes," he answered.

Infuriated, the mother asked the teacher the next day, "What are you teaching my son in math?"

The teacher replied, "Right now, we are learning addition."

The mother asked, "And are you teaching them to say two plus two, that son of a bitch is four?"

After the teacher stopped laughing, she answered, "What I taught them was, two plus two, *the sum of which* is four."

•

One day the first-grade teacher was reading the story of Chicken Little to her class. She came to the part of the story where Chicken Little tried to warn the farmer. She read, ". . . and so Chicken Little went up to the farmer and said, 'The sky is falling, the sky is falling!' "

The teacher paused, then asked the class, "And what do you think that farmer said?"

One little girl raised her hand and said, "I think he said: 'Holy shit! A talking chicken!' "

•

A little girl goes to the barbershop with her father. She stands next to the chair while her dad gets his hair cut, eating a snack cake. The barber says to her, "Sweetheart, you're gonna get hair on your Twinkie."

She says, "Yes, I know, and I'm gonna get boobs, too."

A mother and father took their six-year-old son to a nude beach. As the boy walked along the beach, he noticed that some of the ladies had boobs bigger than his mother's, and asked her why.

She told her son, "The bigger they are, the dumber the person is."

The boy, pleased with the answer, went to play in the ocean but returned to tell his mother that many of the men had larger units than his dad. His mother replied, "The bigger they are, the dumber the person is."

Again satisfied with this answer, the boy returned to the ocean to play. Shortly after, the boy returned again. He promptly told his mother, "Daddy is talking to the dumbest girl on the beach and the longer he talks, the dumber he gets."

•

A little boy was walking down a dirt road after church one Sunday afternoon when he came to a crossroads, where he met a little girl coming from the other direction.

"Hello," said the little boy.

"Hi," replied the little girl.

"Where are you going?" asked the little boy.

"I've been to church this morning and I'm on my way home," answered the little girl.

"Me, too," replied the little boy. "I'm also on my way home from church. Which church do you go to?" he asked.

"I go to the Baptist church back down the road," replied the little girl. "What about you?"

"I go to the Catholic church back at the top of the hill," replied the little boy.

They discovered that they were both going the same way, so they decided that they'd walk together.

They came to a low spot where spring rains had partially flooded the road, so there was no way that they could get across to the other side without getting wet.

"If I get my new Sunday dress wet my mom's going to skin me alive," said the little girl.

"My mom'll tan my hide too if I get my new Sunday suit wet," replied the little boy.

"I tell you what I think I'll do," said the little girl. "I'm gonna pull off all my clothes and hold them over my head and wade across."

"That's a good idea," replied the little boy. "I'm going to do the same thing with my suit."

So they both undressed and waded across to the other side without getting their clothes wet.

They were standing there in the sun waiting to drip-dry before putting their clothes back on when the little boy finally remarked, "You know, I never did realize before just how much difference there really is between a Baptist and a Catholic."

•

I recall my first time with a condom, I was sixteen or so. I went in to buy a package of condoms. There was a beautiful woman behind the counter, and she could see that I was new at it. She handed me the package, and asked if I knew how to wear one.

I honestly answered, "No."

So she unwrapped the package, took one out, and slipped it over her thumb.

She cautioned me to make sure it was on tight and secure.

I apparently still looked confused. So she looked all around the store.

It was empty.

"Just a minute," she said, and walked to the door and locked it.

Taking my hand, she led me into the back room, unbuttoned her blouse and removed it. She unhooked her bra and laid it aside. "Do these excite you?" she asked.

Well, I was so dumbstruck that all I could do was nod my head.

She then said it was time to slip the condom on. As I was slipping it on, she dropped her skirt, removed her panties, and lay down on a desk.

"Well, come on," she said. "We don't have much time."

So I climbed on her. It was so wonderful that unfortunately I could no longer hold back and POW, I was done within a few minutes.

She looked at me with a frown. "Did you put that condom on?"

I said, "I sure did," and held up my thumb to show her.

•

The teacher gave her fifth-grade class an assignment: Get their parents to tell them a story with a moral at the end of it.

The next day the kids came back and one by one began to tell their stories.

"Johnny, do you have a story to share?"

"Yes ma'am. My daddy told a story about my Aunt Barbara. She was a pilot in Desert Storm and her plane got hit. She had to bail out over enemy territory and all she had was a flask of whiskey, a pistol, and a survival knife. She drank the whiskey on the way down so it wouldn't break and then her parachute landed right in the middle of twenty enemy troops. She shot fifteen of them with the gun until she ran out of bullets, killed four more with the knife, till the blade broke, and then she killed the last Iraqi with her bare hands."

"Good heavens," said the horrified teacher. "What kind of moral did your daddy tell you from this horrible story?"

"Stay the f*** away from Aunt Barbara when she's drinking."

•

A mother and her young inquisitive son were flying Southwest Airlines from Kansas City to Chicago.

The son (who had been looking out the window) turned to his mother and asked, "If dogs have baby dogs and cats have baby cats, why don't planes have baby planes?"

The mother (who couldn't think of an answer) told her son to ask the flight attendant.

So the boy dutifully asked the flight attendant, "If dogs have baby dogs and cats have baby cats, why don't planes have baby planes?"

The flight attendant responded, "Did your mother tell you to ask me that?" The little boy admitted that she did.

"Well, then, tell your mother that there are no baby planes because Southwest always pulls out on time. Now, let your mother explain that to you."

•

The teacher asks the children in her class how they think people go to heaven.

Little Johnny puts his hand up but the teacher ignores him. Instead she chooses Jane. Jane says, "Well, Miss, I think that your soul is collected by an angel and it takes you both up to heaven."

Little Johnny shouts out, "Me, Miss, Me, Miss." But again the teacher ignores him. Instead she asks Peter.

"Well, Miss, I think that an elevator door opens and you climb in and go up to heaven."

Little Johnny is still shouting, and the teacher finally gives in and says, "Yes, Johnny, how do you think we go to heaven?" Johnny replies, "Feet first."

The teacher says, "What do you mean?"

"Well, last night I went into my parents' bedroom, and my mother was on the bed with her legs in the air shouting, 'God, I'm coming!' "

•

The pretty teacher was concerned with one of her young students, so she took him aside after class one day.

"Little Johnny, why has your schoolwork been so poor lately?"

"I'm in love," replied Little Johnny.

Holding back an urge to smile, the teacher asked, "With whom?"

"With you!" he said.

"But Little Johnny," said the teacher gently, "don't you see how silly that is? Sure I'd like a husband of my own someday . . . but I don't want a child."

"Oh, don't worry," said Little Johnny reassuringly. "I'll use a rubber!"

•

Little Johnny walked into his parents' bedroom one day only to catch his dad sitting on the side of the bed sliding on a condom. Johnny's father, in an attempt to hide his full erection with a condom on it, bent over as if to look under the bed. Little Johnny asked curiously, "Whatcha doin', Dad?"

His father quickly replied, "I thought I saw a rat go underneath the bed."

Little Johnny replied, "Whatcha gonna do, f*** him?"

•

While in the playground with his friend, Little Johnny noticed that Jimmy was wearing a brand-new, shiny watch. "Did you get that for your birthday?" asked Little Johnny.

"Nope," replied Jimmy.

"Well, did you get it for Christmas then?"

Again, Jimmy said, "Nope."

"You didn't steal it, did you?" asked Little Johnny.

"No," said Jimmy. "I went into Mom and Dad's bedroom the other night when they were 'doing the nasty.' Dad gave me his watch to get rid of me."

Little Johnny was extremely impressed with this idea, and extremely jealous of Jimmy's new watch. He vowed to get one for himself. That night, he waited outside his parents' bedroom until he heard the unmistakable noises of love-making. Just then, he swung the door wide open and boldly strode into the bedroom. His father, caught in mid-stroke, turned and said angrily, "What do you want now?"

"I wanna watch," Johnny replied.

Without missing a stroke, his father said, "Fine. Stand in the corner and watch, but keep quiet."

•

The woman had been away for two days visiting a sick friend in another city. When she returned, her little boy greeted her by saying, "Mommy, guess what! Yesterday I was playing in the closet in your bedroom and Daddy came into the room with the lady next door and they got undressed and got into your bed and then Daddy got on top of her—"

Sonny's mother held up her hand. "Not another word. Wait till your father comes home, and then I want you to tell him exactly what you've just told me."

The father came home. As he walked into the house, his wife said, "I'm leaving you. I'm packing now and I'm leaving you."

"But why?" asked the startled father.

"Go ahead, Sonny. Tell Daddy just what you told me."

"Well," Sonny said, "I was playing in your bedroom closet and Daddy came upstairs with the lady next door and they got undressed and got into bed and Daddy got on top of her and then they did just what you did with Uncle John when Daddy was away last summer."

•

Little Johnny and Susie were only ten years old, but they just knew that they were in love. One day they decided that they wanted to get married, so Johnny went to Susie's father to ask him for her hand. Johnny bravely walked up to him and said, "Mr. Smith, me and Susie are in love and I want to ask you for her hand in marriage."

Thinking that this was the cutest thing, Mr. Smith replied, "Well, Johnny, you are only ten. Where will you two live?"

Without even taking a moment to think about it, Johnny replied, "In Susie's room. It's bigger than mine and we can both fit there nicely."

Still thinking this was just adorable, Mr. Smith said with a huge grin, "OK, then how will you live? You're not old enough to get a job. You'll need to support Susie."

Again, Johnny instantly replied, "Our allowance. Susie makes five bucks a week and I make ten bucks a week. That's about sixty bucks a month, and that'll do us just fine."

By this time, Mr. Smith was a little shocked that Johnny had put so much thought into this. So, he thought for a moment, trying to come up with something that Johnny wouldn't have an answer for. After a second, Mr. Smith said, "Well, Johnny, it seems like you have got everything all figured out. I just have one more question for you. What will you do if the two of you should have little ones of your own?"

Johnny just shrugged his shoulders and said, "Well, we've been lucky so far."

•

Mom walked into the bathroom one day and found young Johnny furiously scrubbing his dick with a toothbrush and toothpaste. "What the hell do you think you're doing, young man?!" she exclaimed.

"Don't try to stop me!" Johnny warned. "I'm gonna do this three times a day, because there's no way I'm gonna get a cavity that looks and smells as bad as my sister's."

•

Two five-year-old boys are standing at the toilet to pee. One says, "Your thing doesn't have any skin on it!"

"I've been circumcised," the other replied.

"What's that mean?"

"It means they cut the skin off the end."

"How old were you when it was cut off?"

"My mom said I was eight days old."

"Did it hurt?" the kid asked inquiringly.

"You bet it hurt, I didn't walk for a year!"

•

Little Johnny was sitting in Beginning Sex Ed class one day when the teacher drew a picture of a penis on the board. "Does anyone know what this is?" she asked.

Little Johnny raised his hand and said, "Sure, my daddy has two of them!"

"Two of them?!" the teacher asked.

"Yeah. He has a little one that he uses to pee with and a big one that he uses to brush Mommy's teeth!"

•

There was a little boy who had just learned to count on his fingers. One day, his uncle came to visit and the boy was anxious to show off his newly acquired skill. He told the uncle to ask him an addition question. So the uncle asked, "What is three plus four?"

The little boy counted it out on his fingers and said, "Seven."

The uncle said, "Listen, kid, you can't count it out on your hands, because someday when you are in school, a teacher will get mad at you for it. Now put your hands in your pockets." So the little boy put his hands in his pockets and his uncle asked, "What is five plus five?"

The uncle saw movement in the boy's pockets, then the boy said, "Eleven."

•

A precious little girl walks into a pet shop and asks in the sweetest little lisp, "Excuthe me, mither, do you keep widdle wabbits?"

As the shopkeeper's heart melts, he gets down on his knees, so that he's on her level, and asks, "Do you want a widdle white wabby or a thoft and fuwwy bwack wabby or maybe one like that cute widdle bwown wabby over there?"

She, in turn, rocks on her heels, puts her hands on her hips, leans forward, and says in a quiet voice, "I don't fink my pet python weally gives a thit."

•

A five-year-old boy was mowing his front lawn and drinking a beer. The preacher who lived across the street saw the beer and came over to harass the kid. "Aren't you a little young to be drinking, son?" he asked.

"That's nothing," the kid said after taking a swig of beer. "I got laid when I was three."

"What? How did that happen?"

"I don't remember, I was drunk."

•

A young female teacher is giving an assignment to her sixth-grade class one day. It's a large assignment, so she starts writing high up on the chalkboard. Suddenly there is a giggle from one of the boys in the class. She quickly turns and asks, "What's so funny, Pat?"

"I just saw one of your garters!"

"Get out of my classroom," she yells, "I don't want to see you for three days!" The teacher turns back to the chalkboard.

Realizing she had forgotten to title the assignment, she reaches to the very top of the chalkboard. Suddenly there is an even louder giggle from another male student. She quickly turns and asks, "What's so funny, Billy?"

"I just saw both of your garters!"

Again, she yells, "Get out of my classroom! This time the punishment is more severe, I don't want to see you for three weeks!" Embarrassed and frustrated, she drops the eraser when she turns around again. So she bends over to pick it up. This time there is a burst of laughter from another male student. She quickly turns to see Little Johnny leaving the classroom. "Where do you think you're going?" she asks.

"From what I just saw, my school days are over!"

•

Three boys received their grades from their female sex education instructor. One got a D+, the second a D−, and the third an F. "One day we should get her for this," said the first boy. "I agree. We'll grab her . . ." said the second. "Yeah," said the third, "and then we'll kick her in the nuts!"

•

A salesman knocks at the door of a home and it's answered by a twelve-year-old boy with a cigar in one hand and a half empty bottle of scotch in the other. The salesman asks the boy, "Excuse me, son, but is your mom or dad in?"

To which the boy replies, "Does it f***ing look like it?"

•

A husband and wife and their two sons are watching TV. She looks at her husband and winks at him; he gets the message and says, "Excuse us for a few minutes, boys, we're going up to our room for a little while."

Pretty soon one of the boys becomes curious, goes upstairs,

and sees the door to his parents' bedroom is ajar. He peeks in for a few minutes, trots downstairs, gets his little brother, and takes him up to peek into the bedroom.

"Before you look in there," he says, "keep in mind this is the same woman who paddled our butts for sucking our thumbs."

•

One day Johnny was sitting in class and had to go to the bathroom, so he raised his hand to ask the teacher's permission. The teacher told Johnny if he could say the alphabet he could go to the bathroom. Johnny stumbled through it and got it all wrong and had to hold it. So Johnny studied and studied and felt as though he knew the alphabet perfectly. The next day when Johnny had to use the bathroom, he raised his hand to ask the teacher could he go. The teacher said if you can say the alphabet, I'll let you go. So Johnny started to say the alphabet: "ABCDEFGHIJKLMNOQRSTUVWXYZ."

The teacher then asked Johnny, "Well, where's the P?" And Johnny responded, "It's running down my leg."

•

The new substitute teacher was introducing herself to the class. "My name is Miss Prussy. That's like pussycat, only with an 'r.'"

The next morning, she began class by asking if anyone remembered her name. Little Johnny's hand shot up from the third row. "Yes," he proudly exclaimed, "you're Miss Crunt."

•

Billy's father had a lot of guns around the house and was always telling Billy things about guns and how to take care of them, etc. Well, one day Billy was in the tub masturbating, and his mother walked in just as he was ejaculating. She stormed out, and Billy chased after her, saying, "I wasn't playing with myself! I was just cleaning it and it went off!"

•

When it was time for milk and cookies at the nursery school, Joey refused to line up with the rest of the class.

"What's the matter, Joey?" the teacher asked. "Don't you want any cookies today?"

"F*** the milk and cookies," Joey answered.

Shocked, the teacher figured the best way to handle the incident was to ignore it. The next day, when it came time for milk and cookies, she asked the same question and got the same reply: "F*** the milk and cookies."

This time the teacher called Joey's mother. She came to class the next day and when milk and cookie time arrived, she hid in the closet. The teacher asked Joey if he wanted his snack and he replied: "F*** the milk and cookies."

The teacher opened the closet door and asked Joey's mother what she thought of that! "Shit," she said, "if the little bastard doesn't want any, then f*** him! Don't give him any!"

•

Two young boys walked into a pharmacy one day, picked out a box of Tampax, and proceeded to the checkout counter. The man at the counter asked the older boy, "Son, how old are you?"

"Eight," the boy replied.

The man continued, "Do you know how these are used?"

The boy replied, "Not exactly, but they aren't for me. They are for my brother—he's four. We saw on TV that if you use these you would be able to swim and ride a bike. He can't do either one."

•

One day, a mother and her two boys, Timmy and Tommy, were riding in their car on the way to church. Timmy leaned over and smacked Tommy across the head, and Tommy yelled out, "Ouch, you f***ing rat!"

Later that day in church, the mom went to talk to the priest. She said, "Father, my boys just won't stop swearing, and I don't know what to do."

The priest said, "Well, have you tried smacking them?"

She said, "No, doesn't the church look down on that?"

The priest said, "Well, yes, but in some cases we'll make an exception."

The next day, the two boys came down for breakfast, and she asked Tommy what he wanted for breakfast. Tommy said, "Well, gimme some f***ing waffles." The mom backhanded Tommy so hard, he flew out of his chair and landed against the door.

Shocked and terrified by this, Timmy became very quiet. His mother asked him what he wanted for breakfast, and his reply was, "Well you can bet your sweet ass I don't want no f***ing waffles!"

●

One day a kindergarten teacher is trying to explain to her class the definition of the word "definitely." To make sure the students have a good understanding of the word, she asks them to use it in a sentence.

The first student raises his hand and says, "The sky is definitely blue."

The teacher says, "Well, that isn't entirely correct, because sometimes it's gray and cloudy."

Another student says, "Grass is definitely green."

The teacher again replies, "If grass doesn't get enough water it turns brown, so that isn't really correct either."

Another student raises his hand and asks the teacher, "Do farts have lumps?"

The teacher looks at him and says, "No, but that isn't really a question you want to ask in class discussion."

So the student replies, "Then I definitely shit my pants."

•

One day, a little boy walks in on his parents having sex and asks what they were doing. The parents' reply is that they are making fish sticks. So the little boy leaves it at that.

A few nights later, the little boy walks in on them again, and this time he asks, "Are you making fish sticks again?"

The parents both reply yes.

The boy remarks, "Well, Mom, you have a little tartar sauce on your mouth."

# Animals

Two fleas from Detroit had an agreement to meet every winter in Miami for a vacation.

Last year, when one flea gets to Miami, he's all blue, shivering and shaking, damn near frozen to death!

The other flea asks him, "What the hell happened to you?"

The first flea says, "I rode down here in the mustache of a guy on a Harley."

The other flea responds, saying, "That's the worst way to travel. Try what I do. Go to the Metro airport bar. Have a few drinks. While you are there, look for a nice stewardess. Crawl up her leg and nestle in where it's warm and cozy. It's the best way to travel that I can think of."

The first flea thanks the second flea and says he will give it a try next winter.

A year goes by. When the first flea shows up in Miami, he is all blue, and shivering and shaking again. Damn near frozen to death. The second flea says, "Didn't you try what I told you?"

Yes," says the first flea, "I did exactly as you said. I went to the Metro airport bar. I had a few drinks. Finally, this nice young stewardess came in. I crawled right up to her warm cozy spot. It was so nice and warm that I fell asleep immediately. When I woke up, I was back in the mustache of the guy on the Harley."

•

A penguin was driving one afternoon when his car broke down. Luckily, he was near a mechanic, so he pushed his car to the mechanic's shop. The mechanic looked at the car and told the penguin, "It's going to be a while, so why don't you go across the street to the shopping mall and come back in an hour."

So the penguin went to the shopping mall and looked around for a while, ate some ice cream, and returned to the mechanic's shop. As he walked up the mechanic said, "Well, it looks like you blew a seal."

The penguin giggled and said, "Oh no, that's just ice cream."

•

Upon reaching his plane seat, a man is surprised to see a parrot strapped into the seat next to him. The man asks the stewardess for a cup of coffee and the parrot squawks, "And why don't you get me a whiskey, you bitch."

The stewardess, flustered by the parrot's outburst, brings back a whiskey for the parrot but inadvertently forgets the man's cup of coffee. As the man nicely points out the omission of his coffee to the stewardess, the parrot downs his drink and shouts, "And get me another whiskey, you slut." Visibly shaken, the stewardess comes back with the parrot's whiskey but still no coffee for the man.

Unaccustomed to such slackness, the man decides that he is going to try the parrot's approach. "I've asked you twice for a cup of coffee, bitch. I expect you to get it for me right now, or I'm going to slap that disgustingly ugly face of yours!" Next thing they know, both the man and the parrot are wrenched up and thrown out of the emergency exit by two burly stewards.

Plunging downward to the ground, the parrot turns to the man and says, "For someone who can't fly, you sure are a lippy bastard."

•

A farmer goes out one day and buys a brand-new stud rooster for his chicken coop. The new rooster struts over to the old rooster and says, "OK, old fart, time for you to retire."

The old rooster replies, "Come on, surely you cannot handle all of these chickens. Look what it has done to me. Can't you just let me have the two old hens over in the corner?"

The young rooster says, "Beat it! You are washed up and I am taking over."

The old rooster says, "I tell you what, young stud. I will race you around the farmhouse. Whoever wins gets the exclusive domain over the entire chicken coop."

The young rooster laughs. "You know you don't stand a chance, old man, so just to be fair I will give you a head start."

The old rooster takes off running. About 15 seconds later the young rooster takes off running after him. They round the front porch of the farmhouse and the young rooster has closed the gap. He is already about 5 inches behind the old rooster and gaining fast. The farmer, meanwhile, is sitting in his usual spot on the front porch when he sees the roosters running by. He grabs up his shotgun and BOOM!, he blows the young rooster to bits.

The farmer sadly shakes his head and says, "Darn it . . . third gay rooster I bought this month."

•

"I hope you can help me, Doctor," said the woman to a podiatrist. "My feet hurt me all the time."

The doctor asked her to walk down the hall and back while he observed, and when she sat back down he pointed out that she was extremely bowlegged. "Do you know if this is a congenital problem?"

"Oh no, it developed quite recently. You see, I've been screwing doggie fashion a lot."

"Well, I'd recommend trying another sexual position," said the doctor, slightly taken aback.

"No way," she replied tartly. "That's the only way my Doberman will f***."

•

A young mother taking her baby to the zoo for the first time made the mistake of passing too close to the great apes. A hairy arm reached out and plucked the baby out of the stroller, and the huge mountain gorilla proceeded to eat the child before her very eyes.

A policeman arrived and spent over an hour trying to calm the hysterical woman, but nothing seemed to work. Finally he put an arm around her shoulders and tried to reason with her: "Lady, don't take it so hard. You and your husband can always have another baby."

"Like hell!" she snapped. "You think I've got nothing better to do than f*** and feed gorillas?"

•

A guy walks into a bar with an octopus. He sits the octopus down on a stool and tells everyone in the bar that this is a very talented octopus. He can play any musical instrument in the world. He hears everyone in the crowd laughing at him, calling him an idiot, etc. So he says that he will wager $50 to anyone who has an instrument that the octopus can't play.

A guy walks up with a guitar and sets it beside the octopus. The octopus starts playing better than Jimi Hendrix, just rippin' it up. So the man pays his $50. Another guy walks up with a trumpet. The octopus plays the trumpet better than Dizzie Gillespie. So the man pays his $50. Then a Scotsman walks up with a bagpipe. He sets it down and the octopus fumbles with it for a minute and sets it down with a confused look.

"Ha!" the Scot says. "Can't you play it?"

The octopus looks up at him and says, "Play it? I'm going to screw it as soon as I figure out how to get its pajamas off."

•

On the farm lived a chicken and a horse, both of whom loved to play together.

One day, the two were playing when the horse fell into a bog and began to sink. Scared for his life, the horse whinnied for the chicken to go get the farmer for help. Off the chicken ran back to the farm. Arriving at the farm, he searched and searched for the farmer, but to no avail for he had gone to town with the only tractor. Running around, the chicken spied the farmer's new Harley. Finding the keys in the ignition, the chicken sped off with a length of rope, hoping he still had time to save his friend's life.

Back at the bog, the horse was surprised, but happy, to see the chicken arrive on the shiny Harley, and he managed to get a hold on the loop of rope the chicken tossed him. After tying the other end to the bumper of the farmer's Harley, the chicken then drove slowly forward, pulling the horse to safety. Happy and proud, the chicken rode the Harley back to the farmhouse, and the farmer was none the wiser when he returned from town.

The friendship between the animals was cemented—best buddies, best pals.

A few weeks later, the chicken fell into a mud pit, and soon he, too, needed help. He cried out for the horse to save his life. The horse thought a moment, walked over, and straddled the puddle. Looking underneath, he told the chicken to grab his hangy-down thing and he would pull him out of the pit. The chicken got a good grip and the horse pulled him out, saving his life.

The moral of the story?

(Yep, you betcha, there IS a moral.)

When you're hung like a horse, you don't need a Harley to pick up chicks.

•

A man was surprised by the sight of a farmer walking down the sidewalk with a three-legged pig on a leash. Unable to restrain his curiosity, he crossed the street and commented, "Quite a pig you have there."

"Let me tell you about this pig," offered its owner eagerly. "It's the most amazing animal in the world. Why, one night my house caught on fire when my wife and I were out, and this pig carried my three children to safety and put the fire out before the firemen could get there."

His listener whistled in admiration. "So why—"

"And that's not all," the farmer continued. "My house was broken into one night, and this pig had the thief tied up and our valuables put back in place before my wife and I got to the bottom of the stairs."

"Pretty impressive," conceded the first man. "But how come—"

"And listen to this," interrupted the proud owner again. "When I fell through the ice on the pond last winter, this pig dove in and pulled me out. This pig saved my life!"

"That's fantastic. But I have to know one thing: How come the pig only has three legs?"

Shaking his head at his listener's stupidity, the farmer explained, "Hey, a pig like this you don't eat all at once."

•

An elephant was having an awful time in the jungle because a horsefly kept biting her near her tail, and there was nothing she could do about it. She kept swinging her trunk, but he was far out of reach. She tried blowing dust at it, but that did no good either. A little male sparrow observed this and suddenly flew down and snipped the horsefly in half with his beak.

"Oh, thank you!" said the elephant. "That was such a relief."

"My pleasure, ma'am," said the sparrow.

"Listen, Mr. Sparrow, if there's anything I can ever do for you, don't hesitate to ask."

The sparrow hesitated. "Well, ma'am . . ." he said.

"What is it?" said the elephant. "You needn't be shy with me."

"Well," said the sparrow, "the truth is that all my life I wondered how it would feel to f*** an elephant."

"Go right ahead," said the elephant. "Be my guest!"

The sparrow flew around behind the elephant, landed on her pussy, and began to f*** away. Up above them in a tree, a monkey watching them began to get very excited. He started to masturbate. This shook a coconut loose and it fell from the tree, hitting the elephant smack on the head.

"Ouch!" said the elephant.

At which point, the sparrow looked up and yelled at the elephant, "What's the matter, babe? Am I hurting you?"

•

A contest was being held at the circus: A thousand-dollar prize was being offered to the first person who could make the elephant nod his head up and down.

Dozens of people tried and failed. Finally, a little old man walked over to the elephant, grabbed his balls, and squeezed as hard as he could. The elephant roared in pain and tossed his head up and down. The old man collected his prize money and departed. The next year a similar contest was held using the same elephant; the only difference was that the winner had to make the elephant shake his head from side to side. Again dozens tried and failed. Finally, the same little old man who walked off with the prize money the previous year appeared. He walked up to the elephant.

"Remember me?" he asked.

The elephant shook his head up and down.

"Want me to do what I did to you last year?"

The elephant shook his head back and forth violently. The old man walked off again with the prize money.

•

Once upon a time there were three little pigs. The straw pig, the stick pig, and the brick pig.

One day, this nasty old wolf came up to the straw pig's house and said, "I'm gonna huff and puff and blow your house down." And he did!

So the straw pig went running over to the stick pig's house and said, "Please let me in, the wolf just blew down my house." So the stick pig let the straw pig in.

Just then the wolf showed up and said, "I'm gonna huff and puff and blow your house down." And he did!

So the straw pig and the stick pig went running over to the brick pig's house and said, "Let us in, let us in, the big bad wolf just blew our houses down!"

So the brick pig let them in just as the wolf showed up. The wolf said, "I'm gonna huff and puff and blow your house down." The straw pig and the stick pig were so scared! But the brick pig picked up the phone and made a call.

A few minutes passed and a big, black Caddy pulled up.

Out stepped two massive pigs in pin-striped suits and fedora hats. These pigs went over to the wolf, grabbed him by the neck, and beat the living crap out of him. Then one of them pulled out a gun, stuck it in the wolf's mouth, and fired, killing him. Then they got back into their Caddy and drove off.

The straw pig and stick pig were amazed! "Who the hell were those guys?" they said.

"Those were my cousins . . . the Guinea Pigs."

•

A man buys several sheep, hoping to breed them for wool. After several weeks, he notices that none of the sheep are getting pregnant, and calls a vet for help. The vet tells him that he should try artificial insemination. The guy doesn't have the slightest idea what this means but, not wanting to display his ignorance, only asks the vet how he will know when the sheep are pregnant. The vet tells him that they will stop standing around and will, instead, lie down and wallow in the grass when they are pregnant.

The man hangs up and gives it some thought. He comes to the conclusion that artificial insemination means he has to impregnate the sheep. So, he loads the sheep into his truck, drives them out into the woods, has sex with them all, brings them back, and goes to bed.

Next morning, he wakes and looks out at the sheep. Seeing that they are all still standing around, he concludes that the first try didn't take, and loads them in the truck again. He drives them out to the woods, bangs each sheep twice for good measure, brings them back, and goes to bed.

Next morning, he wakes to find the sheep still just standing around. One more try, he tells himself, and proceeds to load them up and drive them out to the woods. He spends all day shagging the sheep and, upon returning home, falls listlessly into bed.

The next morning, he cannot even raise himself from the bed to look at the sheep. He asks his wife to look out and tell him if the sheep are lying in the grass. "No," she says, "they're all in the truck and one of them's honking the horn."

•

Farmer Brown had been screwing one of his pigs for four years, when he was suddenly hit by pangs of conscience. It tortured him so much that he decided to tell the priest about it in confession.

The priest was shocked and could only say to Farmer Brown, "Well, tell me, was the pig a male or a female?"

"A female, of course," said Farmer Brown. "What do you think I am—some sort of queer?"

•

There was once an old man and a parrot living all alone together.

One day, the parrot came to the old man and said, "You know, I've never had a woman in my life."

So the old man, as a favor to his best friend, went to the pet store and talked the owner into letting him use a female parrot for one night for the fee of forty dollars.

He took the female home, put it into the cage with his parrot, covered the cage, and went to bed. He was awakened in the middle of the night to the female parrot screaming like she was being killed. He ran over and pulled the cover off the cage. There he saw his male parrot ripping all the feathers off of the female. "What are you doing?" the old man screamed.

The parrot replied, "Are you kidding, for forty dollars, I at least want the bitch naked!"

•

A koala bear decides he wants to get laid, so he picks up a hooker. He goes down on her several times and they are really enjoying themselves. After they are finished, the koala bear starts getting dressed.

The hooker says, "Where's my money?"

The koala bear shrugs his shoulders. The hooker again asks for her money. Again, he shrugs his shoulders. The hooker grabs a dictionary and looks up the word "hooker" and shows it to the koala bear.

It says, "Gets paid for sex."

The koala bear picks up the dictionary and looks up "koala

bear" and shows it to the hooker. It says, "Eats bushes and leaves!"

•

A guy walks into a bar with his pet monkey. He orders a drink and while he's drinking, the monkey jumps all around the place. The monkey grabs some olives off the bar and eats them, then grabs some sliced limes and eats them, then jumps onto the pool table, grabs one of the billiard balls, sticks it in his mouth, and, to everyone's amazement, somehow swallows it whole.

The bartender screams at the guy, "Did you see what your monkey just did?"

The guy says, "No, what?"

"He just ate the cue ball off my pool table—whole!"

"Yeah, that doesn't surprise me," replied the guy, "he eats everything in sight, the little bugger. Sorry. I'll pay for the cue ball and stuff."

He finishes his drink, pays his bill, pays for the stuff the monkey ate, then leaves. Two weeks later he's in the bar again, and has his monkey with him. He orders a drink and the monkey starts running around the bar again.

While the man is finishing his drink, the monkey finds a maraschino cherry on the bar. He grabs it, sticks it up his butt, pulls it out, and eats it. Then the monkey finds a peanut, and again sticks it up his butt, pulls it out, and eats it.

The bartender is disgusted. "Did you see what your monkey did now?" he asks.

"No, what?" replies the guy.

"Well, he stuck a maraschino cherry and a peanut up his butt, pulled them out, and ate them!" said the bartender.

"Yeah, that doesn't surprise me," replied the guy. "He still eats everything in sight, but ever since he had to pass that cue ball, he measures everything first."

•

An Amish lady is trotting down the road in her horse and buggy when she is pulled over by a cop.

"Ma'am, I'm not going to ticket you, but I do have to issue you a warning. You have a broken reflector on your buggy."

"Oh, I'll let my husband, Jacob, know as soon as I get home."

"That's fine. Another thing, ma'am. I don't like the way that one rein loops across the horse's back and around one of his balls. I consider that animal abuse. That's cruelty to animals. Have your husband take care of that right away!"

Later that day, the lady is home telling her husband about her encounter with the cop.

"Well, dear, what exactly did he say?"

"He said the reflector is broken."

"I can fix that in two minutes. What else?"

"I'm not sure, Jacob . . . something about the emergency brake."

•

A guy calls his buddy the horse rancher and says he's sending a friend over to look at a horse.

His buddy asks, "How will I recognize him?"

"That's easy, he's a midget with a speech impediment."

So, the midget shows up, and the guy asks him if he's looking for a male or female horse.

"A female horth."

So he shows him a prized filly.

"Nith-looking horth. Can I thee her eyeth?"

So the guy picks up the midget and he gives the horse's eyes the once-over. "Nith eyeth, can I thee her earzth?"

So he picks the little fella up again, and shows him the horse's ears.

"Nith earzth, can I see her mouf?"

The rancher is gettin' pretty ticked off by this point, but he picks him up again and shows him the horse's mouth.

"Nice mouf, can I see her twat?"

Totally mad as fire at this point, the rancher grabs him under his arms and rams the midget's head as far as he can up the horse's twat, pulls him out, and slams him on the ground.

The midget gets up, sputtering and coughing.

"Perhapth I should rephwase that—can I thee her wun awound a widdle bit?"

# Man/Woman

A man walks into a bar, and after a while picks up a girl. They go back to his place and start a bit of foreplay.

But the guy stops and says, "Listen, give me a sixty-eight."

Bemused, the girl says, "What the f***'s a sixty-eight?"

He says, "Give me a blow job and I'll owe you one!"

•

This man is sitting in a bar and notices two lovely women across the way. He calls the bartender over and says, "I'd like to buy those two ladies a drink."

The bartender replies, "It won't do you any good."

The man, with a confused look on his face, says, "It doesn't matter, I want to buy those women a drink."

The bartender delivers the drinks to the ladies and the ladies acknowledge the drink with a nod of their heads. About a half-hour later, the man approaches the women and says, "I'd like to buy you two another drink."

The women both reply, "It won't do you any good."

The man says, "I don't understand. What do you mean it won't do me any good?"

The first lady says, "We're lesbians."

The man replies, "Lesbians? What are lesbians?"

The second woman replies, "Lesbians . . . We like to lick pussies."

The man says, "Bartender, three beers for us lesbians."

•

A company in the Foreign Legion had spent three years in the Sahara Desert never having seen a woman. They finally decide to send one private on vacation to the nearest town to spend some time with a woman and tell them all about it. After a week the private comes back all happy and relaxed. The whole company crowds around him, waiting to hear of his great escapades.

"And on the third day . . ." he began.

"No! No! Start with the first day," everyone yells out in chorus.

"And on the third day," the private continues, "she asked me to stop so she could go to the bathroom . . ."

•

An old maid wanted to travel by bus to the pet cemetery with the remains of her cat. As she boarded the bus, she whispered to the driver, "I have a dead pussy."

The driver pointed to the woman in the seat behind him and said, "Sit with my wife. You two have a lot in common."

•

## WHAT WOMEN WOULD DO
## IF THEY HAD A PENIS FOR A DAY

10. Get ahead faster in corporate America.

9. Get a blow job.

8. Find out what is so fascinating about beating the meat.

7. Pee standing up while talking to other men at a urinal.

6. Determine *why* you can't hit the bowl consistently.

5. Find out what it's like to be on the other end of a surging orgasm.

4. Touch yourself in public without thought as to how improper it may seem.

3. Jump up and down naked with an erection to see if it feels as funny as it looks.

2. Understand the scientific reason for the light refraction that occurs between a man's eyes and the ruler situated next to his member that causes two inches to be added to the final measurement.

1. Repeat number 9.

•

## WHAT MEN WOULD DO
## IF THEY HAD A VAGINA FOR A DAY

10. Immediately go shopping for zucchini and cucumbers.

9. Squat over a handheld mirror for an hour and a half.

8. See if they could finally do splits.

7. See if it's truly possible to launch a Ping-Pong ball twenty feet.

6. Cross their legs without rearranging their crotch.

5. Get picked up in a bar in less than 10 minutes . . . *before* closing time.

4. Have consecutive multiple orgasms and still be ready for more without sleeping first.

3. Go to the gynecologist for a pelvic exam and ask to have it recorded on video.

2. Sit on the edge of the bed and pray for breasts, too.

1. Finally find that damned G-spot.

•

Late one night a woman was walking home when a man grabbed her and dragged her into the bushes.

"Help me! Help me!" she screamed. "I'm being robbed!"

"You ain't being robbed," her attacker interrupted. "You're being screwed!"

The woman looked down at her attacker as he unzipped his jeans. "If you're screwing me with that," she fumed, "I *am* being robbed!"

•

A farmer has a farm up the coast of California. Unfortunately, there are no women around. He gets rather desperate, and decides to try out an old mule.

He puts a stepladder behind the mule, lowers his pants, but then the mule walks forward. The farmer gets down off the ladder, moves it forward, and tries again, with the same outcome. This process goes on for about five more times, until he finally gets the idea to lead the mule up to the ocean, so the mule can't walk away. When he gets on the ladder again, he hears a cry for help out to sea, and sees a drowning woman flailing her arms.

He jumps off the ladder, swims out to rescue her, and drags her back in. The woman is totally nude, beautiful, and stacked as well.

After he revives her and nurses her back to health, she gazes into his eyes with her limpid blue eyes, and says, "Oh, sir! I'm so thankful to you for saving my life! I'll do anything to repay you! Anything!!"

So he says to her: "Could you hold that mule for me?"

•

After the tourist had been served in a Las Vegas cocktail lounge, he beckoned the waitress back and said quietly, "Miss, y'all sure are a luvly, luvly lady. Can ah persuade y'all to give me a piece of ass?"

"Lord, that's the most direct proposition I've ever had!" gasped the girl.

Then she looked around the room, smiled, and added, "Sure, why not? You're nice-lookin', too, and it's pretty slow here right now, so why don't we just slip away up to my room?"

When the pair returned half an hour later, the man sat down at the same table and the waitress asked, "Will there be anything else, sir?"

"Why yes," replied the southern gentleman. "Ah sure 'preciate what y'all just did for me; it was real sweet and right neighborly, but where ah come from in Tennessee we lack our bourbon real cold, so ah still need to trouble y'all for a piece uh ass for mah drink."

•

A woman and her boyfriend are out having a few drinks. While they're sitting there having a good time together, she starts talking about this really great new drink. The more she talks about it, the more excited she gets, and starts trying to talk her boyfriend into having one. After a while he gives in and lets her order the drink for him. The bartender brings the drink and puts the following on the bar: a saltshaker, a shot of Baileys, and a shot of lime juice. The boyfriend looks at the items quizzically and the woman explains.

"First, you put a bit of the salt on your tongue. Next, you drink the shot of Baileys and hold it in your mouth. And finally, you drink the lime juice."

So, the boyfriend, trying to go along and please her, goes for it. He puts the salt on his tongue—salty but OK. He drinks the shot of Baileys—smooth, rich, cool, very pleasant. He thinks, "This is OK." Finally, he picks up the lime juice and drinks it. In one second, the sharp lime taste hits. At two seconds, the Baileys curdles. At three seconds, the salty, curdled, bitter taste hits. This triggers his gag reflex, but being manly, and not wanting to disappoint his girlfriend, he swallows the now nasty drink.

When he finally chokes it down, he turns to his girlfriend and says, "Jesus, what do you call that drink?"

She smiles widely at him and says, "Blow Job."

•

A man is sitting on a train across from a busty blonde wearing a tiny miniskirt. Despite his efforts, he is unable to stop staring at the top of the woman's thighs. He realizes she has gone without underwear.

The blonde realizes he is staring and inquires, "Are you looking at my pussy?"

"I'm sorry," replies the man, and promises to avert his eyes.

"It's quite all right," replies the woman. "It's very talented. Watch this, I'll make a kiss to you." Sure enough, the pussy blows him a kiss.

The man, who is getting really interested, inquires what else the wonder pussy can do. "I can also make it wink," says the woman. The man stares in amazement as the pussy winks at him.

"Come and sit next to me," suggests the woman, patting the seat. The man moves over and is asked, "Would you like to stick a couple of fingers in?"

Stunned, the man replies, "F*** me! Can it whistle as well?"

•

A professor was giving a lecture on "Involuntary Muscular Contractions" to his first-year medical students. Realizing that this was not the most riveting subject, the professor decided to lighten the mood slightly.

He pointed to a young woman in the front row and said, "Do you know what your asshole is doing while you're having an orgasm?"

She replied, "He's probably golfing with his friends."

•

Pierre, a brave French fighter pilot, takes his girlfriend, Marie, out for a pleasant little picnic by the River Seine.

It's a beautiful day and love is in the air. Marie leans over to Pierre and says: "Pierre, kiss me!" Our hero grabs a bottle of Merlot and splashes it on Marie's lips.

"What are you doing, Pierre?" says the startled Marie.

"I am Pierre the fighter pilot! When I have red meat, I like to have red wine!"

She smiles and they start kissing. When things begin to heat up a little, Marie says, "Pierre, kiss me lower."

Our hero tears her blouse open, grabs a bottle of Chardonnay, and starts pouring it all over her breasts.

"Pierre! What are you doing?" asks the bewildered Marie.

"I am Pierre the fighter pilot! When I have white meat, I like to have white wine!"

They resume their passionate interlude and things really steam up. Marie leans close to his ear and whispers, "Pierre, kiss me lower!"

Our hero rips off her underwear, grabs a bottle of Cognac, and pours it in her lap. He then strikes a match and lights it on fire.

Marie shrieks and dives into the river. Standing waist-deep in the water, she throws her arms upward and screams furiously, "PIERRE, WHAT IN THE HELL DO YOU THINK YOU'RE DOING?"

Our hero stands up, defiantly, and says, "I am Pierre the fighter pilot! When I go down, I go down in flames!"

•

Marty was walking down the street when he saw his friend and yelled to him, "John, how are you?"

John replied, "Don't call me John. Call me Lucky."

"Why should I call you Lucky?"

John proceeded to tell him that he had been standing on the corner of 52nd Street and Third Avenue, when he stepped off the curb just as a two-ton safe fell from the twentieth floor. It landed right where he had been standing an instant earlier.

The man said, "My God, you certainly are lucky. That will be your name from now on."

A few weeks later they bumped into each other again, and Marty said, "Lucky, how are you?"

To which came the reply, "Don't call me Lucky. Call me Lucky, Lucky."

Marty said, "Tell me now, why I should call you Lucky, Lucky?" Then he was told that Lucky had been bumped from a flight to Miami that was later hijacked to Cuba.

Marty agreed, "You certainly are Lucky, Lucky."

The next time they met, Marty shouted, "Lucky, Lucky, how are you?"

To which the reply was, "Don't call me Lucky, Lucky. Call me Lucky, Lucky, Lucky."

Marty said, "Why?"

Lucky, Lucky, Lucky said, "Just last week I took my girlfriend to a hotel room for a matinee, and we made such a commotion that the chandelier over the bed came down and landed right on her cunt."

Marty said, "But what's so lucky about that?"

To which came the reply, "Ten seconds earlier, it would have bashed in my head."

•

A wedding occurred in Ireland. To keep tradition going, everyone gets extremely drunk, and the bride's and groom's families get in a huge fight and begin wrecking the reception room and generally kicking the living daylights out of each other. The police get called in to break up the fight.

The following week, all members of both families appear in court. The fight continues in the courtroom until the judge finally brings calm with the use of his gavel, shouting, "Silence in court!"

The courtroom goes silent and Paddy, the best man, stands up and says, "Judge, I was the best man at the wedding, and I think I should explain what happened."

The judge agrees and asks Paddy to take the stand. Paddy begins his explanation by telling the court that it is traditional in an Irish wedding that the best man gets the first dance with the bride. The judge says, "Okay."

"Well," says Paddy, "after I had finished the first dance, the music kept going, so I continued dancing to the second song, and after that the music kept going and I was dancing to the third song, when all of a sudden the groom leapt over the table, ran toward us, and gave the bride an unmerciful kick right between her legs."

Shocked, the judge instantly responds, "God, that must have hurt!"

"Hurt?!" Paddy replies. "He broke three of my fingers!"

•

Help to Understand the Opposite Sex

This should help you to communicate a little better with the opposite sex. Just so we understand each other better!

### DICTIONARY FOR DECODING
### WOMEN'S PERSONAL ADS:

| | |
|---|---|
| *40-ish* | *49* |
| *Adventurous* | *Slept with everyone* |
| *Athletic* | *No breasts* |
| *Average-looking* | *Moooo* |
| *Beautiful* | *Pathological liar* |
| *Emotionally secure* | *On medication* |
| *Feminist* | *Fat* |
| *Free spirit* | *Junkie* |
| *Friendship first* | *Former slut* |
| *New-Age* | *Body hair in the wrong places* |
| *Old-fashioned* | *No BJs* |
| *Open-minded* | *Desperate* |
| *Outgoing* | *Loud and embarrassing* |

| | |
|---|---|
| *Professional* | *Bitch* |
| *Voluptuous* | *Very fat* |
| *Large frame* | *Hugely fat* |
| *Wants soul mate* | *Stalker* |

## WOMEN'S ENGLISH:

1. Yes = No
2. No = Yes
3. Maybe = No
4. We need = I want
5. I am sorry = You'll be sorry
6. We need to talk = You're in trouble
7. Sure, go ahead = You better not
8. Do what you want = You will pay for this later
9. I am not upset = Of course I am upset, you moron!
10. You're certainly attentive tonight = Is sex all you ever think about?

## MEN'S ENGLISH:

1. I am hungry = I am hungry
2. I am sleepy = I am sleepy
3. I am tired = I am tired
4. Nice dress = Nice cleavage!
5. I love you = Let's have sex now
6. I am bored = Do you want to have sex?
7. May I have this dance? = I'd like to have sex with you
8. Can I call you sometime? = I'd like to have sex with you
9. Do you want to go to a movie? = I'd like to have sex with you
10. Can I take you out to dinner? = I'd like to have sex with you
11. I don't think those shoes go with that outfit = I'm gay

•

A man goes into a pub. The barmaid asks what he wants. "I want to put my head between your tits, and lick the sweat off," he replies.

"You dirty bastard!" shouts the barmaid. "Get out before I get my husband." The man apologizes and says he will never do it again. The barmaid, disgusted, accepts his apology and asks what he wants again.

"I want to pull down your panties, spread cottage cheese between your ass cheeks, and lick it off," he replies.

"What?!" screams the barmaid. "That's it, you're barred, you dirty, filthy, perverted bastard, GET OUT NOW!" Once again the man apologizes, and says he will never, ever do it again.

"Right. I'll give you one last chance," says the barmaid. "Now, what do you want?"

"I want to turn you upside down, fill your pussy with Guinness, and drink it all out of you."

The barmaid screams, starts crying, and runs upstairs to her husband, who is sitting down watching the telly. "What's up, love?" says the husband.

"There's this disgusting man downstairs! When I asked him what he wanted, he said that he wanted to put his head between my tits and lick the sweat off," she says in a flood of tears.

"What?! He's a dead man!" shouts the husband, getting out of his chair.

"Then he said he wanted to pull down my panties, spread cottage cheese between my ass cheeks, and lick it off!" screams the wife.

"Right, he's going to need a body bag, the bastard!" shouts the husband, rolling up his sleeves and picking up a baseball bat.

"Then he said he wanted to turn me upside down, fill

my pussy with Guinness, and drink it out of me," she concludes.

When he hears this, the husband puts the baseball bat down and sits back down in his chair.

"Aren't you going to do something?!" shouts the wife in hysterics.

"Listen, love, I'm not messing with someone who can drink fourteen pints of Guinness . . ."

•

A man is walking down the street and enters a clock and watch shop.

While looking around, he notices a drop-dead gorgeous blond female shop assistant behind the counter.

He walks up to her, unzips his pants, and places his cock on the counter.

"What the hell do you think you are doing?" she asks. "This is a clock shop, not a cock shop!"

The man replies: "Yes, I know it is—I want your two hands and face put on this!"

•

A woman came home just in time to find her husband in bed with another woman.

With superhuman strength borne of fury, she dragged her husband down to the garage and put his manhood in a vise. She then secured it tightly. Next she picked up a hacksaw.

The husband, terrified, screamed, "Stop! Stop! You're not going to cut it off, are you?"

The wife, with a gleam of revenge in her eye, said, "Nope. You are. I'm going to set the garage on fire."

•

Ask any man what a woman's ultimate fantasy is and they will tell you: to have two men at once. According to a recent sociological study, this is true. However, most men do not realize that in this fantasy, one man is cooking and the other is cleaning.

•

George and Harriet decided to celebrate their 25th wedding anniversary with a trip to Las Vegas. When they entered the hotel/casino and registered, a sweet young woman dressed in a very short skirt became very friendly. George brushed her off. Harriet objected, "George, that young woman was nice, and you were so rude."

"Harriet, she's a prostitute."

"I don't believe you. That sweet young thing?"

"Let's go up to our room and I'll prove it."

In their room, George called down to the desk and asked for "Bambi" to come to room 1217. "Now," he said, "you hide in the bathroom with the door open just enough to hear us, OK?"

Soon, there was a knock on the door. George opened it and Bambi walked in, swirling her hips provocatively. George asked, "How much do you charge?"

"One hundred twenty-five dollars basic rate, one hundred dollars tips for special services."

Even George was taken aback. "One hundred twenty-five! I was thinking more in the range of twenty-five dollars."

Bambi laughed derisively. "You must really be a hick if you think you can buy sex for that price."

"Well," said George, "I guess we can't do business. Good-bye."

After she left, Harriet came out of the bathroom. She said, "I just can't believe it!"

George said, "Let's forget it. We'll go have a drink, then eat dinner."

At the bar, as they sipped their cocktails, Bambi came up behind George, pointed slyly at Harriet, and said, "See what you get for twenty-five dollars?"

•

When her husband passed away, the wife put the usual death notice in the newspaper, but added that he had died of gonorrhea. Once the daily newspapers had been delivered, a good friend of the family phoned and complained bitterly, "You know very well that he died of diarrhea, not gonorrhea."

Replied the widow, "Yes, I know that he died of diarrhea, but I thought it would be better for posterity to remember him as a great lover rather than the big shit that he really was."

•

A wife says to her friend, "Our sex life stinks."

Her friend says, "Do you ever watch your husband's face when you're having sex?"

She says, "Once, and I saw rage."

Her friend says, "Why would he be angry during sex?"

The wife says, "Because he was looking through the window at us."

•

Two couples go away for the weekend. The two guys, Jack and Bill, have decided to try to persuade their wives to do a bit of partner swapping for the night. After several drinks that night, they succeed.

Jack knows it's that time of the month for his wife and the thought of Bill not knowing this makes him smile. The guys agree that when they sit around the breakfast table the following morning, they will tap their teaspoon on the side of their coffee mug to indicate the number of times that they did it with the other's wife.

The next morning they are all at the breakfast table, slightly hungover and quite uncomfortable, when Jack proudly taps his teaspoon three times against his coffee mug. After a brief moment of thinking, Bill takes his teaspoon and taps it once on the strawberry jam and three times on the peanut butter!

•

Maria had just gotten married and, being a traditional Italian, she was still a virgin. So, on her wedding night, they were staying at her mother's house and she was nervous. But her mother reassured her. "Don't worry, Maria. Tony's a good man. Go upstairs and he'll take care of you."

So up she went. When she got upstairs, Tony took off his shirt and exposed his hairy chest. Maria ran downstairs to her mother and said, "Mama, Mama, Tony's got a big hairy chest."

"Don't worry, Maria," said the mother, "all good men have hairy chests. Go upstairs. He'll take good care of you."

So up she went again. When she got up in the bedroom, Tony took off his pants, exposing his hairy legs. Again, Maria ran downstairs to her mother. "Mama, Mama, Tony took off his pants and he's got hairy legs!"

"Don't worry. All good men have hairy legs. Tony's a good man. Go upstairs and he'll take good care of you."

So up she went again. When she got up there, Tony took off his socks and on his left foot he was missing three toes. When Maria saw this, she ran downstairs. "Mama, Mama, Tony's got a foot and a half!"

"Stay here and stir the pasta," said the mother. "This is a job for Mama."

•

Every day, a male coworker walks up very close to a lady standing at the coffee machine, inhales a deep breath of air, and tells her that her hair smells nice.

After a week of this, she can't stand it anymore, and takes her complaint to a supervisor in the personnel department to file a sexual harassment grievance against him.

The human resources supervisor is puzzled and asks, "What's sexually threatening about a coworker telling you your hair smells nice?"

The woman replies, "It's Ernie, the midget."

•

An old farmer was having trouble getting his bull to breed with the cows, and was lamenting the fact to a few of his friends down at the local beer hall.

One of them said, "Ya know, Ben, I used to have the same trouble with my bull, but I got it fixed really quickly."

"How did you get it fixed?" asked the farmer.

"Well, I just dipped my finger in the cow's vagina and rubbed it all over the bull's nose and he got right after her," his friend said.

Ben went home to the farm and decided to try it. He grabbed a cow, dipped his fingers in the cow's vagina, and rubbed it all around the bull's nose.

The bull got a rip-roaring boner and jumped on the cow immediately. Ben was impressed. That night, Ben got into bed with his wife and couldn't get the effect on the bull out of his mind. As she lay sleeping, Ben dipped his fingers into his wife's vagina. Feeling that it was nice and wet, he rubbed it all around his nose and got a rip-roaring hard-on. He quickly shook his wife awake and cried out, "Honey, look!"

She rolled over, turned on the light, and said, "You mean you woke me up in the middle of the night just to show me that you have a nosebleed?"

•

Morris wakes up in the morning. He has a massive hangover and can't remember anything he did last night. He picks up his bathrobe from the floor and puts it on. He notices there's something in one of the pockets, and it turns out to be a bra. He thinks, "Hell, what happened last night?" He walks toward the bathroom and finds panties in the other pocket of his robe. Again he thinks, "What happened last night, what have I done? Must have been a wild party." He opens the bathroom door, walks in, and has a look in the mirror. He notices a little string hanging out of his mouth and his only thought is, "Please, if there's a God, please let this be a teabag."

•

"And will there be anything else, sir?" the bellboy asked after setting out an elaborate dinner for two.

"No thank you," the gentleman replied. "That will be all."

As the young man turned to leave, he noticed a beautiful satin negligee on the bed. "Anything for your wife?" he asked.

"Yeah! That's a good idea," the fellow said. "Please bring up a postcard."

•

A young male virgin, a shy college freshman, was lucky enough to have a roommate who was considerably more experienced with the opposite sex. When the bashful boy broke down and explained his predicament, his roommate offered to set him up with the campus floozy. "Just take her out to dinner and a show, and then let nature take its course," he explained. "This girl really knows how to go from there."

The roommate arranged the date as promised, and the freshman took the coed out for a delightful evening of dining and dancing. On the way home, he parked his car in a dark lane, broke out in shakes and a cold sweat, and blurted out: "God, I sure would like to have a little pussy."

"I would, too," the girl sighed. "Mine's the size of a bucket!"

•

Two women were having lunch together, and discussing the merits of cosmetic surgery. The first woman says, "I need to be honest with you, I'm getting a boob job."

The second woman says, "Oh, that's nothing, I'm thinking of having my asshole bleached!"

To which the first replies, "Whoa, I just can't picture your husband as a blond!"

•

Nina and Liz are having a conversation during their lunch break. Nina asks, "So, Liz, how's your sex life these days?"

Liz replies, "Oh, you know. It's the usual, Social Security kind."

"Social Security?" Nina asks quizzically.

"Yeah, you get a little each month, but it's not enough to live on."

•

A guy was on his first date with a notoriously loose girl. She was immediately receptive to his foreplay after they parked. The petting went on and he put his hand in her panties. She seemed to be enjoying it, but suddenly objected, "Ouch! That ring is hurting me!"

"That's no ring. That's my watch!"

•

A guy's eating in a restaurant and spots a gorgeous woman sitting all alone. He calls over his waiter and says, "Send that woman a bottle of your most expensive champagne, on me."

The waiter quickly brings the champagne over to the woman, and says, "Ma'am, this is from the gentleman over there."

She says to the waiter, "Please tell him that for me to accept this champagne, he better have a Mercedes in his garage, a million dollars in the bank, and eight inches in his pants."

The waiter delivers the message, and the guy says, "Please go back and tell her I have two Mercedes in my garage, three million dollars in the bank, but I haven't even met her . . . so why the f*** would I cut off four inches?"

•

In a biology class, the professor was discussing the high glucose levels found in semen. A young female freshman raised her hand and asked, "If I understand, you're saying there is a lot of glucose in male semen?"

"That's correct," responded the professor, going on to add statistical info.

Raising her hand again, the girl asked, "Then why doesn't it taste sweet?"

After a stunned silence, the whole class burst out laughing.

The poor girl's face turned bright red; she picked up her books without a word and walked out of class, never to return. As she was going out the door, the totally straight-faced professor answered her question: "It doesn't taste sweet because the taste buds for sweetness are on the tip of your tongue."

•

### Top ten answers men would love to give to women's stupid questions:

1. No, we can't be friends, I just want you for sex.
2. The dress doesn't make you look fat—it's all that ice cream and chocolate you eat that makes you look fat.
3. You've got no chance of me calling you.
4. No, I won't be gentle.
5. Of course you have to swallow.
6. Well, yes, actually, I do this all the time.
7. I hate your friends.
8. I have every intention of using you, and no intention of speaking to you after tonight.
9. I'd rather watch a porno.
10. Eat it? It took me ten beers to get up the courage to look at it.

•

### FOR WOMEN:

*Penis breath, a lover's dread,*
*Is what you get when you give head.*
*Unpleasant as it tends to be,*

*Be grateful that he doesn't pee.*
*It's times like this, you wonder why*
*You bothered reaching for his fly.*
*But it's too late, can't be a tease,*
*Accept the facts, get on your knees.*
*You know you've got a job to do,*
*So open wide and shove it through.*
*Lick the tip, then take it all.*
*Don't drag your teeth or he might bawl.*
*Slide up and down, use your tongue,*
*And feel the precum start to run.*
*Your jaw it aches, your neck is numb,*
*So when the hell's he gonna cum?*
*Just when you can't take anymore,*
*You hear your lover's mighty roar.*
*And when he hits that real high note,*
*You feel it oozing down your throat.*
*Salty, fishy, sticky stuff,*
*Okay already, that's enough.*
*Let's switch, you say, before you gag,*
*And what revenge, you're on the rag!*

### FOR MEN:

*Eating out and chewing down,*
*But tonight I'm not out on the town.*
*Tonight I'm served a seafood dish,*
*Well at the least it tastes like fish.*
*Time to overcome my fears,*
*As she drags me down there by my ears,*
*To feast upon her hairy pie,*
*Where pubes and stubble jab my eye.*
*She lies back and moans and then softly sighs,*
*I can't help thinking about scampi and fries.*

*Don't lick too low, move up a bit,*
*Got to be careful or I'm in the shit.*
*Nibble, lick, caress, and stroke,*
*The things I do just for a poke.*
*Up, down, and right a bit,*
*Where the hell does she keep her clit?*
*I'll never find it here like this,*
*Fanny design just takes the piss.*
*To find my way around her twat,*
*I'll need a torch and miner's hat.*
*I think my tongue is failing me,*
*Christ, I hope she doesn't pee.*
*I've been licking her minge for years and years.*
*I wish I could breathe through my ears.*
*God, I hope that she comes quick,*
*Since my neck's developing a crick.*
*I'm sweating like I've got a fever,*
*Under the covers, eating beaver,*
*I must have hit the right spot at last,*
*'Cuz her screams are gaining volume fast,*
*Her thighs clamp tight around my head,*
*And her screams scare the neighbors out of their beds.*
*She's coming at last and making a racket,*
*Her thighs crushing my head like a discarded fag packet.*
*I'm choking and spluttering but she doesn't care,*
*That my mouth is full of fish-flavored hair.*
*And that my face is smothered in thick fanny batter*
*And juices that taste like a seafood platter.*
*But she thinks it's funny,*
*And starts taking the piss,*
*But she soon stops her laughing,*
*When I move in for a kiss.*

•

Abie and Rosalie were courting. Rosalie's mother told her daughter that Abie must not touch her until they were wed. One night, Abie said to Rosalie, "Dahlink, every night you kiss me good night and I can't touch you. Won't you give me just one little peekaboo, please?"

So, Rosalie lifted up her skirt, pulled her panties down and back up, and quickly lowered her skirt. Abie said to Rosalie, "Vot a vunder!" Rosalie blushed.

This went on every night for a week. Rosalie would lift up her skirt and Abie would say, "Rosalie, vot a vunder!"

Rosalie, shy, but obviously pleased, would blush.

After a week of it, Rosalie shyly asked Abie, "Every night, Abie, you ask, 'Rosalie, let me have a little peekaboo.' When I give you a little peekaboo, you say, 'Vot a vunder, Rosalie.' Why do you say that, Abie?"

Abie answered: "Rosalie, vot a vunder your guts don't fall out!"

•

A bodybuilder picks up a blonde at a bar and takes her home with him. He takes off his shirt and the blonde says, "What a great chest you have."

The bodybuilder tells her, "That's one hundred pounds of dynamite, baby."

He takes off his pants and the blonde says, "What massive calves you have."

The bodybuilder tells her, "That's one hundred pounds of dynamite, baby."

He then removes his underwear and the blonde goes running out of the apartment, screaming in fear.

The bodybuilder puts his clothes back on and chases after her. He catches up to her and asks why she ran out of the apartment like that.

The blonde replies, "I was afraid to be around all that dynamite after I saw how short the fuse was."

•

A daily newspaper recently conducted a poll of male readers to see what exactly each enjoyed from having oral sex performed on them:

Seven percent said they most enjoyed the sensations.

Five percent confessed that their chief enjoyment came from the sense of domination.

A staggering 88 percent said that they really enjoyed the peace and quiet.

•

The Texas preacher rose with an angry red face. "Someone in this congregation has spread a rumor that I belong to the Ku Klux Klan. This is a horrible lie and one which a Christian community cannot tolerate. I am embarrassed and do not intend to accept this. Now, I want the party who did this to stand and ask forgiveness from God and this Christian family."

No one moved.

The preacher continued, "Do you have the nerve to face me and admit this is a falsehood? Remember, you will be forgiven and in your heart you will feel glory. Now stand and confess your transgression."

Again all was quiet.

Then, slowly, a drop-dead gorgeous blonde with a body that would stop traffic rose from the third pew. Her head was bowed and her voice quivered as she spoke.

"Reverend, there has been a terrible misunderstanding. I never said you were a member of the Klan. I simply told a couple of my friends that you were a wizard under the sheets!"

•

A guy goes into a bar and says, "Gimme a gin and tonic." The bartender reaches under the bar and places an apple on it.

The guys look at the apple skeptically and the bartender says, "Go ahead. Take a bite." The guy takes a bite and incredibly, it tastes like gin. The bartender smiles and says, "Turn it around." He does and it tastes like tonic. He finishes the apple.

A few minutes pass and the guy says, "Gimme a vodka and orange juice." The bartender once again reaches behind the bar and places another apple on it.

The guy eyes the suspicious fruit and the bartender says, "Go ahead. Take a bite." He bites into it and he can't believe it. It tastes like vodka. The bartender smiles and says, "Turn it around." The guys turns the apple and it tastes like orange juice, so he finishes the apple.

Just then, a beautiful woman walks past the two men and the guy says to the bartender, "You know, I could sure go for some pussy about now." The bartender nods, reaches below the bar and produces yet another apple. The guy says, "No way, man."

The bartender says, "Go ahead. Take a bite."

He takes a bite and angrily spits out the apple. "Yuck!! That tastes like shit, man!!!" The bartender smiles and says, "Turn it around."

•

A guy picked this woman up in a nightclub and took her home. While they were walking home he didn't say a thing.

"You're not the communicative type, are you?" she said as they were undressing.

"Nah," he replied, and pulled out his old fella. "I do all my talking with this."

"Damn," said the girl as she leaned forward to look. "You don't have much to say, do you?"

•

A man was carrying two babies, one in each arm, while waiting for a train. Along came this woman and, seeing the two cute babies, she asked the man, "Aren't they cute, what are their names?"

The man, giving the lady an angry look, replied, "I don't know."

The lady asked, "Which is a boy and which is a girl?"

The man looking angrier than before replied, "I don't know."

The woman then started to scold the man, "What kind of a father are you?"

The man replied, "I am not their father. I am just a condom salesman, and these are two complaints that I am taking back to my company!"

•

Her grandmother said: "Sita here ana letame tella you about those-a young boys.

"He's agonna try ana kiss you, you are agonna likea dat, but don'ta let him do that.

"He's agonna try ana kiss your breasts, you are agonna likea dat too, but don'ta let him do that.

"But most important, he's agonna try ana lay on topa you, you are gonna likea dat, but don'ta let him do that. Doing thata willa disgrace the family."

With that bit of advice, the granddaughter went on her date.

The next day she told Grandma that her date went just like she had predicted:

"Gramma, I didn't let him disgrace the family. When he tried, I just turned over, got on top of him, and disgraced *his* family!"

•

This married couple is sitting in a fine restaurant when the wife looks over at a nearby table and sees a man in a drunken stupor.

The husband asks, "I notice you've been watching that man for some time now. Do you know him?"

"Yes," she replies. "He is my ex-husband, and he's been drinking like that since I left him seven years ago."

"Remarkable," the husband replies. "I wouldn't think anybody could celebrate that long."

•

A woman was walking down the street when she was approached by a man.

The man said, "I must have you right now! I'll drop five hundred dollars on the ground at your feet and in the time it takes for you to pick it up, I can have my way with you from behind!"

The woman thought it over, and told the man to wait a minute.

She called her girlfriend on her cell phone and told her about the man's proposition.

Her girlfriend said, "When he drops the five hundred dollars on the ground, I'm sure you can pick it up and run before he gets his pants down. Call me back and tell me what happened."

An hour and a half later the lady called her girlfriend back.

"What happened?" the girlfriend asked.

"The son of a bitch had the five hundred dollars in dimes!"

•

A woman was in bed with her lover when she heard her husband opening the front door.

"Hurry," she said, "stand in the corner."

She rubbed baby oil all over him, then dusted him with talcum powder.

"Don't move until I tell you," she said. "Pretend you're a statue."

"What's this?" the husband inquired as he entered the room.

"Oh, it's a statue," she replied. "The Smiths bought one and I liked it so I got one for us, too."

No more was said, not even when they went to bed. Around 2 A.M. the husband got up, went to the kitchen, and returned with a sandwich and a beer.

"Here," he said to the statue, "have this. I stood like that for two days at the Smiths' and nobody offered me a damned thing."

•

A man walked into the lingerie department of Macy's and shyly walked up to the woman behind the counter and said, "I'd like to buy a bra for my wife."

"What type of bra?" asked the clerk.

"Type?" inquired the man. "There's more than one type?"

"Look around," said the saleslady, as she showed a sea of bras in every shape, size, color, and material imaginable. "Actually, even with all of this variety, there are really only four types of bras to choose from."

Relieved, the man asked about the types. The saleslady replied: "There are the Catholic, the Salvation Army, the Presbyterian, and the Baptist types. Which one would you prefer?"

Now totally befuddled, the man asked about the differences between them.

The saleslady responded, "It is all really quite simple. The Catholic type supports the masses. The Salvation Army type lifts the fallen. The Presbyterian type keeps them staunch and upright. And the Baptist makes mountains out of molehills."

•

Have you ever wondered why A, B, C, D, DD, E, F, G, and H are the letters used to define bra sizes? If you have wondered why, but couldn't figure out what the letters stood for, it is about time you became informed!

{A} Almost Boobs.
{B} Barely There.
{C} Can't Complain!
{D} Dang!
{DD} Double Dang!
{E} Enormous!
{F} Fake.
{G} Get a Reduction.
{H} Help me, I've fallen and I can't get up!

They forgot the German bra. Holtzemfromfloppen!

•

## HOW TO MAKE A WOMAN HAPPY
### *It's not difficult.*
*To make a woman happy, a man only needs to be:*

1. a friend
2. a companion
3. a lover
4. a brother
5. a good father
6. a master
7. a chef
8. an electrician
9. a carpenter
10. a plumber
11. a mechanic
12. a decorator
13. a stylist

14. a sexologist
15. a gynecologist
16. a psychologist
17. a pest exterminator
18. a psychiatrist
19. a healer
20. a good listener
21. an organizer
22. very clean
23. sympathetic
24. athletic
25. warm
26. attentive
27. gallant
28. intelligent
29. funny
30. creative
31. tender
32. strong
33. understanding
34. tolerant
35. prudent
36. ambitious
37. capable
38. courageous
39. determined
40. true
41. dependable
42. passionate

*without forgetting to:*

43. give her compliments regularly
44. love shopping

45. be honest
46. be very rich
47. not stress her out
48. not look at other girls

*and at the same time, must also:*

49. give her lots of attention, but expect little yourself
50. give her lots of time, especially time for herself
51. give her lots of space, never worrying about where she goes

*and finally, it is very important to never forget:*

52. birthdays, anniversaries, arrangements she makes

### HOW TO MAKE A MAN HAPPY

1. Feed him.
2. F*** him.
3. Shut the f*** up.

•

The banker saw his old friend Tom, an eighty-year-old rancher, in town. Tom had lost his wife a year or so before and rumor had it that he was marrying a "mail order" bride.

Being a good friend, the banker asked Tom if the rumor was true. Tom assured him that it was. The banker then asked Tom the age of his new bride-to-be. Tom proudly said, "She'll be twenty-one in November."

Now the banker, being the wise man that he was, could see that the sexual appetite of a young woman could not be satisfied by an eighty-year-old man. Wanting his old friend's remaining years to be happy, the banker tactfully suggested that Tom should consider getting a hired hand to help him out on the ranch, knowing nature would take its own course. Tom thought this was a good idea and said he would look for one that afternoon.

About four months later, the banker ran into Tom in town again. "How's the new wife?" asked the banker.

Tom proudly said, "Oh, she's pregnant."

The banker, happy that his sage advice had worked out, continued, "And how's the hired hand?"

Without hesitating, Tom said, "She's pregnant, too."

•

Researcher: "Excuse me, madam, I'm conducting a survey."

Woman: "Yes, what is it about?"

Researcher: "We are asking people what they think about sex on the television."

Woman: "Very uncomfortable, I would imagine!"

•

A rich man and a poor man have the same wedding anniversary. They're both on Madison Avenue shopping for their wives. The poor man says to the rich man, "What'd you get your wife this year?"

The rich man says, "A Mercedes and a huge diamond ring."

The poor man says, "Why'd you get her both?"

The rich man says, "If she doesn't like the ring, she can take it back happy."

The poor man says, "OK. That works."

The rich man says, "Well, what did you get *your* wife?"

The poor man says, "A pair of slippers and a dildo."

The rich man says, "Why'd you get her a pair of slippers and a dildo?"

The poor man says, "If she doesn't like the slippers, she can go f*** herself!"

•

At the card shop, a woman was spending a long time looking at the cards, finally shaking her head, "No."

A clerk came over and asked, "May I help you?"

"I don't know," said the woman. "Do you have any 'Sorry I laughed at your dick' cards?"

•

A guy calls the hospital. He says, "You gotta send help! My wife's going into labor!"

The nurse says, "Calm down. Is this her first child?"

He says, "No! This is her f***ing husband!"

•

The pretty coed nervously asked the doctor to perform an unusual operation: the removal of a large chunk of green wax from her navel. Looking up from the ticklish task, the physician asked, "How did this happen?"

"Let me put it this way, Doc," the girl began. "My boyfriend likes to eat by candlelight."

•

One day Little Susie got her "monthly bleeding" for the first time in her life. Having failed to understand what was going on and being really frightened, she decided to share her trouble with little Johnny.

Johnny's face grew serious and he said, "You know, I'm not a doctor, but it looks like someone just ripped your balls off!"

•

"Doc, I think my son has gonorrhea," a patient told his urologist on the phone. "The only woman he's screwed is our maid."

"OK, don't be hard on him. He's just a kid," the medic soothed. "Get him in here right away, and I'll take care of him."

"But, Doc. I've been screwing the maid, too, and I've got the same symptoms he has."

"Then you come in with him and I'll fix you both up," replied the doctor.

"Well," the man admitted, "I think my wife now has it, too."

"Son of a bitch!" the physician roared. "That means we've all got it!"

•

A woman with really hairy underarms boards a crowded bus. Unable to find a seat, she settles for hanging on to one of the poles. A drunk man next to her stares at her for three minutes, then tells her, "I love a woman who does aerobics."

The woman replies angrily, "I don't *do* aerobics!"

The drunk man looks at the woman and says, "Then how did you get your leg up so high?"

•

Two coworkers are leaving the office. "I can't wait to get home," says one of them. "As soon as I walk in the door, I'm going to rip my wife's panties right off."

"I know the feeling," the other says. "I've been working so much lately sometimes it feels like I'm not even married any longer."

"No, I'm serious," says the first. "They're killing me."

•

An old man was on the beach and walked up to a beautiful girl in bikini.

"I want to feel your breasts. I'll give you twenty dollars for that," he said.

"Get away from me, you crazy old man!" she said.

"What about one hundred dollars?" he offered.

"Get lost, I say," she fumed.

"I'll give you two hundred dollars," he persisted.

She paused to think about it and then came to her senses. "No, I said."

"Five hundred dollars if you let me feel your breasts," he asked.

She thought, "Well, he is old and seems harmless, and five hundred dollars is a lot of money." She said, "OK, but only for a minute."

She loosened her bikini top, the man slid his hands in and started moaning, "Oh my God! Oh my God!"

She asked, "Why do you keep saying 'Oh my God'?"

"OH MY GOD! OH MY GOD! Where am I ever going to get five hundred dollars?! Oh my God . . . !"

•

A man goes into a cocktail lounge and approaches a blonde sitting by herself.

Man: "May I buy you a cocktail?"

Lady: "No thank you, alcohol is bad for my legs."

Man: "Sorry to hear that. Do they swell?"

Lady: "No, they open!"

•

A man standing in line at a checkout counter of a grocery store was surprised when a very attractive woman standing behind him said, "Hello!" Her face was beaming.

He gave her that "who are you" look and couldn't remember ever having seen her before.

Noticing his look, she figured she had made a mistake and apologized. "Look," she said, "I'm really sorry, but when I first saw you, I thought you were the father of one of my children," and walked out of the store.

The guy was dumbfounded and thought to himself, "What the hell is the world coming to? Here is an attractive woman who can't keep track of who fathers her children!"

Then he got a little panicky. "I don't remember her," he thought but, MAYBE . . . during one of the wild parties he had been to when he was in college, perhaps he did father her child!

He ran from the store, caught up with her in the parking lot, and asked, "Are you the girl I met at a party in college and then we got really drunk and had wild crazy sex on the pool table in front of everyone?"

"No," she said with a horrified look on her face. "I'm your son's second-grade teacher!"

•

A certain young man finally got a date with a female of somewhat questionable morals who lived in his apartment complex. To prepare for his big date, the young man went up onto the roof of his apartment building in order to tan himself. Not wanting any tan lines to show, he sunbathed in the nude.

Unfortunately, he fell asleep while on the roof and managed to get a sunburn on his "tool." But, determined not to miss his date, he put some lotion on his manhood and wrapped it in gauze.

When the hot date showed up at his apartment, the young man treated her to a home-cooked dinner, after which they went into the living room to watch a video. During the video, however, the young man's sunburn started acting up again. He asked to be excused, went into the kitchen, and poured a tall, cool glass of milk. He then placed his sunburned member in the milk and experienced immediate relief of his pain.

The date, meanwhile, wondering what he was doing, wandered into the kitchen, to see him with his penis immersed in a glass of milk. Upon seeing this, she exclaimed, "So that's how you guys load those things!"

•

A man is walking home from work one day, and he sees a new ice cream shop on the street. Since it is a hot day, he goes in.

"Afternoon, dear, what flavors of ice cream do you sell?"

"Oh, we sell every flavor. Even ones you have never heard of. You name it, we sell it!" the shopkeeper replies.

Deciding to test this claim, he asks for a fish-flavored ice cream, and he is presented with exactly that, a definite fish flavor, yet still nice. Amazed, he walks home eating his fish-flavored ice cream!

The next day the man passes the shop again and can't resist going in again.

"Afternoon, I'll have a curried egg–flavored ice cream, please," says the man.

"Right you are," replies the shopkeeper.

The shopkeeper turns around, picks up a cone, and fills it with ice cream. Handing it to the man, she says, "Try that."

The man tastes it and replies, "That's incredible, it tastes just like curried egg."

The man goes home and thinks all night of a flavor the shopkeeper will not be able to reproduce. So the next day the man goes into the shop again.

"Hi, today I want a pussy-juice-flavored ice cream, please," says the man.

"Right you are," replies the shopkeeper.

The shopkeeper turns around, picks up a cone, and fills it with ice cream. Handing it to the man, she says, "Try that."

The man tastes it and replies, "Yuck, that's terrible, it tastes just like shit."

The shopkeeper replies, "Try again, but this time take shorter licks."

•

A man goes to a bar in London for a couple of drinks. As he is sitting alone and drinking, he notices a sexy woman sitting in a corner, alone and staring at him. He gulps down a couple of whiskeys and, gathering courage, goes up to her and says, "Excuse me. . . . My name is Harvey. Can I sit here and buy you a drink?"

The woman agrees and soon both of them are drinking away like good old friends. Then, after everything is through, Harvey and the lady walk out of the bar. Again gathering courage, and slightly drunk, he asks her, "Eschcuse me, can we have sex please?"

The lady says, "Well I don't mind, but you see I'm on my menstrual cycle."

"No problem," says Harvey. "You proceed on your menstrual cycle, I will follow you in my Honda Accord!"

•

A girl had invented a device to cause any car that passed in front of her house to suddenly break down, but couldn't find any practical way to profit from it. So, thinking clearly, she set up the device, and as the cars passed the house and broke down, she'd offer the man in the car a place to stay for the night.

Then, as soon as the man was asleep, he'd be jarred awake by her with his penis in her mouth, and she'd hold a sign up that read "$50 or I'll bite hard!" Of course, usually the guy would pay and she'd let him go.

Well, one day a Scotsman broke down, and had to stay the night. Sure enough, he felt something between his legs at night, and there she was with him in her mouth and holding the sign—"$50 or I'll bite hard!"

The Scotsman just smiled and said, "You pay me one hundred dollars or I'll piss."

•

A woman sends her clothing out to the Chinese laundry. When it comes back, there are still stains in her panties. The next week she encloses a note to the Chinaman that says, "Use more soap on panties."

This goes on for several weeks, the woman sending the same note to the laundry. Finally, fed up, the Chinaman responds with his own note that says, "Use more paper on ass."

•

At a news conference, a journalist said to the politician running for the presidency, "Your secretary said publicly that you have a small penis. Would you please comment on this?"

"The truth is," replied the politician, "that she has a big mouth."

•

A woman finally got divorced from a rather nasty and egotistical man. She then married someone whom she felt would treat her with more love and kindness.

When her ex-husband happened to meet her on the street one day, he couldn't overcome his usual tendencies, and asked her sarcastically, "So, how does that new husband of yours like screwing a used pussy?"

"He likes it just fine," she replied, "once he gets past the used part."

•

A concerned patient visited his physician and asked him if masturbation was harmful.

"No," the doctor said. "Not if you don't do it too often."

"How about three times a day?"

"That seems a little excessive. Why don't you get yourself a girl?"

"I've got a girl," the patient said.

"I mean a girl you can live with and sleep with."

"I've got one like that."

"Then why in heaven's name do you masturbate three times a day?"

"Oh," said the patient disgustedly, "she doesn't like it during mealtimes."

•

A woman decides to have a face-lift for her fiftieth birthday. She spends $15,000 and feels pretty good about the results. On her way home, she stops at a newsstand to buy a paper. Before leaving, she says to the clerk, "I hope you don't mind my asking, but how old do you think I am?"

"About thirty-two," is the reply.

"Nope! I'm exactly fifty," the woman says happily.

A little while later she goes into a restaurant and asks the counter girl the very same question. The girl replies, "I'd guess about twenty-nine."

The woman replies with a big smile, "Nope, I'm fifty."

Now she's feeling really good about herself. She stops in a drugstore on her way down the street. She goes up to the counter to get some mints and asks the clerk this burning question. The clerk responds, "Oh, I'd say thirty."

Again she proudly responds, "I'm fifty, but thank you!"

While waiting for the bus to go home, she asks an old man waiting next to her the same question. He replies, "Lady, I'm seventy-eight and my eyesight is going. Although, when I was young, there was a surefire way to tell how old a woman was. It sounds very forward, but it requires you to let me put my hands under your bra. Then, and only then, can I tell you *exactly* how old you are."

They wait in silence on the empty street until her curiosity gets the best of her. She finally blurts out, "What the hell, go ahead." He slips both of his hands under her blouse and begins to feel around very slowly and carefully. He bounces and weighs each breast and he gently pinches each nipple.

He pushes her breasts together and rubs them against each other. After a couple of minutes of this, she says, "Okay, okay . . . How old am I?"

He completes one last squeeze of her breasts, removes his hands, and says, "Madam, you are fifty."

Stunned and amazed, the woman says, "That was incredible, how could you tell?"

The old man says, "Promise you won't get mad?"

"I promise I won't," she says.

"I was behind you in line at the restaurant."

•

An Amish woman and her daughter were riding in an old buggy one cold, blustery January day. The daughter said to the mother, "My hands are freezing cold."

The mother replied, "Put your hands between your legs. The body heat will warm them up."

So the daughter did, and her hands warmed up. The next day, the daughter was riding in the buggy with her boyfriend. The boyfriend said, "My hands are freezing cold."

The daughter replied, "Put them between my legs, they'll warm up."

The next day, the boyfriend was again driving in the buggy with the daughter. He said, "My nose is freezing cold."

The daughter replied, "Put it between my legs. It will warm up."

He did, and his nose warmed up. The next day, the boyfriend was once again driving with the daughter and he said, "My penis is frozen solid."

The daughter replied, "Put it between my legs. It will warm up."

The next day, the daughter was driving in the buggy with

her mother, and she said to her mother, "Have you ever heard of a penis?"

The slightly concerned mother said, "Sure, why do you ask?"

The daughter said, "Well, they make one hell of a mess when they thaw out!"

•

A man took his girlfriend to bed for the first time. He was working away very hard, but she was not responding at all. Finally, in exasperation, he asked her, "What's the matter?"

She said, "It's your organ. I don't think it's big enough."

To which the man replied, "Well, I didn't think I'd be playing in a cathedral!"

•

A wealthy man had been having an affair with an Italian woman for several years.

One night, during one of their rendezvous, she confided in him that she was pregnant.

Not wanting to ruin his reputation or his marriage, he said he would pay her a large sum of money if she would go to Italy to secretly have the child. If she stayed in Italy to raise the child, he would also provide child support until the child turned 18. She agreed, but asked how he would know when the baby was born. To keep it discreet, he told her to simply mail him a postcard and write "spaghetti" on the back. He would then arrange for child support payments to begin.

One day, about nine months later, he came home to his confused wife.

"Honey," she said. "You received a very strange postcard today."

"Oh, just give it to me and I'll explain it," he said.

The wife obeyed and watched as her husband read the card, turned white, and fainted.

On the card was written: "Spaghetti, Spaghetti, Spaghetti. Two with meatballs, one without."

•

A businessman returned home from the office with some startling gossip. He informed his wife that he'd heard that their neighbor in apartment 4-G had f***ed every woman in the building except one.

"That's right," replied the wife. "It's that stuck-up Mrs. Jones on the eighth floor!"

•

The sexy housewife was built so well the TV repairman couldn't keep his eyes off her. Every time she came in the room, he'd nearly jerk his neck right out of joint looking at her.

When he'd finished, she paid him and said, "I'm going to make an unusual request. But you have to first promise me you'll keep it a secret."

The repairman quickly agreed and she went on.

"Well, it's kind of embarrassing to talk about, but while my husband is a kind, decent man, he has a certain physical weakness. A certain disability. Now, I'm a woman and you're a man . . ."

The repairman salivated in anticipation, "Yes, yes!"

"And since I've been wanting to, ever since you came in the door . . ."

"Yes, yes!"

"Would you please help me move the refrigerator?"

•

Two guys, one old and one young, are pushing their carts around Home Depot when they collide.

The old guy says to the young guy, "Sorry about that. I'm looking for my wife, and I guess I wasn't paying attention to where I was going."

The young guy says, "That's OK. It's a coincidence. I'm looking for my wife, too. I can't find her and I'm getting a little desperate."

The old guy says, "Well, maybe we can help each other. What does your wife look like?"

The young guy says, "Well, she is twenty-seven years old, tall, with red hair, blue eyes, long legs, big boobs, and she's wearing tight white shorts. What does your wife look like?"

The old guy says, "Doesn't matter—let's look for yours."

•

A man proposes a one-dollar bar bet to a well-endowed young lady that, despite her dress being buttoned to the neck, he can touch her breasts, without touching her clothes.

Since this doesn't seem remotely possible, she is intrigued and accepts the bet. He steps up, cups his hands around her breasts, and squeezes firmly.

With a baffled look, she says, "Hey, you touched my clothes."

And he replies, "OK, here's your dollar . . ."

•

Jack was enthusiastic over the new girl he had found at the neighborhood massage parlor. "You like three-way broads," he told his friend. "Well, this one knows four ways."

"What's the fourth way?" asked his friend.

"She lets you go down on her."

•

One Monday morning a mailman is walking the neighborhood on his usual route. As he approaches one of the homes, he notices that both cars are in the driveway. His wonder is cut short by Bob the homeowner coming out with a load of empty beer and liquor bottles.

"Wow, Bob, looks like you guys had a hell of a party last night," the mailman comments.

Bob, in obvious pain, replies, "Actually we had it Saturday

night; this is the first I have felt like moving since four Sunday morning. We had about fifteen couples from around the neighborhood over for some holiday cheer and got a bit wild. Hell, we even got so drunk that around midnight we started playing WHO AM I."

The mailman thinks a moment and says, "How do you play that?"

Bob continues between hungover gasps, "Well, all the guys go in the bedroom and we come out one at a time with a sheet covering us and only our 'units' showing through a hole in the sheet. Then the women try to guess who it is."

The mailman laughs and says, "Damn, I am sorry I missed that."

"Probably a good thing you did," Bob responds, "since your name was guessed at least four or five times."

•

A woman walks into her doctor's office, scared of the strange development that appeared on the inside of her thighs—a green spot on each. "They won't wash off, they won't scrape off, and they seem to be getting worse."

The doctor assures her he'll get to the bottom of this, and that she needn't worry until tests come back. He sends her home.

A few days later, the woman's phone rings. Much to her relief, it's the doctor. She immediately begs to know what's going on with those spots.

"You're perfectly healthy—there's no problem. But I'm wondering: Is your boyfriend a Harley guy?" the doctor asks.

"Yes, how did you know?"

"Tell him his earrings aren't real gold."

•

A young man, anxious for some sexual exercise, picked up a hot little number in Central Park, not realizing that she was a nymphomaniac. He took her to a hotel. After six times, she was screaming for more. After the seventh, exhausted, he slipped out of the room on the pretense of buying cigarettes. He stopped in the men's room, unzipped his fly, and couldn't find anything.

In a panic, he reached inside his shorts. It was still there, but tiny and all drawn up. In a soothing voice he whispered, "It's all right. You can come out now. She's not here!"

•

And God created Woman, and gave her three breasts.

God spoke, saying to her, "I have created thee as I see fit. Is there anything about thee that thou would prefer differently?"

And Woman spoke, saying, "Lord, I am not made to birth whole litters. I need but two breasts."

And God said, "Thou speak wisely, as I have created thee with wisdom."

There was a crack of lightning and a lingering odor of ozone, and it was done, and God stood holding the surplus breast in His hands.

"What are you going to do with that useless boob?" Woman exclaimed.

And so it was, God created Man.

•

Adam was hanging around the Garden of Eden feeling very lonely.

So God asked him, "What's wrong with you?"

Adam said he didn't have anyone to talk to.

God said that He was going to make Adam a companion and that it would be a woman.

He said, "This pretty lady will gather food for you, she will cook for you, and when you discover clothing, she will wash it for you. She will always agree with every decision you make and she will not nag you, and will always be the first to admit she was wrong when you've had a disagreement. She will praise you! She will bear your children, and never ask you to get up in the middle of the night to take care of them. She will *never* have a headache, and will freely give you love and passion whenever you need it."

Adam asked God, "What will a woman like this cost?"

God replied, "An arm and a leg."

Then Adam asked, "What can I get for a rib?"

Of course, the rest is history . . .

•

Girl in movie theater: "The man next to me is masturbating!"

Girlfriend: "Ignore him."

"I can't; he's using my hand!"

•

Boudreaux fell in love with Marie and asked her to marry him. Marie was very naive and uninformed about the birds and the bees.

Boudreaux was a poor fisherman and could not afford to take time off for a honeymoon.

So, the night that they were married, they retired to his little shack on the bayou.

When Boudreaux was undressing, Marie said, "Oh, Boudreaux! What dat is?"

Boudreaux, thinking very quickly and being sensitive to Marie's naiveté, said, "Marie, my love, I am the only man in the world wit one of dese." And then he proceeded to show her what it was for, and Marie was happy!

The next morning Boudreaux went off to fish as usual. When he returned home that evening, Marie was on the front porch obviously upset about something.

"Boudreaux, you told me that you were the only man in the world with one of those, and I saw Thibodeaux, our friend, changing his clothes behind the fish shed, and he had one, too."

Thinking fast, Boudreaux said, "Oh, Marie, darling, Thibodeaux is my very best friend. I had two of dem things, so I gave him one. He is the only other man in the world with one of doze."

Marie, being very very naive, accepted his answer and they did their thing again that night.

Boudreaux went off to fish again the next morning, and when he returned home, Marie was very upset, and stamping her foot on the porch. Boudreaux said, "Marie, what is the matter now?"

"Boudreaux, you gave Thibodeaux the best one of dem thangs!!"

•

## THE GUYS' RULES

*At last a guy has taken the time to write this all down—*
*finally, the guys' side of the story.*
*We always hear "The Rules."*
*Now here are the rules from the male side.*
*These are our rules!*
*Please note . . . These are all numbered "1" on purpose!*

1. Men are not mind readers.
1. Learn to work the toilet seat. You're a big girl. If it's up, put it down. We need it up, you need it down. You don't hear us complaining about you leaving it down.
1. Sunday sports. It's like the full moon or the changing of the tides. Let it be.
1. Shopping is not a sport. And no, we are never going to think of it that way.
1. Crying is blackmail.
1. Ask for what you want. Let us be clear on this one:

Subtle hints do not work! Strong hints do not work!
Obvious hints do not work! Just say it!

1. Yes and no are perfectly acceptable answers to almost
   every question.
1. Come to us with a problem only if you want help solv-
   ing it. That's what we do. Sympathy is what your girlfriends are for.
1. A headache that lasts for 17 months is a problem. See
   a doctor.
1. Anything we said 6 months ago is inadmissible in an
   argument. In fact, all comments become null and void
   after 7 days.
1. If you won't dress like the Victoria's Secret girls, don't
   expect us to act like soap opera guys.
1. If you think you're fat, you probably are. Don't ask us.
1. If something we said can be interpreted two ways and
   one of the ways makes you sad or angry, we meant the
   other one.
1. You can either ask us to do something or tell us how
   you want it done. Not both. If you already know best
   how to do it, just do it yourself.
1. Whenever possible, please say whatever you have to
   say during commercials.
1. Christopher Columbus did not need directions and neither do we.
1. All men see in only 16 colors, like Windows default set-
   tings. Peach, for example, is a fruit, not a color. Pump-
   kin is also a fruit. We have no idea what mauve is.
1. If it itches, it will be scratched. We do that.
1. If we ask what is wrong and you say "nothing," we will
   act like nothing's wrong. We know you are lying, but it
   is just not worth the hassle.

1. If you ask a question you don't want an answer to, expect an answer you don't want to hear.
1. When we have to go somewhere, absolutely anything you wear is fine. Really.
1. Don't ask us what we're thinking about unless you are prepared to discuss such topics as sex, cars, the shotgun formation, or basketball.
1. You have enough clothes.
1. You have too many shoes.
1. I am in shape. Round is a shape!
1. Thank you for reading this. Yes, I know, I have to sleep on the couch tonight; but did you know men really don't mind that? It's like camping.

•

What were the first words Eve used when she beheld Adam?

"Don't stick that thing in me!"

•

A young man went into a sex shop to buy some condoms and a salesgirl approached him.

Salesgirl: "Can I help you, sir?"

Young man: "Yes, I want to buy some condoms."

Salesgirl: "What size do you need, sir?"

Young man: "I didn't realize they came in different sizes. I don't know what size I would need."

Salesgirl: "May I hold your penis to tell what size you would need?"

As she was holding the penis, she called for assistance:

"Give me a SMALL one . . ."

"Wait! Make it MEDIUM . . ."

"Wait! Make it LARGE . . ."

"Shit! Give me a TISSUE!!!"

•

The subway car was packed. It was rush hour, and many people were forced to stand. One particularly cramped woman turned to the man behind her and said, "Sir, if you don't stop poking me with your thing, I'm going to the cops!"

"I don't know what you're talking about, miss—that's just my paycheck in my pocket."

"Oh really," she spat. "Then you must have some job, because that's the fifth raise you've had in the last half hour!"

•

This couple is in bed getting busy when the girl places the guy's hand onto her pussy. "Put your finger in me," she asks him. So he does without hesitation, and she starts moaning. "Put two fingers in," she says. So in goes another one. She's really starting to get worked up when she says, "Put your whole hand in!"

The guy's like, "OK!"

So he has his entire hand in, when she says, moaning aloud, "Put both your hands inside of me!!!" So the guy puts both of his hands in! "Now clap your hands," commands the girl.

"I can't," says the guy.

The girl looks at him and says, "See, I told you I had a tight pussy!"

•

A guy walking down the street sees a woman with perfect breasts.

He says to her, "Hey, miss, would you let me bite your breasts for one hundred dollars?"

"Are you nuts?" she replies. And keeps walking away.

He turns around, runs around the block, and gets to the corner before she does.

"Would you let me bite your breasts for one thousand dollars?" he asks again.

"Listen, sir, I'm not that kind of woman. Got it?"

So the guy runs again around the next block and faces her again: "Would you let me bite your breasts just once for ten thousand dollars?"

She thinks about it for a while and says, "Hmmm, ten thousand dollars, eh? OK, just once, but not here. Let's go to that dark alley over there."

So they go to that alley and she takes off her blouse to reveal the most perfect breasts in the world. As soon as he sees them he jumps on them and starts caressing them, fondling them, kissing them, burying his face in them . . . but not biting.

In the end the woman gets all annoyed and asks: "Are you gonna bite them or what?"

"Nah," he replies. "Costs too much."

•

## PEEING

(Written to a woman who accidentally walked into a men's restroom . . .)

Please don't feel bad, lady. It wasn't you entering the men's washroom that caused that guy to pee on the guy next to him. Hell, we do that all the time. It's rare for us guys to ever hit what we're aiming for. Sometimes I go into the washroom, start to pee, and then just start spinning around; just so I'll make sure I hit something.

You see, something you ladies should understand by now is that men's penises have a mind of their own. A guy can go into a bathroom stall because all the urinals are being used, take perfect aim at the toilet, and his penis will still manage to pee all over the roll of toilet paper, down his left pant leg, and onto his shoe. I'm telling ya, those little buggers can't be trusted.

After being married 28 years, my wife has me trained.

I'm no longer allowed to pee like a man, standing up. I am required to sit down and pee. She has convinced me that this is a small price to pay. Otherwise, if she had gone to the toilet one more time at night and either sat on a pee-soaked toilet seat, or fell right into the toilet because I forgot to put the seat down, she was going to kill me in my sleep.

Now another thing us guys don't usually like to talk about is a real problem, and you ladies need to be understanding. It's the dreaded "morning wood."

Most mornings us guys wake up with two things: a tremendous desire to pee, and a penis so hard you could cut diamonds with it. Well, no matter how hard you try, you can't get that thing to bend, and if it don't bend you can't aim. Well, hell, if you can't aim you have no choice but to pee all over the wallpaper and that damn fuzzy toilet seat cover you women insist on putting on the toilet.

And by the way, when you use those damn fuzzy toilet seat covers, the friggin' toilet seat won't stay up by itself. So that means we have to use one hand to hold up the toilet seat and the other hand to try to control ourselves for that perfect aim.

Now sometimes, when you're newly married, you think you can get the toilet seat with that damn fuzzy thing to stay up. You jam it back and compress that fuzzy thing until the seat stays there. OK, so you start to pee, but then that compressed fuzz starts to decompress and without warning that damn toilet seat comes flying down and tries to whack off your weenie.

So us guys will not lift a toilet seat with a fuzzy, it's just not safe. I tried to delicately explain this morning situation to my wife. I told her, "Look, it won't bend." She said, "Sit down like I told you to do all the rest of the time." OK. I tried sitting down on the toilet with "morning wood."

Well, it's very hard to get it bent under the toilet seat, and before I could manage it, I had peed all over the bath towels hanging on the wall across the room. Now, even if you are sitting and you can get it forced down under the toilet seat, when you start to pee the pee shoots out from the crack between the bottom of the toilet seat and the top of the bowl. You pee all over the back of your knees and it runs down the back of your legs onto that damn matching fuzzy horseshoe rug you keep putting on the floor in front of the toilet.

I have found the only effective maneuver to deal with this morning urinary dilemma is to assume the flying Superman position lying over the toilet seat.

This takes a great deal of practice, perfect balance, and split-second precision but it's the only sure way to get all the pee in the bowl during the first morning pee.

So you ladies have to understand that we men are not totally to blame. We are sensitive to your concerns about hygiene and bathroom cleanliness, but there are times when things just get beyond our control.

It's not our fault, it's just Mother Nature.

Now, if it was Father Nature, there wouldn't have been a problem!

# Drunks

Two drunks are trying to figure out how to get some alcohol for free. They only have a dollar in change between them. "I've got it, follow me," says the first man.

They go to a hot dog stand and buy a hot dog and throw away the bun.

"We'll go into a bar and order drinks, and when the bartender asks for money, I'll unzip my fly and pull out the hot dog. You drop to your knees and pretend to suck me off."

The second man agrees to this and they start their rounds.

When they get to the bar, they sit down and have a beer. The bartender tells them, "That will be three dollars."

The first man stands up and upzips his fly. The second man drops to his knees and starts sucking on the hot dog.

"Get the hell out of here!" screams the bartender.

They run out and go to another bar and order drinks and when the bartender asks for money, the first man unzips his fly, and the second man drops to his knees. The bartender throws them out.

After the sixth bar, the second man complains, "Man, this isn't working out so well, my knees are killing me!"

"You think you've had it bad," the first man exclaims. "I lost the hot dog four bars ago!"

•

Two drunks are standing at a whorehouse door. The first drunk says, "I heard half these broads have the clap and that

none of them would think twice about stealing
we've got."

The second drunk says, "Not so loud, or ~~they~~
us in."

·

A large woman wearing a sleeveless sundress walked into a
bar in Dublin, Ireland.

She raised her right arm, revealing a huge, hairy armpit
as she pointed to all the people sitting at the bar and asked,
"What man here will buy a lady a drink?"

The bar went silent as the patrons tried to ignore her. But
down at the end of the bar, a pie-eyed drunk slammed his
hand down on the counter and bellowed, "Give the ballerina
a drink!"

The bartender poured the drink and the woman chugged
it down. She turned to the patrons and again pointed around
at all of them, revealing the same hairy armpit, and asked,
"What man here will buy a lady a drink?"

Once again, the same little drunk slapped his money down
on the bar and said, "Give the ballerina another drink!"

The bartender approached the little drunk and said, "Tell
me, it's your business if you want to buy the lady a drink, but
why do you keep calling her the ballerina?"

The drunk replied, "Any woman who can lift her leg that
high has got to be a ballerina!"

·

A drunk is in a bar, lying on the floor and looking the worse
for wear. Other patrons decide to be Good Samaritans and
take him home.

They pick him up off the floor, and drag him out the door.
On the way to the car, he falls down three times.

When they get to his house, they help him out of the car

he falls down four more times. Mission accomplished, they prop him against the doorjamb and ring the doorbell.

"Here's your husband!" they exclaim proudly.

"Where's his wheelchair?" asks the puzzled wife.

•

A drunk walks out of a bar with a key in his hand, stumbling back and forth.

A cop on the beat sees him and approaches. "Can I help you, sir?"

"Yessh! Ssssomebody ssstole my car," the man replies.

The cop asks, "Where was your car the last time you saw it?"

"It wasss on the end of thisshh key," the man replies.

About that time, the cop looks down and sees the man's wiener is hanging out of his fly for all the world to see.

He asks the man, "Sir, are you aware that you are exposing yourself?"

Momentarily confused, the drunk looks down at his crotch and, without missing a beat, blurts out, "I'll be damned! My girlfriend's gone, too!!!!"

•

Paddy staggered home very late after another evening with his drinking buddy. He took off his shoes to avoid waking his wife, Brigid.

He tiptoed as quietly as he could toward the stairs leading to their upstairs bedroom, but misjudged the bottom step. As he caught himself by grabbing the banister, his body swung around and he landed heavily on his rump. A whiskey bottle in each back pocket broke and made the landing especially painful.

Managing not to yell, Paddy sprang up, pulled down his pants, and looked in the hall mirror to see that his butt cheeks were cut and bleeding. He managed to quietly find a full box of Band-Aids and began putting a Band-Aid as best he could on each place he saw blood. He then hid the now almost empty Band-Aid box and shuffled and stumbled his way to bed.

In the morning, Paddy woke up with searing pain in both his head and butt to find Brigid staring at him from across the room. She said, "You were drunk again last night, weren't you, Paddy?"

Paddy said, "Why do you say such a mean thing?"

"Well," Brigid said, "it could be the open front door, it could be the broken glass at the bottom of the stairs, it could be the drops of blood trailing through the house, it could be your bloodshot eyes, but mostly . . . it's all those Band-Aids stuck on the hall mirror."

# Political

I miss Bill Clinton! He was the closest thing we ever got to having a black man as President.

  Number 1—He played the sax.

  Number 2—He smoked weed.

  Number 3—He had his way with ugly white women.

  Even now? Look at him . . . his wife works, and he doesn't! And he gets a check from the government every month.

•

Manufacturers announced today that they will be stocking America's shelves this week with "Clinton Soup," in honor of one of the nations' most distinguished men. It consists primarily of a weenie in hot water.

•

Chrysler Corporation is adding a new car to its line to honor Bill Clinton. The Dodge Drafter will be built in Canada.

•

When asked what he thought about foreign affairs, Clinton replied, "I don't know, I never had one."

•

The Clinton-revised judicial oath: "I solemnly swear to tell the truth as I know it, the whole truth as I believe it to be, and nothing but what I think you need to know."

•

Clinton will be recorded in history as the only president to do hanky-panky between Bushes.

•

*A plan to save bankrupt airlines . . .*

*Replace all female flight attendants with some good-looking strippers! What the hell, the attendants have gotten old and haggard-looking.*

*They don't even serve food anymore, so what's the loss?*

*The strippers would double, triple, perhaps quadruple the alcohol consumption and get a "party atmosphere" going in the cabin. And, of course, every heterosexual businessman in this country would start flying again, hoping to see naked women.*

*Muslims would be afraid to get on the planes for fear of seeing naked women. Hijackings would come to a screeching halt, and the airline industry would see record revenues.*

*Why the hell didn't Bush think of this?*

*Why do I still have to do everything myself?*

*Sincerely,*

*Bill Clinton*

•

One day in the future, Dick Cheney had a heart attack and died.

He immediately went to hell, where the devil was waiting for him.

"I don't know what to do here," said the devil. "You are on my list, but I have no room for you. You definitely have to stay here, so I'll tell you what I'm going to do. I've got a couple of folks here who weren't quite as bad as you. I'll let one of them go, but you have to take their place. I'll even let *you* decide who leaves."

Cheney thought that sounded pretty good, so the devil opened the door to the first room.

In it was Ted Kennedy and a large pool of water. He kept diving in and surfacing empty-handed. Over, and over, and over, he dove in and surfaced with nothing. Such was his fate in hell.

"No," Cheney said. "I don't think so. I'm not a good swimmer, and I don't think I could do that all day long."

The devil led him to the door of the next room.

In it was Al Gore with a sledgehammer and a room full of rocks. All he did was swing that hammer, time after time after time.

"No, this is no good, I've got this problem with my shoulder. I would be in constant agony if all I could do was break rocks all day," commented Al.

The devil opened a third door.

Through it, Dick saw Bill Clinton, lying on the floor with his arms tied over his head, and his legs restrained in a spread-eagle pose.

Bent over him was Monica Lewinsky, doing what she did best.

Cheney looked at this in shocked disbelief, and finally said, "Yeah, man, I can handle this."

The devil smiled and said:

"OK, Monica, you're free to go."

•

Official Announcement:

The government today announced that it is changing its emblem from the eagle to a condom because it more accurately reflects the government's political stance. A condom allows for inflation, halts production, destroys the next generation, protects a bunch of pricks, and gives you a sense of security while you're actually being screwed.

Damn, it just doesn't get more accurate than that!

# Religion

A new young monk arrives at the monastery. He is assigned to help the other monks in copying the old canons and laws of the church by hand. He notices, however, that all of the monks are copying from copies, not from the original manuscript.

So the new monk goes to the head abbot to question this, pointing out that if someone makes even a small error in the first copy, it would never be noticed. In fact, that error would be continued in all of the subsequent copies.

The head monk says, "We have been copying from the copies for centuries, but you make a good point, my son."

So he goes down into the dark caves underneath the monastery where the original manuscript is held in archives in a locked vault that hasn't been opened for hundreds of years.

Hours go by and nobody sees the old abbot. The young monk gets worried and goes downstairs to look for him.

He sees him banging his head against the wall, and wailing, "We forgot the 'R,' we forgot the 'R.' " His forehead is all bloody and bruised and he is crying uncontrollably.

The young monk asks the old abbot, "What's wrong, Father?"

With a choking voice, the old abbot replies, "The word is celebrate. The word is celebRate."

•

An Irish daughter had not been home for over five years. Upon her return, her father cussed her. "Where have ye been all this time? Why'd ye not write to us, not even a line? Why didn't ye call? Can ye not understand what ye put yer old mum thru?"

The girl, crying, replied, "(*Sniff, sniff*) . . . Dad . . . I became a prostitute. . . ."

"Ye what!!? Out of here, ye shameless harlot! Sinner! You're a disgrace to this family."

"OK, Dad. . . . As ye wish. I just came back to give Mum this luxurious fur coat, title deed to a ten-bedroom mansion, plus a savings certificate for five million dollars. For me little brother this gold Rolex, and for ye, Daddy, the sparkling new Mercedes limited-edition convertible that's parked outside plus a membership to the country club. . . . (*takes a breath*) An invitation for ye all to spend New Year's Eve on board my new yacht in the Riviera, and . . ."

"Now what was it ye said ye had become?" says Dad.

Girl, crying again, "(*Sniff, sniff*) . . . A prostitute, Dad! (*Sniff, sniff*)"

"Oh! Be Jesus! Ye scared me half to death, girl! I thought ye said 'a Protestant.' Come here and give yer old man a big hug!"

•

An American golfer playing in Ireland hooked his drive into the woods. Looking for his ball, he found a little leprechaun flat on his back, a big bump on his head, and the golfer's ball beside him.

Horrified, the golfer got his water bottle from the cart and poured it over the little guy, reviving him.

"Arrgh! What happened?" the leprechaun asked.

"I'm afraid I hit you with my golf ball," the golfer says.

"Oh, I see. Well, ye got me fair and square. Ye get three wishes, so whaddya want?"

"Thank God, you're all right!" the golfer answers in relief. "I don't want anything, I'm just glad you're OK, and I apologize." And the golfer walks off.

"What a nice guy," the leprechaun says to himself. "I have to do something for him. I'll give him the three things I would want . . . a great golf game, all the money he ever needs, and a fantastic sex life."

A year goes by (as it does in stories like this), and the American golfer is back. On the same hole, he again hits a bad drive into the woods and the leprechaun is there waiting for him.

" 'Twas me that made ye hit the ball here," the little guy says. "I just want to ask ye, how's yer golf game?"

"My game is fantastic!" the golfer answers. "I'm an internationally famous golfer now." He adds, "By the way, it's good to see you're all right."

"Oh, I'm fine now, thank ye. I did that fer yer golf game, you know. And tell me, how's yer money situation?"

"Why, it's just wonderful!" the golfer states. "When I need cash, I just reach in my pocket and pull out hundred-dollar bills I didn't even know were there!"

"I did that fer ye also. And tell me, how's yer sex life?"

The golfer blushes, turns his head away in embarrassment, and says shyly, "It's OK."

"C'mon, c'mon now," urges the leprechaun, "I'm wanting to know if I did a good job. How many times a week?"

Blushing even more, the golfer looks around, then whispers, "Once, sometimes twice a week."

"What?" responds the leprechaun in shock. "That's all? Only once or twice a week?"

"Well," says the golfer, "I figure that's not bad for a Catholic priest in a small parish."

•

It was time for Father John's Saturday night bath, and the young nun, Sister Magdalene, had prepared the bathwater and towels just the way the old nun had instructed.

Sister Magdalene was also instructed not to look at Father John's nakedness if she could help it, do whatever he told her to do, and pray. The next morning, the old nun asked Sister Magdalene how the Saturday night bath had gone.

"Oh, Sister," said the young nun dreamily, "I've been saved."

"Saved? And how did that come about?" asked the old nun.

"Well, when Father John was soaking in the tub, he asked me to wash him, and while I was washing him, he guided my hand down between his legs where he said the Lord keeps the Key to Heaven."

"Did he now?" said the old nun evenly.

Sister Magdalene continued, "And Father John said that if the Key to Heaven fitted my lock, the portals of Heaven would be opened to me and I would be assured salvation and eternal peace. And then Father John guided his Key to Heaven into my lock."

"Is that a fact?" said the old nun more evenly.

"At first it hurt terribly, but Father John said the pathway to salvation was often painful and that the glory of God would soon swell my heart with ecstasy. And it did, it felt so good being saved."

"That wicked old bastard," said the old nun. "He told me it was Gabriel's Horn, and I've been blowing it for forty years."

•

Four Catholic ladies are having coffee together, discussing how important their children are. The first one tells her friends, "My son is a priest. When he walks into a room, everyone calls him 'Father.' "

The second Catholic woman chirps, "Well, my son is a bishop. Whenever he walks into a room, people say, 'Your Grace.' "

The third Catholic woman says smugly, "Well, not to put you down, but my son is a cardinal. Whenever he walks into a room, people say, 'Your Eminence.' "

The fourth Catholic woman sips her coffee in silence. The other three women give her this subtle, "Well . . . ?" She replies, "My son is a gorgeous, six foot two inch, hardbodied, well-hung, male stripper. Whenever he walks into a room, women say, 'My God. . . .' "

•

The new priest is nervous about hearing confessions, so he asks an older priest to sit in on his sessions. The new priest hears a couple of confessions, then the old priest asks him to step out of the confessional for a few suggestions.

The old priest suggests, "Cross your arms over your chest and rub your chin with one hand." The new priest tries this. The old priest suggests, "Try saying things like, 'I see,' 'Yes,' 'Go on,' 'I understand,' and 'How did you feel about that?' "

The new priest says those things, trying them out. The old priest says, "Now, don't you think that's a little better than slapping your knee and saying, 'No shit! What happened next?' "

•

The Internal Revenue Service sent their auditor (a nasty little man) to audit a synagogue. The auditor was doing all the checks, and then turned to the rabbi and said, "I noticed that you buy a lot of candles."

"Yes," answered the rabbi.

"Well, Rabbi, what do you do with the candle drippings?" he asked.

"A good question," noted the rabbi. "We actually save them up. When we have enough, we send them back to the candle maker. And every now and then, they send us a free box of candles."

"Oh," replied the auditor, somewhat disappointed that his question actually had a practical answer. So he thought he'd try another question, in his obnoxious way. "Rabbi, what about all these matzo purchases? What do you do with the crumbs from the matzo?"

"Ah, yes," replied the rabbi calmly, "we actually collect up the crumbs and send them in a box back to the manufacturer, and every now and then, they send a box of matzo balls."

"Oh," replied the auditor, thinking hard how to fluster the rabbi. "Well, Rabbi," he went on, "what do you do with all the foreskins from the circumcisions?"

"Yes, here, too, we do not waste," answered the rabbi. "What we do is save up all the foreskins. And when we have enough we actually send them to the Internal Revenue Service."

"Internal Revenue Service?" questioned the auditor in disbelief.

"Ah, yes," replied the rabbi, "Internal Revenue Service. And about once a year, they send us a little prick like you."

•

A married Irishman went into the confessional and said to his priest, "I almost had an affair with another woman."

The priest said, "What do you mean, almost?"

The Irishman said, "Well, we got undressed and rubbed together, but then I stopped."

The priest said, "Rubbing together is the same as putting it in. You're not to see that woman again. For your penance, say five Hail Mary's and put fifty dollars in the poor box."

The Irishman left the confessional, said his prayers, and

then walked over to the poor box. He paused for a moment and then started to leave. The priest, who was watching, quickly ran over to him, saying, "I saw that. You didn't put any money in the poor box!"

The Irishman replied, "Yeah, but I rubbed the fifty dollars on the box, and according to you, that's the same as putting it in."

•

Mother Superior was on her way to late morning prayers when she passed two novices just leaving early morning prayers, on their way to classes. As she passed the young ladies, Mother Superior said, "Good morning, ladies."

The novices replied, "Good morning, Mother Superior, may God be with you."

But after they had passed, Mother Superior heard one say to the other, "I think she got out of the wrong side of the bed this morning."

This startled Mother Superior, but she chose not to pursue the issue. A little farther down the hall, Mother Superior passed two of the sisters who had been teaching at the convent for several years. She greeted them with, "Good morning, Sister Martha, Sister Jessica, may God give you wisdom for our students today."

"Good morning, Mother Superior. Thank you, and may God be with you."

But again, after passing, Mother Superior overheard, "She got out of the wrong side of bed today." Baffled, she started to wonder if she had spoken harshly, or with an irritated look on her face. She vowed to be more pleasant. Looking down the hall, Mother Superior saw retired Sister Mary approaching, step by step, with her walker.

As Sister Mary was rather deaf, Mother Superior had plenty of time to arrange a pleasant smile on her face before greeting Sister Mary. "Good morning, Sister Mary. I'm so happy to see you up and about. I pray God watches over you today, and grants you a wonderful day."

"Ah, good morning, Mother Superior, and thank you. I see you got up on the wrong side of bed this morning." Mother Superior was floored!

"Sister Mary, what have I done wrong? I have tried to be pleasant, but three times already today people have said that about me."

Sister Mary stopped her walker, and looked Mother Superior in the face. "Oh, don't take it personally, Mother Superior. It's just that you're wearing Father Murphy's slippers."

•

Two Irishmen were sitting at a pub having beer and watching the brothel across the street.

They saw a Baptist minister walk into the brothel, and one of them said, "Aye, 'tis a shame to see a man of the cloth goin' bad."

Then they saw a rabbi enter the brothel, and the other Irishman said, "Aye, 'tis a shame to see that the Jews are fallin' victim to temptation as well."

Then they see a Catholic priest enter the brothel, and one of the Irishmen said, "What a terrible pity . . . one of the girls must be dying."

•

Drunk Ole Mulvihill staggers into a Catholic church, enters a confessional box, and sits down, but says nothing.

The priest coughs a few times to get his attention but Ole just sits there.

Finally, the priest pounds three times on the wall.

The drunk mumbles, "Ain't no use knockin', there's no paper on this side either."

•

Sister Margaret had been a model nun all her life. Then she was called to her reward. As she approached the pearly gates, Saint Peter said, "Hold on, Sister Margaret. Not so fast!"

"But I have been good all my life and dedicated to the work of the Lord from the time I was taken in as an infant by the sisters at the convent to my dying breath. I have lived for this moment!" Sister Margaret exclaimed in disbelief.

"That is just the problem," replied Saint Peter. "You never learned right from wrong, and to get into heaven, you must know the difference between right and wrong."

"Well, what can I do? I will do anything to get into heaven!" Sister Margaret pleaded.

"I am going to have to send you back down to Earth. When you get there, I want you to smoke a cigarette and call me when you are finished. We will discuss your situation then," ordered Saint Peter.

Sister Margaret returned to Earth, smoked a Camel, and then immediately called Saint Peter, coughing and hacking. "Saint Peter," she gasped, "I can hardly breathe, my mouth tastes terrible, my breath stinks, I feel dizzy, and I think I am going to throw up."

"Good!" replied the old saint. "Now you are finally getting a feel for right and wrong. Now go out tonight and drink some hard liquor and call me when you are ready."

Sister Margaret phoned Saint Peter immediately after taking several belts of Jack Daniel's. "Saint Peter . . . I feel woozy. That vile liquid burned my throat and nauseated me. It is all I can do to keep it down."

"Good, good! Now you are starting to see the difference between right and wrong," said Saint Peter with delight. "Tomorrow, I want you to seek out a man and know him in the Biblical sense. Afterward, call me."

A week passed before Sister Margaret called Saint Peter and left a message: "Yo, Pete, it's Peggy . . . it's gonna be a while."

•

A man wonders if having sex on the Sabbath is a sin because he is not sure if sex is work or play. He asks a priest for his opinion on this question.

The priest says, after consulting the Bible, "My son, after an exhaustive search I am positive sex is work and is not permitted on Sundays."

The man thinks, "What does a priest know of sex?"

He goes to a minister, a married man, experienced, for the answer. He queries the minister and receives the same reply, "Sex is work and not for the Sabbath!"

Not pleased with the reply, the man seeks out the ultimate authority, a man of thousands of years of tradition and knowledge—a rabbi.

The rabbi ponders the question and states, "My son, sex is definitely play."

The man replies, "Rabbi, how can you be so sure when so many others tell me sex is work?"

The rabbi softly speaks: "If sex were work, my wife would have the maid do it!"

•

An Arab had spent many days crossing the desert without finding a source of water. It got so bad that his camel died of thirst. He crawled through the sands, certain that he was breathing his last breath, when suddenly he saw a shiny object sticking out of the sand several yards ahead of him. He crawled to the object, pulled it out of the sand, and discovered that he had a Manischewitz wine bottle.

It looked like there might have been a drop or two left in the bottle, so he unscrewed the top—and out popped a genie.

But this was no ordinary genie.

This genie appeared to be a Hasidic rabbi, complete with black alpaca coat, black hat, side curls, and *tzitzies* (prayer shawl).

"Vell, kid," said the genie. "You know how it voiks. You got three wishes."

"I'm not going to trust you," said the Arab. "I'm not going to trust a Jewish genie!"

"Whaddya got to lose? Looks ta me you're a goner any-vay!"

The Arab thought about this for a minute, and decided that the genie was right.

"Okay, I wish I were in a lush oasis with plentiful food and drink."

*POOF*

The Arab found himself in the most beautiful oasis he had ever seen and he was surrounded with jugs of wine and plat-ters of delicacies.

"Okeydokey, kiddo, vat's your second vish?"

"My second wish is that I were rich beyond my wildest dreams."

*POOF*

The Arab found himself surrounded by treasure chests filled with rare old coins and precious gems.

"Okay, kid, you got just one more wish. Better should make it a good one!"

After thinking for a few minutes, the Arab said, "I wish that no matter where I go, beautiful women will always need and want me!"

*POOF*

He is turned into a tampon.

THE MORAL OF THE STORY:

If you do business with a Jewish genie, there's going to be a string attached.

•

There was a church that had a very big-busted organist. Her breasts were so huge that they bounced and jiggled while she played. Unfortunately, she distracted the congregation considerably.

The very proper church ladies were appalled. They said something had to be done about this or they would have to get another organist.

One of the ladies approached her very discreetly and told her to mash up some green persimmons (if you eat them they make you pucker, because they are so sour) and rub them on her breasts and maybe they would shrink in size. She agreed to try it.

The following Sunday morning the minister got up on the pulpit and said, "Dew to thircumsthanthis bewond my con-twol, we will not hath a thermon tewday."

•

When the Mother Superior answered the knock at the convent door, she found two leprechauns shuffling their feet on the doorsill. "Aye an' begorrah, Mother Superior," said the foremost one after an awkward pause, "would ye be havin' any leprechaun nuns in your church?"

The nun shook her head solemnly.

The little man shuffled his feet a bit more, then piped up, "An' would there be any leprechaun nuns in the convent?"

"No, my boys," said the Mother Superior gravely.

"Ye see, laddy," cried the leprechaun, whirling around to his companion triumphantly. "I told you ye been f***in' a penguin!"

•

A pompous minister was seated next to a hillbilly on a flight across the country. After the plane was airborne, drink orders were taken.

The hillbilly asked for a whiskey and soda, which was brought and placed before him.

The flight attendant then asked the minister if he would like a drink.

He replied in disgust, "I'd rather be savagely raped by brazen whores than let liquor touch these lips."

The hillbilly then handed his drink back to the flight attendant and said, "Shit, me, too! I didn't know we got a choice."

•

In a small town in the old country the rabbi died. His widow was so disconsolate that the people of the town decided that she ought to get married again.

But the town was so small that the only eligible bachelor was the town butcher. The poor rabbi's wife was somewhat dismayed because she had been wed to a scholar, and the butcher had no great formal education. However, she agreed and they were married.

After the marriage, Friday came. She went to the ritual bath. Then home to prepare to light the candles. The butcher leaned over to her and said, "My mother told me that after the ritual bath and before lighting the candles, it's a blessing to have sex." So they did. She lit the candles. He leaned over again and said, "My father told me that after lighting the candles it's good to have sex." So they did.

They went to bed after prayers to get ready for Sabbath. When they awoke he said to her, "My grandmother said that before you go to the synagogue it's a mitzvah to have sex." So they did.

After praying all day, they came home to rest, and again he whispers in her ear, "My grandfather says after praying it's a blessing to have sex." So they did.

On Sunday she goes out to shop for food and meets a friend who asks, "Nu, so how is the new husband?"

She replies, "Well, he is no scholar, but he comes from a wonderful family."

•

A Christian, a Muslim, and a Jew, all very pious, met at an interfaith congress and got to talking about the experiences that had inspired their religious devotion.

The Christian recounted being on a plane when it ran into a terrible storm over a remote wilderness area.

"There was lightning and thunder all around us, and the pilot told us to brace for the crash. I dropped to my knees and prayed to God to save us—and then for one thousand feet all around us, the wind calmed and the rain stopped. We made it to the airport, and since then my faith has never wavered."

The Muslim then told of a terrifying incident on his pilgrimage to Mecca. "A tremendous sandstorm came up out of nowhere, and within minutes my camel and I were almost buried. Sure I was going to die, I prostrated myself toward Mecca and prayed to Allah to deliver me. And suddenly, for one thousand feet all around me, the swirling dust settled and I was able to make my way safely across the desert. Since then I have been the devoutest of believers."

Nodding respectfully, the Jew then told his tale. "One Sabbath I was walking back from the temple when I saw a huge sack of money just lying there at the edge of the road. It had clearly been abandoned, and I felt it was mine to take, but obviously this would have been a violation of the Sabbath. So I dropped to my knees and prayed to Yahweh—and suddenly, for one thousand feet all around me, it was Tuesday."

•

A local preacher was dissatisfied with the small amount in the collection plates each Sunday. Someone suggested to him that perhaps he might be able to hypnotize the congregation into giving more. "And just how would I go about doing that?" he asked.

"It is very simple. First you turn down the air conditioner so that the auditorium is warmer than usual. Then you preach in a monotone. Meanwhile, you dangle a watch on a chain and swing it in a slow arc above the lectern and suggest they put twenty dollars in the collection plate."

So the very next Sunday, the reverend did as suggested, and lo and behold the plates were full of twenty-dollar bills. Now, the preacher did not want to take advantage of this technique each and every Sunday. So therefore, he waited for a couple of weeks and then tried his mass hypnosis again.

Just as the last of the congregation was becoming mesmerized, the chain on the watch broke and the watch hit the lectern with a loud thud and springs and parts flew everywhere.

"Shit!" exclaimed the pastor.

It took them a week to clean up the church.

•

An ambitious new sales rep for Budweiser traveled all the way to Rome and managed to finagle an audience with the pope himself. As soon as the two were alone together, he leaned over and whispered, "Your Holiness, I have an offer I think might interest you. I'm in a position to give you a million dollars if you'll change the wording in the Lord's Prayer to 'our daily beer.' Now whaddaya say?"

"Absolutely not," said the shocked pontiff.

"Hey, I understand; it's a big decision," sympathized the salesman. "How about five million to make it easier?"

"I couldn't think of it," sputtered the pope.

"I know it's a tough one. Tell you what—I can go up to fifty million dollars," proposed the salesman.

Asking him to leave the room, the pope called in a cardinal and whispered, "When does our contract with Pillsbury expire?"

•

One day God decided He was overdue for a vacation. "I hear Mars is nice," suggested Saint Peter.

God shook His head. "I'm still sore from the sunburn I got there ten thousand years ago."

"I had a good time on Pluto," said the Archangel Gabriel.

"No way," said God. "I nearly broke my neck skiing there last millennium."

"There's always Earth," suggested a cherub meekly.

"Are you nuts?" yelled God. "I dropped by there two thousand years ago, and they're still sore at me for knocking up some Jewish chick."

•

A young couple met with their pastor to set a date for their wedding.

When he asked whether they preferred a contemporary or a traditional service, they opted for the contemporary.

On the big day, a major storm forced the groom to take an alternate route to the church. The streets were flooded, so he rolled up his pants legs to keep his trousers dry.

When he finally reached the church, his best man rushed

him into the sanctuary and up to the altar, just as the ceremony was starting. "Pull down your pants," whispered the pastor.

"Uh, Reverend, I've changed my mind," the groom responded. "I think I would prefer the traditional service."

•

A Hasidic man is standing by a hotel bar about an hour before Shabbat, all dressed up in his special Shabbat clothes.

A magnificent-looking blond airline hostess, with legs that go on forever and breasts that are just waiting to envelop you, has just finished checking in, and is on her way to the elevator, when she sees the Hasid. She stops dead in her tracks and walks over to him.

"Hi," she says.

"Hullo," he answers.

"I have a confession to make to you," she says.

He nods.

"I have a sexual fantasy."

He nods.

"I've always wanted to be with a Hasidic man. I want to run my hands up and down his white silk socks, run my hands over his *tzitzis*, play with his *gartel*, run my fingers through his beautiful beard, and play with his *payess*. In fact, I want you now, and I have a room upstairs. Will you join me for half an hour?"

He looks at her thoughtfully and says, "And what's in it for me??"

•

A visitor to the Vatican needs to relieve himself. Imagine his surprise when in the restroom he sees the pope sitting on a toilet masturbating.

As this was a sight few people saw, he quickly takes a few photos.

The pope recovers his composure and buys the camera for $100,000.

As it was a nice camera, the pope decided to keep it and use it on his travels. One of his entourage sees it and asks how much it cost.

"One hundred thousand dollars," says the pope.

"Wow! That guy must have seen you coming!"

# Golf

George dropped by the course wanting to play an impromptu round of golf. The golf pro explained that they're pretty busy, but there was a woman about to tee off by herself, and if George hurried, he could play with her.

George rushed down, and asked the woman if he could join her. Sally introduced herself, and said, "Yes."

Well, George and Sally immediately hit it off. They were golfing, talking, laughing, having the time of their lives. When they got to the 17th tee, Sally invited George into the woods for a blow job. Of course, George agreed.

When the game was over, George asked Sally if she would like to play again the following week. The two of them started having a regular weekly game, with Sally's special bonus for George just off the 17th tee.

One day, after a few months of this, Sally told George, "I have something very important to tell you."

"What is it?" George asked nervously. "Has someone found out about us?"

"Actually," Sally said, "my real name is Sam. I'm not really a woman, I'm a man."

George was stunned and angered. "Do you mean to tell me that all this time you've been a man, yet you've been hitting from the woman's tee?"

•

## Bedroom Golf

* Each player shall furnish his own equipment for play. Normally one club and two (2) balls.

* Play on a course must be approved by the owner of the holes.

* Owner of the course must approve the equipment before play begins.

* For most effective play, the club must have a firm shaft. Course owners are permitted to check the shaft stiffness before play begins.

* Course owners reserve the right to restrict the shaft length to avoid any damage to the course.

* Unlike outdoor golf, the goal is to get the club into the hole, while keeping the balls out.

* The object of the game is to take as many strokes as deemed necessary until the course owner is satisfied that play is complete. Failure to do so may result in being denied permission to play the course in the future.

* It is considered bad form to begin playing the hole immediately upon arrival at the course. The experienced player will normally take time to admire the entire course, with special attention being given to the well-formed bunkers.

* Players are cautioned not to mention other courses they may have played or are currently playing to the owner of the course being played. Upset course owners have been known to damage a player's equipment for this reason.

* Players should assure themselves that their match has been properly scheduled, particularly when a new course is being played for the first time. Previous players have been known to become irate if they discover someone else playing what they consider to be a private course.

* Players should not assume a course is in shape for play at all times. Some players may be embarrassed if they find the course to be temporarily under repair.

*\* Players are advised to be extremely tactful in this situation.
More advanced players will find alternate means of play
when this is the case. Players are encouraged to have proper
rain gear along, just in case.*

*\* Players are advised to obtain the course owner's permission
before attempting to play the back nine.*

*\* Slow play is encouraged; however, players should be pre-
pared to proceed at a quicker pace, at least temporarily, at the
request of the course owner.*

*\* It is considered outstanding performance, time permitting,
to play the same hole several times in one match.*

*\* The course owner will be the sole judge as to who is the best
player.*

*\* Players are advised to think twice before considering mem-
bership at a given course. Additional assessments may be lev-
ied by the course owner, and the rules are subject to change.
For this reason many players prefer to continue to play several different courses.*

•

Smedley walked up to the groundskeeper. "Sorry, old sport,
but I'm afraid . . . Well, I had a little accident on the seventh
hole."

"An accident, sir?"

"Yes, I . . . I moved my bowels."

"I see," said the groundskeeper. "Well, not to worry. It'll
only take me a moment to clean it up."

"I'm afraid it'll take longer than a moment," Smedley continued. "You see, I followed through."

•

A young woman dressed in shorts had been taking golf les-
sons.

She had just started playing her first round of golf when
she suffered a bee sting. Her pain was so intense that she de-

cided to return to the clubhouse for help and to complain. Her golf pro saw her come into the clubhouse and asked, "Why are you back in so early? What's wrong?"

"I was stung by a bee," she said.

"Where?" he asked.

"Between the first and second hole," she replied.

He nodded knowingly and said, "Then your stance is too wide."

•

A golfer was involved in a terrible car crash and was rushed to the hospital. Just before he was put under, the surgeon popped in to see him. "I have some good news and some bad news," says the surgeon. "The bad news is that I have to remove your right arm!"

"Oh God, no!" cries the man. "My golfing is over! Please, Doc, what's the good news?"

"The good news is, I have another one to replace it with, but it's a woman's arm. I'll need your permission before I go ahead with the transplant."

"Go for it, Doc" says the man. "As long as I can play golf again."

The operation went well and a year later the man is out on the golf course when he bumps into the surgeon. "Hi, how's the new arm?" asks the surgeon.

"I'm playing the best golf of my life. My new arm has a much finer touch and my putting has really improved."

"That's great," says the surgeon.

"Not only that," continues the golfer, "my handwriting has improved, I've learned how to sew my own clothes, and I've even taken up painting landscapes in watercolors."

"Unbelievable!" says the surgeon. "I'm so glad to hear the transplant was such a great success. Are you having any side effects?"

"Well, just one problem," says the golfer. "Every time I get an erection, I also get a headache!"

•

Here is an actual sign posted at a golf club:

1. BACK STRAIGHT, KNEES BENT, FEET SHOULDER-WIDTH APART.
2. FORM A LOOSE GRIP.
3. KEEP YOUR HEAD DOWN!
4. AVOID A QUICK BACKSWING.
5. STAY OUT OF THE WATER.
6. TRY NOT TO HIT ANYONE.
7. IF YOU ARE TAKING TOO LONG, LET OTHERS GO AHEAD OF YOU.
8. DON'T STAND DIRECTLY IN FRONT OF OTHERS.
9. QUIET PLEASE . . . WHILE OTHERS ARE PREPARING.
10. DON'T TAKE EXTRA STROKES. WELL DONE. NOW FLUSH THE URINAL, GO OUTSIDE, and TEE OFF.

•

Two men are playing golf, and are being held up by a pair of women playing very slowly ahead. As the day drags on, they get increasingly frustrated, and one of them says, "I'm going to go up there and ask them to hurry up, or let us play through."

He goes up, but comes back a few minutes later, looking very sheepish.

"You'll never believe this: when I got up closer, I realized that one is my wife, and the other is my lover! So I took off before they saw me, and came back."

The other guy says, "Oh, well, I'll go up there and hurry them along."

He heads off, and comes back a few minutes later, looking very sheepish, too.

"Gee," he says, "it's a small world isn't it?"

# Lawyers

A young associate was romantically ambushed in a darkened room of the law firm. After months of the social isolation that comes from eighty-hour workweeks, the associate was happy to reciprocate. However, when asked by a friend to identify the lover, the associate was puzzled.

"All I know for sure is that it was a partner—I had to do all the work."

•

A grade-school teacher was asking students what their parents did for a living. "Tim, you be first," she said. "What does your mother do all day?"

Tim stood up and proudly said, "She's a doctor."

"That's wonderful. How about you, Amie?"

Amie shyly stood up, scuffed her feet, and said, "My father is a mailman."

"Thank you, Amie," said the teacher. "What about your father, Billy?"

Billy proudly stood up and announced, "My daddy plays piano in a whorehouse."

The teacher was aghast and promptly changed the subject to geography. Later that day she went to Billy's house and rang the bell. Billy's father answered the door. The teacher explained what his son had said and demanded an explanation. Billy's father said, "I'm actually an attorney. How can I explain a thing like that to a seven-year-old?"

•

Q: What do you have if you have six lawyers buried up to their necks in pig shit?
A: Not enough pig shit.

•

Q: What do you call 5,000 dead lawyers at the bottom of the ocean?
A: A good start!

•

Q: How can you tell when a lawyer is lying?
A: His lips are moving.

•

Q: What's the difference between a dead dog in the road and a dead lawyer in the road?
A: There are skid marks in front of the dog.

•

Q: Why won't sharks attack lawyers?
A: Professional courtesy.

•

A father walks into a market with his young son. The boy is holding a quarter. Suddenly, the boy starts choking, going blue in the face. The father realizes the boy has swallowed the quarter and starts panicking, shouting for help.

An attractive, serious-looking woman in a blue business suit is sitting at a coffee bar in the market, reading her newspaper and sipping a cup of coffee. At the sound of the commotion, she looks up, puts her coffee cup down, neatly folds the newspaper and places it on the counter, gets up from her seat, and makes her way, unhurried, across the market. Reaching the boy, the woman carefully drops his pants, takes hold of the boy's testicles, and starts to squeeze and twist, gently at first and then ever so firmly.

After a few seconds the boy convulses violently and coughs up the quarter, which the woman deftly catches in her free hand. Releasing the boy's testicles, the woman hands the coin to the father and walks back to her seat in the coffee bar without saying a word.

As soon as he is sure that his son has suffered no ill effects, the father rushes over to the woman and starts thanking her, saying, "I've never seen anybody do anything like that before, it was fantastic. Are you a doctor?"

"No," the woman replies. "Divorce attorney."

•

Two lawyers had been stranded on a desert island for several months. The only thing on the island was a tall coconut tree that provided them their only food. Each day one of the lawyers would climb to the top to see if he could spot a rescue boat coming.

One day the lawyer yelled down from the tree, "*Wow*, I just can't believe my eyes. There is a woman out there floating in our direction."

The lawyer on the ground was most skeptical and said, "You're hallucinating; you've finally lost your mind."

But within a few minutes, up to the beach floated a stunning redhead, totally naked, unconscious, without even so much as a ring or earrings on her person.

The two lawyers went down to the water, dragged her up on the beach, and discovered, yes, she was alive, warm, and breathing.

One said to the other, "You know, we've been on this godforsaken island for months now without a woman. It's been such a long, long time. . . . So do you think we should, well . . . you know . . . screw her?"

"Out of *what*?" asked the other.

•

Q: How do you get a lawyer out of a tree?
A: Cut the rope.

•

Q: Do you know how to save a drowning lawyer?
A: Take your foot off his head.

•

Q: What's the difference between a lawyer and a bucket of shit?
A: The bucket.

•

Q: What is the definition of a shame (as in "that's a shame")?
A: When a busload of lawyers goes off a cliff.

•

Q: What is the definition of a "crying shame"?
A: There was an empty seat.

•

Q: What can a goose do, a duck can't, and a lawyer should?
A: Stick his bill up his ass.

•

Q: What do you get when you cross the Godfather with a lawyer?
A: An offer you can't understand.

•

Q: Why is it that many lawyers have broken noses?
A: From chasing parked ambulances.

•

Q: Where can you find a good lawyer?
A: In the cemetery.

•

Q: What's the difference between a lawyer and a gigolo?
A: A gigolo only screws one person at a time.

•

Q: What's the difference between a lawyer and a vampire?
A: A vampire only sucks blood at night.

•

Q: Why do lawyers wear neckties?
A: To keep the foreskin from crawling up their chins.

•

Q: If you see a lawyer on a bicycle, why don't you swerve to hit him?
A: It might be your bicycle.

# Old Age

A ninety-seven-year-old man comes to his doctor looking depressed. He says, "Doc, I think I'm impotent." The doctor sits him down and begins the standard speech he gives to senior citizens, about how as the body ages bodily functions slow down and it is completely normal to suffer some decrease in sexual desire. How the man shouldn't worry or become upset about it, but should just relax and things will probably be completely fine and blah blah blah.

Finally the doctor asks, "When did you first begin to think you were impotent?"

"Three times last night, and again this morning."

•

In the nursing home one evening, the old man looked over and said to the old lady, "I know just what you're wanting. For five dollars, I'll have sex with you right over there in that rocking chair."

The old lady looked surprised, but didn't say a word. The old man continued, "For ten dollars I'll do it with you on that nice soft sofa over there, but for twenty dollars I'll take you back to my room, light some candles, and give you the most romantic evening you've ever had in your life."

The old lady still said nothing, but after a couple minutes, she started digging down in her purse. She pulled out a wrinkled $20 bill and held it up. "So you want the nice romantic evening in my room," said the old man.

"Get serious," she replied. "Four times in the rocking chair."

•

Grandma and Grandpa were visiting their kids overnight. When Grandpa found a bottle of Viagra in his son's medicine cabinet, he asked about using one of the pills. The son said, "I don't think you should take one, Dad, they're very strong and very expensive."

"How much?" asked Grandpa.

"Ten dollars a pill," answered the son.

"I don't care," said Grandpa, "I'd still like to try one, and before we leave in the morning, I'll put the money under the pillow." Later the next morning, the son found $110 under the pillow. He called Grandpa and said, "I told you each pill was ten dollars, not a hundred and ten."

"I know," said Grandpa. "The hundred is from Grandma."

•

Two old ladies are sitting in their rocking chairs at the nursing home, reminiscing. One turns to the other and says, "Mildred, do you remember the minuet?"

"Good lordy, no," Mildred replied, "I can't even remember the ones I screwed."

•

Three old guys are sitting around complaining. The first guy says, "My hands shake so bad that when I shaved this morning I almost cut my ear off."

The second guy says, "My hands shake so bad that when I ate breakfast today, I spilled half my coffee on my toast."

The third guy says, "My hands shake so bad that the last time I went to pee, I came taking my cock out."

•

An old man in the nursing home got a bottle of wine for his birthday. He talked the old lady in the next room into sharing it with him.

After they were both totally bombed, he started groping

the old lady and pulling at her clothes. He managed to get her blouse and bra off before she stopped him.

She said, "I can't do this, I have acute angina."

The old guy said, "God, I hope so. You've got the ugliest tits I've ever seen."

•

It was the stir of the town when an eighty-year-old man married a twenty-year-old girl. After a year she went into the hospital to give birth. The nurse came out to congratulate the fellow. "This is amazing. How do you do it at your age?"

He answered, "You've got to keep that old motor running."

The following year she gave birth again. The same nurse said, "You really are amazing. How do you do it?"

He again said, "You've got to keep the old motor running."

The same thing happened the next year. The nurse said, "You must be quite a man."

He responded, "You've got to keep that old motor running."

The nurse then said, "Well, you had better change the oil—this one's black."

•

A young teenage girl was a prostitute and, for obvious reasons, kept it a secret from her grandma. One day, the police raided a brothel and arrested a group of prostitutes, including the young girl. The prostitutes were instructed to line up in a straight line on the sidewalk. Well, who should be walking in the neighborhood but little old Grandma. The young girl was frantic.

Sure enough, Grandma noticed her young granddaughter and asked curiously, "What are you lining up for, dear?" Not willing to let Grandma in on her little secret, the young girl told her that some people were passing out free oranges and that she was lining up for some.

"Mmm, sounds lovely," said Grandma. "I think I'll have

some myself," she continued as she made her way to the back of the line.

A police officer made his way down the line, questioning all of the prostitutes. When he got to Grandma at the end of the line, he was bewildered. "But you're so old . . . how do you do it?"

Grandma replied, "Oh, it's quite easy, sonny . . . I just remove my dentures and suck 'em dry!"

•

Grandma and Grandpa were watching a religious healing program on TV.

The evangelist called for all who wanted to be healed to put one hand on the TV and the other on the body part they wanted healed.

Grandma hobbled to the TV and put one hand on the TV and the other on her arthritic hip . . .

Grandpa made his way to the set and put one hand on the TV and the other on his crotch . . .

Grandma looked at him with disgust: "You just don't understand, you old coot . . . the purpose of this program is to heal the sick, not raise the dead."

•

Mrs. Murphy and Mrs. Cohen had been longtime close friends. But being old-fashioned, each went to a retirement home of her own respective religion.

It was not long before Mrs. Murphy felt very lonesome for Mrs. Cohen, so one day she asked to be driven to the Jewish home to visit her old friend. When she arrived she was greeted with open arms, hugs, and kisses.

Mrs. Murphy said, "Don't be holding back, Mrs. Cohen. How do you like it here?"

Mrs. Cohen went on and on about the wonderful food, the facility, and the caretakers. Then, with a twinkle in her eye, she said, "But the best thing is that I now have a boyfriend."

Mrs. Murphy said, "Now isn't that wonderful! Tell me all about it."

Mrs. Cohen said, "After lunch we go up to my room and sit on the edge of the bed. I let him touch me on the top, and then on the bottom, and then we sing Jewish songs."

Mrs. Murphy said, "For sure it's a blessing. I'm so glad for you, Mrs. Cohen."

Mrs. Cohen said, "And how is it with you, Mrs. Murphy?"

Mrs. Murphy said it was also wonderful at her new facility, and that she also had a boyfriend.

Mrs. Cohen said, "Good for you! So what do you do?"

Mrs. Murphy says, "We also go up to my room after lunch and sit on the edge of the bed. I let him touch me on top, and then I let him touch me down below."

Mrs. Cohen said, "Yes? And then . . . ?"

Mrs. Murphy said, "Well, since we don't know any Jewish songs, we just f***!"

•

## LOVEMAKING TIPS FOR SENIORS

1. Put on your glasses. Double-check that your partner is actually in bed with you.
2. Set timer for 3 minutes, in case you doze off in the middle.
3. Set the mood with lighting. Turn them ALL OFF!
4. Make sure you put 911 on your speed dial before you begin.
5. Write partner's name on your hand in case you can't remember it.
6. Keep extra PoliGrip close by so your teeth don't end up under the bed or between the thighs.
7. Have Tylenol ready in case you actually complete the act.

8. Make all the noise you want. The neighbors are deaf, too.
9. If it works, call everyone you know with the good news.
10. Don't even think about trying it twice.

•

There is an eighty-year-old virgin who suddenly gets an itch in her crotch area. She goes to the doctor, who checks her out and tells her she has crabs. She explains that she can't have crabs because she is a virgin, but the doctor doesn't believe her, so she goes to get a second opinion.

The second doctor gives her the same answer. So she goes to a third doctor and says, "Please help me. This itch is killing me and I know that I don't have crabs because I'm a virgin."

The doctor checks her out and says, "I have good news and bad news. The good news is you don't have crabs. The bad news is that your cherry rotted and you have fruit flies."

•

Two medical students were walking along the street when they saw an old man walking with his legs spread apart.

One of the students said to his friend: "I'm sure he has Petry Syndrome. Those people walk just like that."

The other student said: "No, I don't think so. The old man surely has Zovitzki Syndrome. He walks just as we learned in class."

Since they couldn't agree they decided to ask the old man. They approached and one of the students said to him: "We're medical students and couldn't help but notice the way you walk, but we couldn't agree on the syndrome you might have. Could you tell us what it is?"

The old man said: "I'll tell you, but first tell me what you think."

One of the students said: "I think it's Petry Syndrome."

The old man said: "You thought . . . but you're wrong."

Then the other student said: "I think you have Zovitzki Syndrome."

The old man said: "You thought . . . but you're wrong."

So they asked him: "Well, what do you have?"

And the old man said: "I thought it was a fart . . . but I was wrong."

•

An eighty-year-old man went to his doctor for his quarterly checkup. The doctor asked him how he was feeling and the eighty-year-old said, "Things are great and I've never felt better. I now have a twenty-year-old bride who is pregnant with my child. So what do you think about that?"

The doctor considered his question for a minute and then began, "I have an older friend, much like you, who is an avid hunter. One day when he was setting off hunting, he was in a bit of a hurry and accidentally picked up his walking cane instead of his gun. As he neared a lake, he came across a very large beaver sitting at the water's edge. He realized he'd left his gun at home and so couldn't shoot the magnificent creature, but out of habit he raised his cane, aimed it at the animal as if it were his favorite hunting rifle, and went, 'bang, bang.'

"Miraculously, two shots rang out and the beaver fell over dead. Now, what do you think of that?" asked the doctor.

The eighty-year-old said, "If you ask me, I'd say somebody else pumped a couple of rounds into that beaver."

The doctor replied, "My point exactly."

•

A salesman drove into a small town where a circus was in process.

A sign read: DON'T MISS THE AMAZING ITALIAN.

The salesman bought a ticket and sat down. There, on center stage, was a table with three walnuts on it.

Standing next to it was an old Italian. Suddenly, the old man dropped his pants, whipped out his huge male member, and smashed all three walnuts with three mighty swings!

The crowd erupted in applause as the elderly Italian was carried off on the shoulders of the crowd.

Ten years later the salesman visited the same little town and saw the faded sign for the same circus and the same sign: DON'T MISS THE AMAZING ITALIAN.

He couldn't believe the old guy was still alive, much less still doing his act! He bought a ticket. Again, the center ring was illuminated.

This time, however, instead of walnuts, three coconuts were placed on the table. The Italian stood before them, then suddenly dropped his pants and smashed the coconuts with three swings of his amazing member.

The crowd went wild!

Flabbergasted, the salesman requested a meeting with him after the show. "You're incredible!" he told the Italian. "But I have to know something. You're older now, why switch from walnuts to coconuts?"

"Well," said the Italian, "my eyesa no whata they used to be!"

•

There is a family gathering, with all the generations around the table. The teenagers smuggle in a Viagra tablet and put it in Grandpa's drink.

After a while, Grandpa excuses himself to go to the bathroom. When he returns, however, his trousers are wet all over.

"What happened, Grandpa?" ask his concerned children.

"Well," he answers, "I had to go to the bathroom. So I took it out, but then I saw that it wasn't mine, so I put it back."

•

An elderly couple is attending church services. About halfway through she leans over and says, "I just let a silent fart. What do you think I should do?"

He replies, "Put a new battery in your hearing aid."

•

An Italian-American family was considering putting their grandfather in a nursing home. All the Catholic facilities were completely full, so they had to put him in a Jewish home.

After a few weeks in the Jewish facility, they came to visit Grandpa. "How do you like it here?" asks the grandson.

"It's wonderful!! Everyone here is so courteous and respectful," says Grandpa.

"We're so happy for you. We were worried that this was the wrong place for you."

"Let me tell you about how wonderfully they treat the residents here," Grandpa says with a big smile. "There's a musician here—he's eighty-five years old. He hasn't played the violin in twenty years, and everyone still calls him 'Maestro.' And there's a physician here—ninety years old. He hasn't been practicing medicine for twenty-five years, and everyone still calls him 'Doctor'!! Also a federal judge, retired for over thirty years, is still addressed as 'Your Honor.' And me, I haven't had sex for thirty years, and they still call me 'the F***ing Italian'!"

•

At a senior citizens' luncheon, an elderly gentleman and an elderly lady struck up a conversation and discovered that they both loved to fish.

Since both of them were widowed, they decided to go fishing together the next day.

The gentleman picked the lady up, and they headed to the river to his fishing boat and started out on their adventure.

They were riding down the river when there was a fork in the river, and the gentleman asked the lady, "Do you want to go up or down?"

All of a sudden the lady stripped off her shirt and pants and made mad passionate love to the man right there in the boat.

When they finished, the man couldn't believe what had just happened, but he had just experienced the best sex that he'd had in years.

They fished for a while and continued on down the river, when soon they came upon another fork in the river.

He again asked the lady, "Up or down?"

There she went again, stripped off her clothes, and made wild passionate love to him again.

This really impressed the elderly gentleman, so he asked her to go fishing again the next day.

She said yes and there they were the next day, riding in the boat when they came upon the fork in river, and the elderly gentleman asked, "Up or down?"

The woman replied, "Down."

A little puzzled and disappointed, the gentleman guided the boat down the river. When he came upon another fork in the river he asked the lady, "Up or down?"

She replied, "Up."

This really confused the gentleman, so he asked, "What's the deal? Yesterday, every time I asked you if you wanted to go up or down you made passionate love to me. Now today, nothing!"

She replied, "Well, yesterday I wasn't wearing my hearing aid and I thought the choices were f*** or drown."

•

An eight-year-old boy and his father were walking through a drugstore when the boy noticed the condom display. He said, "Daddy, what are those?"

His father replied, "Those are condoms, son, and they are used for safe sex."

The boy said, "Oh, OK, I've heard of that in school."

He noticed the three-pack and said to his father, "Daddy, who uses those?"

His father replied, "Those are for high school boys, one for Friday, one for Saturday, and one for Sunday."

Then the boy looked at the six-pack and said, "Daddy, who uses those?"

His father replied, "Son, those are for college boys. Two for Friday, two for Saturday, and two for Sunday."

"Oh," the boy says. Then the boy looks at a big twelve-pack and says, "And Daddy, who uses these?"

His father looks at him one last time and says, "Son, those are for married men. One for January, one for February, one for March . . ."

•

An elderly gentleman went to the local drug store and asked the pharmacist for Viagra. The pharmacist said, "That's no problem. How many do you want?"

The man replied, "Just a few, maybe a half dozen, but can you cut each one into four pieces?"

The pharmacist said, "That's too small a dose. That won't get you through sex."

The gentleman said, "Oh, that's all right. I'm past eighty years old, and I don't even think about sex anymore. I just want it to stick out far enough so I don't pee on my shoes."

•

A seventy-five-year-old woman went to the doctor for a checkup. The doctor told her she needed more cardiovascular activity and recommended that she engage in sexual activity three times a week. A bit embarrassed, she said to the doctor, "Please tell my husband."

The doctor went out into the waiting room and told the husband that his wife needed sex three times a week. The seventy-eight-year-old husband replied, "Which days?"

The doctor answered, "Monday, Tuesday, and Friday would be ideal."

The husband said, "I can bring her on Mondays, but on Tuesdays and Fridays I golf, so she'll have to take the bus."

•

A son was placing his father into a nursing home. "Please don't put me in there, son!" cried the old man.

The son said, "Pop, I can't take care of you and work, too. I've checked the place out and it is the best one there is. I think you'll love it."

The next day the father called his son and said, "Son, you were right! I LOVE this place. It is so great here. Thank you so much for making the decision!"

"That's swell, Dad," said the son. "What makes it so great?"

"Well," replied the dad, "last night I was in my room and from out of nowhere, I got an erection. A nurse came in, saw me, and gave me a blow job! I haven't had one of those in thirty or forty years! I'd almost forgotten what it was like! It was fantastic!"

"That's great, Dad," said the son.

A few days later the father called his son again and said,

"You have to get me out of here! I hate this place! I can't live here anymore!"

"What's wrong, Pop?" asked the son.

"Last night I fell down in the hallway. I was getting up and when I was on my hands and knees, a male nurse came along and sodomized me! I CAN NOT and WILL NOT live like this!"

The son said, "Dad, I know that's terrible and we'll get it straightened out, but until then, you have to understand, we have to take the good with the bad. Just hang in there."

"No, son," said the dad. "You don't understand! I get an erection maybe once a year! I fall down two or three times a day!"

•

An old man vacationing in Las Vegas decides to visit a brothel, as it has been a long time since he's had any. After paying the madam, he picks out a cute little blond girl, and they go upstairs. After the preliminaries, he climbs on and starts humping away, and hollers out, "How am I doing, honey?"

She replies, "About three nots."

He says, "Three knots? What does that mean?"

She says, "You're not in, you're not hard, and you're not getting your money back!"

•

What is the difference between girls/women aged: 8, 18, 28, 38, 48, 58, 68?

*At 8—You take her to bed and tell her a story.*

*At 18—You tell her a story and take her to bed.*

*At 28—You don't need to tell her a story to take her to bed.*

*At 38—She tells you a story and takes you to bed.*

*At 48—She tells you a story to avoid going to bed.*

*At 58—You stay in bed to avoid her story.*

*At 68—If you take her to bed, that'll be a story!*

•

The old couple were planning to go on a second honeymoon for their 50th wedding anniversary.

The old woman said, "We will go to all the same places that we did on our first honeymoon."

"Uh-huh," agreed the old man.

"We will do all the things that we did on our first honeymoon," said the old woman.

"Uh-huh," agreed the old man.

"And we will make love like we did on our first honeymoon," said the old woman.

"That's right," said the old man, "except this time I get to sit on the side of the bed and cry, 'It's too big, it's too big!' "

•

One day Grandpa says to Grandma, "Why don't we go to the motel like we used to do when we were young and get kinky?" So they get to the motel and go into the room. Grandpa takes off his glasses and says he's going into the shower to freshen up. In the meantime Grandma takes off her clothes and gets into bed. She does some leg stretches to limber up (it's been a while). Well, she throws her legs over her head and they get caught in the headboard.

Right then Grandpa walks out of the bathroom and sees her that way. "My God, woman," he says, "you need to put your teeth in and comb your hair, you look like an asshole!"

•

An old man in a nursing home awoke one day and trundled down the hallway to the community breakfast room looking rather forlorn. Ms. Smith, a nurse, met him in the hallway. She greeted him smilingly and asked how he was this day.

Mr. Jones allowed that not all was well; in fact, his penis

had died during the night. Ms. Smith knew that Mr. Jones was occasionally a little off mentally, so she merely replied that she was sorry to hear the bad news and went on her way. The next morning Mr. Jones was on his way to breakfast again, but on this day he was dressed in a coat and tie, and his penis was hanging out of his pants. Sure enough, he met Ms. Smith, whereupon—although somewhat startled—she calmly reminded him that the day before he had told her his penis had died and asked why it was hanging out of his pants. Mr. Jones replied simply, "Today is the viewing."

•

The girls in the whorehouse were frankly skeptical when a ninety-year-old man came in and put his money down on the front desk, but finally a good-hearted hooker took him up to her room. Imagine her surprise when he proceeded to make love to her with more energy and skill than any man she had ever known. "I've never come so many times," she gasped. "How about once more, on the house?"

"All right," conceded the old geezer, "but I have to take a five-minute nap and you must keep your hands on my penis, just so, while I'm asleep." She agreed eagerly, and as soon as he woke up he gave her an even better lesson in lovemaking.

"Oh God," gasped the hooker ecstatically, "I can't get enough of you. Please, just once more—I'll pay you."

The old man agreed, subject to the same conditions. Just before he nodded out the hooker said, "Excuse me, but would you mind explaining about the nap and why I have to keep my hands on your privates?"

"I'm ninety years old," retorts the man, "so is it so surprising I need a little rest? As for the other, it's because the last time while I was napping they took my wallet."

•

At his annual checkup Bernie was given an excellent bill of health. "It must run in your family," commented the doctor. "How old was your dad when he died?"

"What makes you think he's dead?" asked Bernie. "He's eighty-six and going strong."

"Aha! And how long did your grandfather live?"

"What makes you think he's dead, Doc? He's one hundred and ten years old and getting married to a twenty-two-year-old in two weeks," retorted Bernie.

"At his age!" exclaimed the doc. "Why's he want to marry a twenty-two-year-old?"

"Doc," said Bernie, "what makes you think he wants to?"

•

A teenager was riding in an elevator with a very old woman when a horrible smell filled the car. Finally the kid said, "Excuse me for asking, lady, but did you fart?"

"Of course I did, sonny," she replied sharply. "Think I always smell like that?"

•

At one point during a game, the coach called one of his nine-year-old baseball players aside and asked, "Do you understand what cooperation is and what the word 'team' means?" The little boy nodded in the affirmative. "Do you understand that what matters is whether we win or lose together as a team?" The little boy nodded yes. "So," the coach continued, "I'm sure you know, when an out is called, you shouldn't argue, curse, attack the umpire, or call him a peckerhead. Do you understand all that?" Once again the little boy nodded. He continued, "And when I take you out of the game so another boy gets a chance to play, it's not good sportsmanship to call your coach a 'dumb ass,' is it?"

Again the little boy nodded. "Good," said the coach. "Now go over there and explain all that to your grandmother."

•

After retiring, I went to the Social Security office to apply for Social Security. The woman behind the counter asked me for my driver's license to verify my age.

I looked in my pockets and realized I had left my wallet at home. I told the woman that I was very sorry, but I would have to go home and come back later.

The woman said, "Unbutton your shirt."

So I opened my shirt, revealing my curly silver hair.

She said, "That silver hair on your chest is proof enough for me," and she processed my Social Security application.

When I got home, I excitedly told my wife about my experience at the Social Security office.

She said, "You should have dropped your pants . . . you might have gotten disability, too."

•

Two old men decide they are close to their final days and decide to have a last night on the town. After a few drinks, they end up at the local brothel.

The madam takes one look at the two old geezers and whispers to her manager, "Go up to the first two bedrooms and put an inflated doll in each bed. These two are so old and drunk, I'm not wasting two of my girls on them. They won't know the difference."

The manager does as he is told and the two old men go upstairs and take care of their business. As they are walking home the first man says, "You know, I think my girl was dead!"

"Dead?" says his friend, "why would you say that?"

"Well, she never moved or made a sound all the time I was loving her."

His friend says, "I think mine was a witch."

"A witch, why the hell would you say that?"

"Well, I was making love to her, kissing her on the neck, and I gave her a little bite, then she farted and flew out the window."

•

An elderly man really took care of his body. He lifted weights and jogged six miles every day. One morning he looked into the mirror, admiring his body, and noticed that he was sun-tanned all over with the exception of his penis. So he decided to do something about that. He went to the beach, undressed completely, and buried himself in the sand, except for his penis, which he left sticking out of the sand. A bit later, two little old ladies came strolling along the beach, one using a cane to help her get along. Upon seeing the thing sticking out of the sand, the lady with the cane began to move the penis around with her cane. Remarking to the other little old lady, she said, "There really is no justice in the world."

The other little old lady asked, "What do you mean by that?"

The first little old lady replied, "Look at that.

"When I was twenty, I was curious about it.

"When I was thirty, I enjoyed it.

"When I was forty, I asked for it.

"When I was fifty, I paid for it.

"When I was sixty, I prayed for it.

"When I was seventy, I forgot about it.

"Now that I'm eighty, the damned things are growing wild, and I'm too old to squat."

•

An elderly couple sit through a porno movie twice. They don't get up to leave until the theater is ready to close for the night. "You folks must've enjoyed the show," the usher says.

"Disgusting," says the old lady.

"It was revolting," her husband adds.

"Then why did you sit through it twice?" the usher asks.

"We had to wait until you turned up the house lights," the old lady replies. "We couldn't find my panties, and his teeth were in them!"

•

Ma and Pa were rocking on the front porch when Pa turned and slapped Ma. Ma said, "What was that for?" Pa said, "For forty years of bad sex." Ma said, "Oh," and continued rocking. Then Ma reached over and slapped Pa. Pa said, "What was that for?" Ma said, "For knowing the difference."

# Prostitutes

This guy has a spare $10 that he decides to spend on his first hooker ever.

He goes out, he gets one, then he brings her home.

They have hours of hardcore sex. Then she leaves when he falls asleep.

The next morning, he wakes up and discovers that he has crabs. He goes and finds the hooker again and says, "Hey, bitch, you gave me crabs!"

She replies, "Well, for ten dollars what did you expect, lobsters?"

•

Two prostitutes were riding around town with a sign on the roof of their car that read, "TWO PROSTITUTES . . . $150.00."

A policeman noticed the car, and quickly pulled them over. He approached the ladies and told them they'd have to remove the sign. Otherwise, they'd be arrested and taken to jail. Just then, another car passed by with a sign that read, "JESUS SAVES."

The two ladies asked the policeman why he let the other car drive by without pulling it over. "Well, that's a little different since it pertains to religion." The two ladies were furious, but nonetheless they removed the sign and drove away.

The next day, the same policeman noticed the same two ladies riding around town with a sign on the roof of their car. He figured he had an easy bust, so he pulled them over once again.

As he approached the car, though, he noticed the sign now read, "TWO ANGELS SEEKING PETER . . . $150.00"

•

This guy goes into a whorehouse and tells the mistress he wants to eat out a girl for the first time. She sends him up and he meets this deadly blond chick. She whips down her pants and he starts licking her twat. Minutes later he feels something in his mouth and spits out a corn niblet. Thinking this is normal, as he has never done it before, he continues eating her out. Minutes pass and he finds a piece of carrot in his mouth. Still thinking this is normal he continues. Soon after he finds a piece of meat and stands up. "Excuse me, miss, but are you sick?"

She looks at him and replies, "No, but the last guy was!"

•

Three friends decide to visit a prostitute. It's a slow night, so she gives the guys a deal. "You can pay by the inch."

When the first man comes back out, his friends ask, "How much did she charge you?"

"Seventy-five dollars," says the first.

The second guy goes in and returns with a fee of $85. The first two are proud of their prowess.

The third man goes in and returns. "How much did she charge you?" ask the first two.

"Twenty dollars," replies the third.

The first two start laughing hysterically.

"Hey, guys," replies the third, "I'm not so stupid. I paid on the way out instead of on the way in!"

•

Sam, from the garment center in New York, went to Miami Beach for a winter vacation. While walking down Collins Avenue, he was approached by a luscious blonde, who whispered into his ear, "I'm selling—are you buying?"

Sam said, "Sure, I'm buying."

So they went to a hotel room and made love for the entire night.

A week or so later, when Sam went back to New York, he came down with syphilis. After weeks and weeks of painful treatment, Sam was released by the hospital. As he was walking along Fifth Avenue, the same blonde came over to him and whispered, "I'm selling, mister—are you buying?"

Sam looked her straight in the eye and asked, "So what are you selling now, cancer?"

•

A man approached a prostitute and asked, "How much for a blow job?"

"Hundred bucks."

"OK," he said and began to jerk off.

"What the hell are you doing that for?"

"For a hundred bucks, you don't think I'm going to give you the easy one, do you?"

•

A guy walks into a whorehouse. On his dick it says, "Shortie's." One of the whores feels bad for him, so she gives him a blow job.

All the other whores laugh at her until they come out of the room. It turns out that his dick says, "Shortie's Bar and Grill in Albuquerque, New Mexico."

# Stupid People

Bubba died in a fire and his body was burned pretty badly.

The morgue needed someone to identify the body, so they sent for his two best friends, Darryl and Gomer.

The three men had always done everything together.

Darryl arrived first, and when the mortician pulled back the sheet, Darryl said, "Yup, his face is burned up pretty bad. You better roll him over."

The mortician rolled him over, and Darryl said, "Nope, ain't Bubba."

The mortician thought this was rather strange. Then he brought Gomer in to identify the body. Gomer looked at the body and said, "Yup, he's pretty well burnt up. Roll him over."

The mortician rolled him over and Gomer said, "No, it ain't Bubba."

The mortician asked, "How can you tell?"

Gomer said, "Well, Bubba had two assholes."

"What! He had two assholes?" asked the mortician.

"Yup, I've never seen 'em, but everyone knew he had two assholes. Every time we went to town, folks would say, 'Here comes Bubba with them two assholes.' "

•

Bubba, a furniture dealer from Arkansas, decided to expand the line of furniture in his store, so he went to Paris to see what he could find.

After arriving in Paris, he met with some manufacturers

and selected a line that he thought would sell well back home in Arkansas.

To celebrate the new acquisition, he decided to visit a small bistro and have a glass of wine. As he sat enjoying his wine, he noticed that the small place was quite crowded, and that the other chair at his table was the only vacant seat in the house.

Before long, a very beautiful young Parisian girl came to his table, asked him something in French (which he did not understand), and motioned toward the chair. He invited her to sit down.

He tried to speak to her in English, but she did not speak his language so, after a couple of minutes of trying to communicate with her, he took a napkin and drew a picture of a wineglass and showed it to her.

She nodded, and he ordered a glass of wine for her.

After sitting together at the table for a while, he took another napkin, and drew a picture of a plate with food on it, and she nodded. They left the bistro and found a quiet cafe that featured a small group playing romantic music.

They ordered dinner, after which he took another napkin and drew a picture of a couple dancing. She nodded, and they got up to dance.

They danced until the cafe closed and the band was packing up.

Back at their table, the young lady took a napkin and drew a picture of a four-poster bed.

To this day, Bubba has no idea how she figured out he was in the furniture business.

•

A condom saleswoman was stranded in the countryside and had to put up for the night with a farmer and his two hillbilly sons.

In the middle of the night, she felt a bit horny and crept into the room where the two brothers were sleeping and woke them up for a bout of passionate lovemaking. She explained that the condoms were to ensure that she did not get pregnant.

The next morning she bade them farewell and started off from the farm.

Days passed and then one brother spoke to the other: "It has been some time now that she's gone and I don't think she'll ever get pregnant. Let's take these damn things off, I gotta take a piss!"

•

A girl came skipping home from school one day. "Mommy, Mommy," she yelled, "we were counting today and all the other kids could only count to four, but I counted to ten. See? One, two, three, four, five, six, seven, eight, nine, ten!"

"Very good!" said her mother.

"Is it because I'm blond?"

"Yes, it's because you're blond," said the mommy.

The next day the girl came skipping home from school.

"Mommy, Mommy," she yelled, "we were saying the alphabet today, and all the other kids could only say it to D, but I said it to G. See? A, B, C, D, E, F, G!"

"Very good!" said her mother.

"Is it because I'm blond, Mommy?"

"Yes, honey, it's because you're blond!"

The following day the girl came skipping home from school.

"Mommy, Mommy," she yelled, "we were in gym class today, and when we showered, all the other girls had flat chests, but I have these!"

She lifted her tank top to reveal a pair of 36Cs.

"Very good," said her embarrassed mother.

"Is it because I'm blond, Mommy?"

"No, honey, it's because you're twenty-four."

•

A guy gets home early from work and hears strange noises coming from the bedroom. He rushes upstairs to find his wife naked on the bed, sweating and panting. "What's up?" he says.

"I'm having a heart attack," cries the woman.

He rushes downstairs to grab the phone, but just as he's dialing, his four-year-old son comes up and says, "Daddy! Daddy! Uncle Ted's hiding in your closet and he's got no clothes on."

The guy slams the phone down and storms upstairs into the bedroom, past his screaming wife, and rips open the wardrobe door. Sure enough, there is his brother, totally naked, cowering on the closet floor.

"You rotten s.o.b.," says the husband. "My wife's having a heart attack and you're running around naked scaring the kids!"

•

Did you hear about the Polish girl who thought that a sanitary belt was a drink out of a clean shot glass?

•

Did you hear about the Polack who thought *Moby-Dick* was a venereal disease?

•

Did you hear about the two Polacks who were hunting deer and other wild game in the north woods when they came upon a naked woman sitting on a stump? One said to her, are you game? She smiled and said she was; so the other Polack shot her!

•

The redneck and his gal were embracing passionately in the front seat of the car.

"Want to go in the backseat?" she asked.

"Nope," he replied.

A few minutes later she asked, "Now do you want to get in the backseat?"

"No, I don't," he said again, "I wanna stay here in the front seat with you."

•

There were three lunatics who were walking down the road when they came across a huge pile of shit.

The first loony put his eye in it and said, "Looks like shit."

The next one put his nose in it and said, "Smells like shit."

The last one put his tongue in it and said, "Tastes like shit."

They all looked at one another and said, "Lucky we didn't stand in it!"

# One-Liners

*Man who run in front of car get tired.*

*Man who run behind car get exhausted.*

*Man who walk through airport turnstile sideways going to Bangkok.*

*Man with one chopstick go hungry.*

*Man who scratch ass should not bite fingernails.*

*Man who eat many prunes get good run for money.*

*Baseball is wrong: Man with four balls cannot walk.*

*Panties not best thing on earth! But next to best thing on earth.*

*War does not determine who is right, war determine who is left.*

*Wife who put husband in doghouse soon find him in cat-house.*

*Man who fight with wife all day get no piece at night.*

*It take many nails to build crib, but one screw to fill it.*

*Man who drive like hell, bound to get there.*

*Man who stand on toilet is high on pot.*

*Man who live in glass house should change clothes in basement.*

*Man who fish in other man's well often catch crabs.*

*Man who fart in church sit in own pew.*

*Crowded elevator smell different to midget.*

•

"Having sex is like playing bridge. If you don't have a good partner, you'd better have a good hand."

—Woody Allen

"Bisexuality immediately doubles your chances for a date on Saturday night."

—Rodney Dangerfield

"There are a number of mechanical devices which increase sexual arousal, particularly in women. Chief among these is the Mercedes-Benz 380SL."

—Lynn Lavner

"Sex at age ninety is like trying to shoot pool with a rope."

—Camille Paglia

"Sex is one of the nine reasons for incarnation. The other eight are unimportant."

—George Burns

"Women might be able to fake orgasms. But men can fake a whole relationship."

—Sharon Stone

"Hockey is a sport for white men. Basketball is a sport for black men. Golf is a sport for white men dressed like black pimps."

—Tiger Woods

"My mother never saw the irony in calling me a son-of-a-bitch."

—Jack Nicholson

"Ah, yes, divorce, from the Latin word meaning to rip out a man's genitals through his wallet."

—Robin Williams

"Women need a reason to have sex. Men just need a place."

—Billy Crystal

"There's a new medical crisis. Doctors are reporting that many men are having allergic reactions to latex condoms. They say they cause severe swelling. So what's the problem?"

—Dustin Hoffman

"See, the problem is that God gives men a brain and a penis, and only enough blood to run one at a time."

—Robin Williams

"It's been so long since I've had sex, I've forgotten who ties up whom."

—Joan Rivers

"Sex is one of the most wholesome, beautiful, and natural experiences money can buy."

—Steve Martin

"You don't appreciate a lot of stuff in school until you get older. Little things like being spanked every day by a middle-aged woman. Stuff you pay good money for in later life."

—Elmo Phillips

"Bigamy is having one wife too many. Monogamy is the same."

—Oscar Wilde

"It isn't premarital sex if you have no intention of getting married."

—George Burns

•

## THE GOOD, THE BAD, AND THE UGLY

*Good: Your wife is pregnant.*
*Bad: It's triplets.*
*Ugly: You had a vasectomy five years ago.*

*Good: Your wife's not talking to you.*
*Bad: She wants a divorce.*
*Ugly: She's a lawyer.*

*Good: Your son is finally maturing.*
*Bad: He's involved with the woman next door.*
*Ugly: So are you.*

*Good: Your son studies a lot in his room.*
*Bad: You find several porn movies hidden there.*
*Ugly: You're in them.*

*Good: Your hubby and you agree, no more kids.*
*Bad: You can't find your birth control pills.*
*Ugly: Your daughter borrowed them.*

*Good: Your husband understands fashion.*
*Bad: He's a cross-dresser.*
*Ugly: He looks better than you.*

*Good: You just gave "the birds and the bees" talk to your
daughter.*
*Bad: She keeps interrupting.*
*Ugly: With corrections.*

*Good: Your son is dating someone new.*
*Bad: It's another man.*
*Ugly: He's your best friend.*

*Good: Your daughter got a new job.*
*Bad: As a hooker.*
*Ugly: Your coworkers are her best clients.*
*Way ugly: She makes more money than you do.*

•

There was a beautiful young woman knocking on my hotel room door all night! I finally had to let her out.

•

A car hit an elderly Jewish man. The paramedic says, "Are you comfortable?" The man says, "I make a good living."

•

I just got back from a pleasure trip. I took my mother-in-law to the airport.

•

I've been in love with the same woman for forty-nine years. If my wife ever finds out, she'll kill me!

•

What are three words a woman never wants to hear when she's making love? "Honey, I'm home!"

•

Someone stole all my credit cards, but I won't be reporting it. The thief spends less than my wife did.

•

We always hold hands. If I let go, she shops.

•

My wife and I went back to the hotel where we spent our wedding night, only this time *I* stayed in the bathroom and cried.

•

My wife and I went to a hotel where we got a waterbed. My wife called it the Dead Sea.

•

The doctor gave a man six months to live. The man couldn't pay his bill, so the doctor gave him another six months.

•

The doctor called Mrs. Cohen saying, "Mrs. Cohen, your check came back." Mrs. Cohen answered, "So did my arthritis!"

•

Doctor: "You'll live to be sixty!"
Patient: "I AM sixty!"
Doctor: "See! What did I tell you?"

•

A doctor held a stethoscope up to a man's chest. The man asks, "Doc, how do I stand?" The doctor says, "That's what puzzles me!"

•

Patient: "I have a ringing in my ears."
Doctor: "Don't answer!"

•

A drunk was in front of a judge. The judge says, "You've been brought here for drinking."

The drunk says, "Okay, let's get started."

•

Why do Jewish divorces cost so much? They're worth it.

•

Why do Jewish men die before their wives? They want to.

•

The Harvard School of Medicine did a study of why Jewish women like Chinese food so much. The study revealed that this is due to the fact that Won Ton spelled backward is Not Now.

•

Q: Why don't Jewish mothers drink?
A: Alcohol interferes with their suffering.

•

Q: Have you seen the newest Jewish American Princess horror movie?
A: It's called "Debbie Does Dishes."

•

Q: Why do Jewish mothers make great parole officers?
A: They never let anyone finish a sentence.

•

Q: What's a Jewish American Princess's favorite position?
A: Facing Bloomingdale's.

•

A Jewish boy comes home from school and tells his mother he has a part in the play. She asks, "What part is it?"

The boy says, "I play the part of the Jewish husband."

The mother scowls and says, "Go back and tell the teacher you want a speaking part."

•

Q: Where does a Jewish husband hide money from his wife?
A: Under the vacuum cleaner.

•

Q: How many Jewish mothers does it take to change a lightbulb?
A: (Sigh) "Don't bother. I'll sit in the dark. I don't want to be a nuisance to anybody."

•

Short summary of every Jewish holiday: They tried to kill us, we won, let's eat.

•

Did you hear about the bum who walked up to a Jewish mother on the street and said, "Lady, I haven't eaten in three days."

"Force yourself," she replied.

•

1. Jim Bakker and Jimmy Swaggert have written an impressive new book. It's called *Ministers Do More Than Lay People*.

2. Transvestite: A guy who likes to eat, drink, and be Mary.

3. The difference between the pope and your boss . . . the pope only expects you to kiss his ring.

4. My mind works like lightning. One brilliant flash and it is gone.

5. The only time the world beats a path to your door is if you're in the bathroom.

6. I hate sex in the movies. Tried it once. The seat folded up, the drink spilled, and that ice, well, it really chilled the mood.

7. It used to be only death and taxes were inevitable. Now, of course, there's shipping and handling, too.

8. A husband is someone who, after taking the trash out, gives the impression that he just cleaned the whole house.

9. My next house will have no kitchen—just vending machines and a large trash can.

10. A blonde said, "I was worried that my mechanic might try to rip me off. I was relieved when he told me all I needed was turn signal fluid."

11. I'm so depressed. My doctor refused to write me a prescription for Viagra. He said it would be like putting a new flagpole on a condemned building.

12. My neighbor was bitten by a rabid stray dog. I went to see how he was and found him writing frantically on a piece of paper. I told him rabies could be treated, and he didn't have to worry about a will. He said,

"Will? What will? I'm making a list of the people I want to bite."

13. Definition of a teenager? God's punishment for enjoying sex.

•

## Rodney Dangerfield's Best One-Liners

*I was so poor growing up . . . if I wasn't a boy . . . I'd have had nothing to play with.*

*A girl phoned me the other day and said, "Come on over; nobody's home." I went over. Nobody was home.*

*During sex, my girlfriend always wants to talk to me. Just the other night she called me from a hotel.*

*One day I came home early from work. I saw a guy jogging naked. I said to the guy, "Hey, buddy, why are you doing that?"*

*He said, "Because you came home early."*

*It's been a rough day. I got up this morning. I put a shirt on and a button fell off. I picked up my briefcase, and the handle came off. I'm afraid to go to the bathroom.*

*I was such an ugly kid . . . When I played in the sandbox, the cat kept covering me up.*

*I could tell my parents hated me. My bath toys were a toaster and radio.*

*I was such an ugly baby . . . My mother never breast-fed me. She told me that she only liked me as a friend.*

*I'm so ugly . . . My father carried around a picture of the kid who came with his wallet.*

*When I was born, the doctor came into the waiting room and said to my father, "I'm sorry. We did everything we could, but he pulled through."*

*I'm so ugly . . . My mother had morning sickness after I was born.*

*I remember the time that I was kidnapped and they sent a piece of my finger to my father. He said he wanted more proof.*

*Once when I was lost, I saw a policeman and asked him to help me find my parents. I said to him, "Do you think we'll ever find them?" He said, "I don't know, kid. There's so many places they can hide."*

*My wife made me join a bridge club. I jump off next Tuesday.*

*I'm so ugly . . . I worked in a pet shop, and people kept asking how big I'd get.*

*I went to see my doctor. "Doctor, every morning when I get up and I look in the mirror . . . I feel like throwing up. What's wrong with me?" He said, "I don't know, but your eyesight is perfect."*

*I went to the doctor because I'd swallowed a bottle of sleeping pills. My doctor told me to have a few drinks and get some rest.*

*With my old man I got no respect. I asked him, "How can I get my kite in the air?" He told me to run off a cliff.*

*Some dog I got. We call him Egypt because in every room he leaves a pyramid. His favorite bone is in my arm. Last night he went on the paper four times; three of those times I was reading it.*

One year they wanted to make me poster boy for birth control.

My uncle's dying wish was to have me sitting in his lap; he was in the electric chair.

I'm so ugly, when I was born the doctor slapped my mother.

# X-Rated Riddles

Q: What is the difference between a drug dealer and a hooker?
A: A hooker can wash her crack and sell it again.

•

Q: What's the height of conceit?
A: Having an orgasm and calling out your own name.

•

Q: What's the definition of macho?
A: Jogging home from your vasectomy.

•

Q: What's the difference between a G-spot and a golf ball?
A: A guy will actually search for a golf ball.

•

Q: Do you know how New Zealanders practice safe sex?
A: They spray-paint Xs on the back of the sheep that kick!

•

Q: What is a Yankee?
A: The same as a quickie, but a guy can do it alone.

•

Q: What do Tupperware and a walrus have in common?
A: They both like a tight seal.

•

Q: What do a Christmas tree and priests have in common?
A: Their balls are just for decoration.

•

Q: What is the difference between "ooooooh" and "aaaaaaah"?
A: About three inches.

•

Q: Why do gay men wear ribbed condoms?
A: For traction in the mud.

•

Q: What's the difference between purple and pink?
A: The grip.

•

Q: How do you find a blind man in a nudist colony?
A: It's not hard.

•

Q: How do you circumcise a hillbilly?
A: Kick his sister in the jaw.

•

Q: What's the difference between a girlfriend and a wife?
A: Forty-five pounds.

•

Q: What's the difference between a boyfriend and a husband?
A: Forty-five minutes.

•

Q: Why do men find it difficult to make eye contact?
A: Breasts don't have eyes.

•

Q: If the dove is the bird of peace, what is the bird of true love?
A: The swallow.

•

Q: What is the difference between medium and rare?
A: Six inches is medium, eight inches is rare.

•

Q: Why do women rub their eyes when they get up in the morning?
A: They don't have balls to scratch!

•

Q: What did Spock find in the commode?
A: The captain's log.

•

Q: Why did Captain Kirk piss on the ceiling?
A: To boldly go where no man has gone before.

•

Q: What do the U.S.S. *Enterprise* and toilet paper have in common?
A: They both circle Uranus in search of Klingons.

•

Q: What's the difference between a lightbulb and a pregnant woman?
A: You can unscrew a lightbulb.

•

Q: What do you get an eighty-year-old woman for her birthday?
A: Mikey. He'll eat anything.

•

Q: What's the difference between a midget con artist and a woman with herpes?
A: One is a cunning runt.

•

Q: What's the difference between a rubber and a coffin?
A: One is to come in and one is to go in.

•

Q: What has a thousand teeth and eats weenies?
A: A zipper.

•

Q: What is the difference between a JAP (Jewish American Princess) and Jell-O?
A: Jell-O moves when you eat it.

•

Q: What is the modern woman's idea of the perfect man?
A: One who's two-and-a-half-feet tall, has a ten-inch tongue, and can breathe through his ears.

•

Q: Where is an elephant's sex organ?
A: In his feet. If he steps on you, consider yourself f***ed.

•

Q: Why is a Polish woman like a hockey team?
A: Because they both take showers after three periods.

•

### SOMETHING TO OFFEND EVERYONE!

Q: What do you call two Mexicans playing basketball?
A: Juan on Juan.

•

Q: What is the difference between a Harley and a Hoover?
A: The position of the dirt bag.

•

Q: What do you see when the Pillsbury Doughboy bends over?
A: Doughnuts.

•

Q: Why is air a lot like sex?
A: Because it's no big deal unless you're not getting any.

•

Q: What do you call a smart blonde?
A: A golden retriever.

•

Q: What do attorneys use for birth control?
A: Their personalities.

•

Q: What's the fastest way to a man's heart?
A: Through his chest with a sharp knife.

•

Q: Why do men want to marry virgins?
A: They can't stand criticism.

•

Q: Why is it so hard for women to find men who are sensitive, caring, and good-looking?
A: Because those men already have boyfriends.

•

Q: What's the difference between a new husband and a new dog?
A: After a year, the dog is still excited to see you.

•

Q: What makes men chase women they have no intention of marrying?
A: The same urge that makes dogs chase cars they have no intention of driving.

•

Q: Why don't bunnies make noise when they have sex?
A: Because they have cotton balls.

•

Q: What's the difference between a porcupine and BMW?
A: A porcupine has the pricks on the outside.

•

Q: What did the blonde say when she found out she was pregnant?
A: "Are you sure it's mine?"

•

Q: Why does Mike Tyson cry during sex?
A: Mace will do that to you.

•

Q: Why did O.J. Simpson want to move to West Virginia?
A: Everyone has the same DNA.

•

Q: Did you hear about the dyslexic rabbi?
A: He walks around saying, "Yo."

•

Q: Why do drivers' education classes in redneck schools use the car only on Mondays, Wednesdays, and Fridays?
A: Because on Tuesday and Thursday, the Sex Ed class uses it.

•

Q: Where does an Irish family go on vacation?
A: A different bar.

•

Q: What would you call it when an Italian has one arm shorter than the other?
A: A speech impediment.

•

Q: What does it mean when the flag at the post office is flying at half-mast?
A: They're hiring.

•

Q: What's the difference between a southern zoo and a northern zoo?
A: A southern zoo has a description of the animal on the front of the cage along with a "recipe."

•

Q: How do you get a sweet little eighty-year-old lady to say the F-word?
A: Get another sweet little eighty-year-old lady to yell BINGO!

•

Q: What's the difference between a northern fairy tale and a southern fairy tale?

A: A northern fairy tale begins, "Once upon a time . . ." A southern fairy tale begins, "Y'all ain'tgonnabelievethis-shit. . . ."

•

Q: What do you say to a dirty blonde with no arms and no legs?
A: "Great Tits!"

•

Q: Why is a dirty blonde like a stamp?
A: Both get licked, then stuck, and finally sent on their way.

•

Q: Why is a dirty blonde like railway tracks?
A: 'Cause she's been laid all over the country.

•

Q: What does a dirty blonde say after having multiple orgasms?
A: Way to go, team.

•

Q: How can you tell if a dirty blonde has been playing with your computer?
A: Your joystick will be soaking wet.

•

Q: Why do saunas remind some people of dirty blondes?
A: 'Cause both are steamy and wet on entry, and hey, they don't mind if you bring friends.

•

Q: Did you hear about the dirty blonde who tried to blow up her husband's car?
A: She scorched her lips on the exhaust pipe.

•

Q: What's the difference between a mosquito and a dirty blonde?
A: If a mosquito gets slapped, it will stop sucking.

•

Q: Why is a dirty blonde like a shotgun?
A: Give her a cock and she'll be ready to blow.

•

Q: What does a dirty blonde look like after sex?
A: No idea, friend, I'm already long gone.

•

Q: What's a dirty blonde's favorite nursery rhyme?
A: HumpMe DumpMe.

•

Q: What's the difference between a dirty blonde and a rooster?
A: A rooster says, "Cockll-doodlle-doooooo," while a dirty blonde shouts, "Any-cock'll-doooo."

•

Q: What is the best secretary in the world to have?
A: The one that never misses a period.

•

Q: What do dirty blondes say after sex?
A: "Thanks, guys!"

•

Q: What's the difference between a dirty blonde and the *Titanic*?
A: They know how many men went down on the *Titanic*.

•

Q: What's the difference between a dirty blonde and the Atlantic Coast?
A: There're fewer crabs in the Atlantic.

•

Q: What's the difference between a dirty blonde and the Grand Old Duke of York?
A: The Duke only had ten thousand men.

•

Q: How does a horny guy spell relief?
A: B-L-O-N-D-E.

•

Q: Why was the dirty blonde girl smiling as she walked down the aisle?
A: 'Cause she knew she'd given her last blow job.

•

Q: Why was the dirty blonde upset when she got her driver's license?
A: Because she got an F in sex.

•

Q: What do a Boeing and a dirty blonde have in common?
A: Both contain a cockpit.

•

Q: What would you call a dirty blonde with brain cells?
A: Pregnant.

•

Q: Why did they call the dirty blonde "twinkie"?
A: She loved to get filled with cream.

•

Q: Why does a dirty blonde have an IQ one point higher than a cop's horse?
A: So she won't shit on the street during a rally.

•

Q: Why is it good to have a dirty blonde passenger?
A: Allows you to park in the handicap zone.

•

Q: What's a dirty blonde's idea of safe sex?
A: Locking the car door.

•

Q: Did you hear the one about the dirty blonde lesbian?
A: Well, she kept having affairs with men.

•

Q: What is the difference between a dirty blonde and most men?

A: The dirty blonde has the higher sperm count.

•

Q: What's the definition of the perfect woman?

A: A deaf and dumb dirty blonde nymphomaniac whose father owns a bar.

•

Q: What does a dirty blonde do if she is not in bed by midnight?

A: She picks up her purse and goes home.

•

Q: Why don't dirty blondes eat pickles?

A: Because they can't get their head in the jar.

•

Q: What would a dirty blonde use for protection during sex?

A: A bus shelter.

# Miscellaneous

A couple was watching a Discovery Channel special about an African bush tribe whose men all had penises 24 inches long. When a male reaches a certain age, a string is tied around his penis; on the other end is a weight. After a while, the weight stretches the penis to 24 inches.

Later that evening as the husband was getting out of the shower, his wife looked down at him and said, "How about we try the African string-and-weight procedure?"

The husband agreed and they tied a string and weight to his penis.

A few days later, the wife asked the husband, "How is our little tribal experiment coming along?"

"Well, it looks like we're about halfway there," he replied.

"Wow, you mean it's grown to twelve inches?"

"No, it's turned black."

•

Superman is on his way to a large reunion of superheroes being held in Miami Beach. He arrives two hours late; his clothes are a mess and he has definitely been in a fight. As he approaches his table, his good friend Batman yells, "Hey, Man of Steel, what happened to you?"

"Well, this is gonna sound crazy, but I was zipping along the coastline, making great time, when suddenly I look down and there, lying naked on the Jacksonville beach, was Wonder Woman!"

"Wow!" says Robin. "What did you do?"

"What do you think I did, kid? Her legs were spread, so I figured I was in like Flynn. I dove down like an eagle and jumped her bones!"

"Boy, I bet she was surprised," said Batman.

Superman smiles weakly and says, "Yeah, she was; but not as surprised as the Invisible Man was."

•

One day, the wife comes home with a spectacular diamond ring.

"Where did you get that ring?" her husband asks.

"Well," she replies, "my boss and I played the lotto and we won, so I bought it with my share of the winnings."

A week later, his wife comes home with a long, shiny fur coat.

"Where did you get that coat?" her husband asks.

She replies, "My boss and I played the lotto and we won again, so I bought it with my share of the winnings."

Another week later, his wife comes home, driving a red Ferrari. "Where did you get that car?" her husband asks.

Again she repeats the same story about the lotto and her share of the winnings.

That night, his wife asks him to draw her a nice warm bath while she gets undressed. When she enters the bathroom, she finds that there is barely enough water in the bath to cover the plug at the far end.

"What's this?" she asks her husband.

"Well," he replies, "we don't want to get your lotto ticket wet, do we?"

•

A man painting the inner walls of an outhouse fell through the opening and landed in the muck at the bottom. He shouted, "Fire! Fire! Fire!" at the top of his lungs.

The local fire department responded with sirens roaring as they approached.

"Where's the fire?" called the chief.

"No fire," replied the painter as they pulled him out of the hole. "But if I had yelled, 'Shit! Shit! Shit!' who would have rescued me?"

•

Jim and Edna were both patients in a mental hospital. One day while they were walking past the hospital swimming pool, Jim suddenly jumped into the deep end. He sank to the bottom of the pool and stayed there.

Edna promptly jumped in to save him. She swam to the bottom and pulled Jim out. When the director of nursing became aware of Edna's heroic act, she considered her to be mentally stable. When she went to tell Edna the news, she said, "Edna, I have good news and bad news. The good news is you're being discharged; since you were able to rationally respond to a crisis by jumping in and saving the life of another patient, I have concluded that your act displays sound-mindedness. The bad news is that Jim, the patient you saved, hanged himself in his bathroom with the belt of his robe right after you saved him. I am sorry, but he's dead."

Edna replied, "He didn't hang himself, I put him there to dry. How soon can I go home?"

•

## THE CRUISE

*Dear Diary. Day One*
I am all packed and ready to get on the cruise ship. I've packed all my pretty dresses and makeup. I'm really excited.

*Dear Diary. Day Two*
We spent the entire day at sea. It was beautiful and we saw some whales and dolphins. What a wonderful vacation this

has started to be. I met the captain today and he seems like a very nice man.

*Dear Diary. Day Three*

I spent some time in the pool today. I also did some shuffle-board and hit some golf balls off the deck. The captain invited me to join him at his table for dinner. I felt honored and we had a wonderful time. He is a very attractive and attentive gentleman.

*Dear Diary. Day Four*

Went to the ship's casino . . . did OK . . . won about $80. The captain invited me to have dinner with him in his stateroom. We had a luxurious meal complete with caviar and Champagne. He asked me to stay the night but I declined. I told him there was no way I could be unfaithful to my husband.

*Dear Diary. Day Five*

Went back to the pool today and got a little sunburned. I decided to go to the piano bar and spend the rest of the day inside. The captain saw me and bought me a couple of drinks. He really is a charming gentleman. He again asked me to visit him for the night and again I declined. He told me that if I didn't let him have his way with me he would sink the ship.

I was appalled.

*Dear Diary. Day Six*

I saved 1,600 lives today.

Twice.

•

A guy walks into a bar. He's a rather large, menacing chap. He chugs back a beer and says, "All the guys on this side of the bar are cocksuckers! Anyone got a problem with that?"

Everyone is understandably silent.

He then chugs back another beer and says, "All the guys

on the other side of the bar are motherf***ers! Anyone got a problem with that?"

Everyone is silent, again.

Then one man gets up from his stool and starts to walk toward the man.

"You got a problem, buddy?"

"No, I'm just on the wrong side of the bar."

•

An eminent teacher and thinker once expressed his philosophy of life succinctly. "When it all boils down to the essence of truth," the philosopher said, "one must live by a dog's rule of life: If you can't eat it or f*** it, piss on it!"

•

A man notices a sign in a window that reads "Singing Blow Jobs! $10." Intrigued, he goes into the building. He walks up to a woman sitting behind a counter and asks about the singing blow jobs. She leads him into the next room. There are no windows, only a chair and a small table with a clean ashtray on it. The woman tells him to have a seat and wait. Soon, a good-looking brunette walks into the room and shuts off the light. She unzips his pants, pulls out his dick, and he soon feels her warm, wet mouth sliding up and down. As she does this, she starts singing. Her voice is clear as a bell as she's giving him a blow job. It's over soon, and the man goes home. He can't stop wondering how she could have done it, singing so clearly with a dick in her mouth . . . so he goes back the next day armed with a flashlight. As soon as she starts singing, he pulls out the flashlight and takes a look.

Her head is bobbing up and down like it should, there's nobody else in the room, and her hands are on his legs so she's not tricking him. Then he notices a glint of light . . . in the ashtray is a glass eye!

•

Did you hear about the man who had five penises?

Well, they said his pants fit him like a glove.

•

A couple of women were playing golf one sunny Saturday morning. The first of the twosome teed off and watched in horror as her ball headed directly toward a foursome of men playing the next hole.

The ball hit one of the men, and he immediately clasped his hands together at his groin, fell to the ground, and proceeded to roll around in evident agony.

The woman rushed down to the man and immediately began to apologize. "Please allow me to help. I'm a physical therapist and I know I could relieve your pain if you'd allow me," she told him earnestly.

"Ummph, oooh, nnooo, I'll be all right. I'll be fine in a few minutes," he replied breathlessly as he remained in the fetal position still clasping his hands together on his groin.

But she persisted, and he finally allowed her to help him. She gently took his hands away and laid them to the side, she loosened his pants, and she put her hands inside. She began to massage him. She then asked him, "How does that feel?"

He replied, "It feels great, but my thumb still hurts like hell."

•

How can you tell when your girlfriend's horny?

You stick your hands in her panties and it feels like you're feeding a horse.

•

A man is driving down a deserted stretch of highway when he notices a sign out of the corner of his eye. It reads: SISTERS OF ST. FRANCIS HOUSE OF PROSTITUTION—10 MILES.

He thinks it was just a figment of his imagination and drives on without a second thought. Soon he sees another sign that says: SISTERS OF ST. FRANCIS HOUSE OF PROSTITUTION— 5 MILES.

Suddenly, he begins to realize that these signs are for real. Then he drives past a third sign saying: SISTERS OF ST. FRANCIS HOUSE OF PROSTITUTION—NEXT RIGHT.

His curiosity gets the best of him and he pulls into the drive. On the far side of the parking lot is a somber stone building with a small sign next to the door reading: SISTERS OF ST. FRANCIS.

He climbs the steps and rings the bell. The door is answered by a nun in a long black habit who asks: "What may we do for you, my son?"

He answers, "I saw your signs along the highway, and was interested in possibly doing business."

"Very well, my son. Please follow me." He is led through many winding passages and is soon quite disoriented. The nun stops at a closed door, and tells the man, "Please knock on this door."

He does as he is told and this door is answered by another nun in a long habit, holding a tin cup.

This nun instructs, "Please place fifty dollars in the cup, then go through the large wooden door at the end of this hallway."

He gets fifty dollars out of his wallet and places it in the second nun's cup.

He trots eagerly down the hall and slips through the door, pulling it shut behind him.

As the door locks behind him, he finds himself back in the parking lot, facing another small sign: PEACE—YOU HAVE JUST BEEN SCREWED BY THE SISTERS OF ST. FRANCIS.

•

The farmer and his wife had worked hard, scrimped, and saved to send their son to college.

As soon as he had enrolled, he started to grow a beard. Next he grew a large mustache and sideburns.

Being pleased with his new facial adornment, he had his picture taken and sent it off to his parents.

On the back of the photo he scrawled, "How do you like it? Don't I look like a count?"

Shortly after, the son received this terse note: "You idiot, it cost us a fortune to send you to college, and you can't even spell!"

•

"Hello?"

"Hi, honey. This is Daddy. Is Mommy near the phone?"

"No, Daddy. She's upstairs in the bedroom with Uncle Paul."

After a brief pause, Daddy says, "But honey, you haven't got an Uncle Paul."

"Oh yes I do, and he's upstairs in the room with Mommy, right now."

Brief pause.

"Uh, okay then. This is what I want you to do. Put the phone down on the table, run upstairs, and knock on the bedroom door and shout to Mommy that Daddy's car just pulled into the driveway."

"Okay, Daddy, just a minute."

A few minutes later the little girl comes back to the phone.

"I did it, Daddy."

"And what happened, honey?" he asked.

"Well, Mommy got all scared, jumped out of bed with no clothes on, and ran around screaming. Then she tripped over the rug, hit her head on the dresser, and now she isn't moving at all!"

"Oh my God! What about your Uncle Paul?"

"He jumped out of the bed with no clothes on, too. He was all scared and he jumped out of the back window and into the swimming pool. But I guess he didn't know that you took out the water last week to clean it. He hit the bottom of the pool and I think he's dead."

\* \*Long pause\* \*

\* \*Longer pause\* \*

\* \*Even longer pause\* \*

Then Daddy says, "Swimming pool? . . . Is this 696-4230?"

•

Two men are sitting at the bar at the top of the Empire State Building drinking when the first man turns to the other one and says, "You know, last week I discovered that if you jump from the top of this building, by the time you fall to the tenth floor, the wind around the building is so intense that it carries you around the building and back into the window."

The bartender just shakes his head in disapproval while wiping the bar, but says nothing.

The second guy says, "What? Are you insane? There's no way in hell that could happen!"

"No, it's true," said the first man. "Let me prove it to you."

He gets up from the bar, jumps over the balcony, and plummets toward the street below.

When he passes the tenth floor, the high wind whips him around the building and back into a window, and he takes the elevator back up to the bar. He meets the second man, who is astonished.

"You know, I saw that with my own eyes, but that must've been a one-time fluke. That was scientifically impossible!"

"No, I'll prove it again," says the first man as he jumps. Again, just as his body hurtles toward the street, the tenth-floor wind gently carries him around the building and into the window. He takes the elevator back to the bar. Once upstairs, he successfully urges his dubious fellow drinker to try it.

"Well, what the heck," the second guy says, "I've seen that it works, so I'll try it!"

He immediately jumps over the balcony—plunges downward—rapidly passes the eleventh, tenth, ninth, eighth floors . . . his body hits the sidewalk with a loud "splat."

Back upstairs, the bartender who had been silent the whole time turns to the first drinker and shakes his head. He says, "You know, Superman, you're a real asshole when you're drunk."

•

This guy just started at his new job working at a porno shop. His boss comes out and tells him that he has to leave for a while, and asks if he can handle it. The new employee is somewhat reluctant, but with the boss's positive comments he finally agrees.

A few minutes later a white woman walks in and asks, "How much for the white dildo?"

He answers, "Thirty-five dollars."

She: "How much for the black one?"

He: "Thirty-five dollars for the black one, they are the same price."

She: "I think I'll take the black one. I've never had a black one before." She pays him, and off she goes.

A little bit later a black woman comes in and asks, "How much for the black dildo?"

He: "Thirty-five dollars."

She: "How much for the white one?"

He: "Thirty-five dollars for the white one also, they are the same price."

She: "Hmmm . . . I think I'll take the white one. I've never had a white one before." She pays him, and off she goes.

About an hour later a young blond woman comes in and asks, "How much are your dildos?"

He: "Thirty-five for the white, thirty-five for the black."

She: "Hmmmmm . . . how much is that plaid one on the shelf?"

He: "Well, that's a very special dildo . . . it'll cost you one hundred fifty dollars."

She thinks for a moment and answers, "I'll take the plaid one, I've never had a plaid one before." She pays him, and off she goes.

Finally, the guy's boss returns and asks, "How did you do while I was gone?"

The salesman responded, "I think I did pretty good. I sold one white dildo, one black dildo, and I sold your thermos for one hundred fifty dollars!"

•

There's this guy who loves his girlfriend so much he decides to have her name tattooed on his dick.

It said "WY" when it was soft, and "Wendy" when it was hard.

A few months later the couple get married. For their honeymoon they take a trip to a Caribbean island resort. Once there, they decide to go to a nude beach.

While strolling on the beach, the guy sees a local man with the letters "WY" on his dick, too.

The tourist walks up to the local, points at the tattoo on his unit, and asks, "Hey, is your girlfriend's name Wendy, too?"

The man says with a thick island accent, "No, mon, mine says, 'Welcome to the Island, Have a Nice Day.' "

•

A man who was called to testify at the income tax department asked his accountant for advice on what to wear. "Wear your shabbiest clothing. Let him think you are a pauper," the accountant replied.

Then he asked his lawyer the same question, but got the opposite advice. "Do not let them intimidate you. Wear your most elegant suit and tie."

Confused, the man went to his rabbi, told him of the conflicting advice, and requested some resolution of the dilemma.

"Let me tell you a story," replied the rabbi. "A woman, about to be married, asked her mother what to wear on her wedding night. 'Wear a heavy, long flannel nightgown that goes right up to your neck.'

"But when she asked her best friend, she got conflicting advice. 'Wear your sexiest negligee, with a V-neck right down to your navel.' "

The man protested: "What does all this have to do with my problem with the visit to the tax department?"

The rabbi replied, "No matter what you wear, you are going to get screwed."

•

These two friends are enjoying a few drinks when Joe asks Harry, "Tell me, Harry, in all honesty, what do you think of a woman with a growth of black hair under her nose?"

Harry replies, "Shit, no, I would never be turned on by a woman like that."

Joe says, "OK, so tell me, what about a woman with big black hairs growing under her arms?"

Harry says, "For shit's sake, what are you talking about? I couldn't even get it up with a woman like that."

Joe says, "OK, but let me ask you another question. What

about a woman with long black hairs growing on her legs, never shaves her legs?"

Harry replies, "Shit, man, give me a break, I would never get into bed with a lady like that."

Joe says, "OK, so answer me one last question. If all you say is true, why the hell are you f***ing my wife?"

•

Q: What's the definition of a real bastard?
A: A guy who f***s you all night long with a two-inch penis and kisses you the next morning with a nine-inch tongue!

•

Sheila the Aussie housewife got out of the shower and slipped on the bathroom floor. Instead of slipping forward or backward, she somehow did the splits and suctioned herself to the floor.

She yelled out for her husband, Bruce.

"Bruce, Bruce," she yelled. Bruce came running in.

"Bruce, I've bloody suctioned myself to the floor," she said.

"Strewth," Bruce said and tried to pull her up. "You're stuck fast, girl. I'll go across the road and get Joe." (His friend.)

They came back and they both tried to pull her up.

"No way. We can't do it."

Joe said, "Let's try plan B."

"Plan B?" exclaimed Bruce. "What's that?"

"I'll go home and get my hammer and chisel and we'll break the tiles under her," replied Joe.

"Right on," Bruce said. "While you're doing that, I'll stay here and play with her tits."

"Play with her tits?" Joe said. "Not exactly a good time for that, mate."

"No," Bruce replied, "but I reckon if I can get her wet

enough, we can slide her into the kitchen where the tiles aren't so expensive."

•

There was a Jewish man who did circumcisions on Jewish baby boys. He had been doing it for years and all the time collected the foreskins from all the babies.

He had quite a lot. One day he walked past a shop that had the following sign in the window: WE CAN MAKE ANYTHING OUT OF ANYTHING—JUST BRING THE MATERIAL.

So the Jewish man went in and asked them to make a purse from the foreskins he had collected. He was told to return in a week's time when it would be ready.

A week later, he returned to the shop to collect the purse. He complimented the shopkeeper for doing such a fine job and asked how much he owed him.

"Three hundred dollars," said the shopkeeper.

"Three hundred dollars, for such a small purse, you must be joking! How come it's so expensive?"

The shopkeeper replied, "Ah, you see this is no ordinary purse . . . if you rub it, it turns into a suitcase."

•

The National Poetry Contest had come down to two, a Yale graduate and a redneck from Texas. They were given a word, then allowed two minutes to study the word and come up with a poem that contained the word.

The word they were given was "Timbuktu."

First to recite his poem was the Yale graduate.

He stepped to the microphone and said:

*"Slowly across the desert sand*
*Trekked a lonely caravan;*
*Men on camels, two by two*
*Destination Timbuktu."*

The crowd went crazy! No way could the redneck top that, they thought.

The redneck calmly made his way to the microphone and recited:

*"Me and Tim a-huntin' went.*
*Met three whores in a pop-up tent.*
*They was three, and we was two,*
*So I bucked one, and Timbuktu."*

The redneck won hands down!

•

A man went to a strip club. When he got inside he noticed a conspicuously unoccupied seat in the front row. Seizing the opportunity, he took the seat.

As soon as the first dancer walked out, the guy directly behind him yelled, "Yeah, baby! That's what I've been waiting for!"

The man in the front row turned around and gave him a dirty look. A few minutes into the show, the dancer did a move and snatched off her top, revealing two pasties. The guy behind our friend goes off again. "Yeah baby! Shake those things."

Our friend turned around and said, "Hey buddy, calm down!"

After a few moments, the dancer did another move, and snatched off her skirt, revealing a very thin G-string.

Again the man behind our friend yelled out, "Oh baby! You're almost there!"

Our friend again turned around and said, "Hey buddy, shut the hell up, will ya!"

A few minutes later, the dancer stretched out on the floor and snatched off both the pasties and the G-string, and the whole club went wild, except for the man behind our friend.

Curious, our friend turned around and asked, "Say, buddy, where's your enthusiasm now?"

The guy responded, "It's all over your back, dude."

•

At dawn, the telephone rings.

"Hello, Señor Lucky? This is Ernesto . . . the caretaker at your country house."

"Ah yes, Ernesto. What can I do for you? Is there a problem?"

"Uh . . . I'm just calling to advise you, señor, that your parrot died."

"My parrot? Dead? The one that won the international speaking competition?"

"*Si*, señor . . . that's the one."

"Damn! That's a pity! I spent a small fortune on that bird. What did he die from?"

"From eating rotten meat, señor."

"Rotten meat? Who the hell fed the parrot rotten meat?"

"Nobody, señor. He ate the meat of your dead horse!"

"Dead horse? What dead horse?!"

"The Thoroughbred that won the Breeder's Cup, Señor Lucky. He died from a heart attack pulling the big water cart."

"Are you insane? What water cart?"

"The one we used to put out the fire, señor!"

"Good Lord! What fire are you talking about, man?"

"The one at your house, señor! A candle fell and the curtains caught on fire."

"What the f***!! There's electricity at the house! What the hell was the candle for?"

"For the funeral, señor."

"WHAT BLOODY FUNERAL?!"

"Your wife's, señor . . . She showed up one night out of the blue and I thought she was a thief. So I hit her with your new Tiger Woods Nike driver."

A long pause of complete silence . . .

"Ernesto, if you broke that driver, you're in deep shit!"

•

Once upon a time there lived a king. The king had a beautiful daughter, the princess.

But there was a problem. Everything the princess touched would melt. No matter what; metal, wood, stone, anything she touched would melt. Because of this, men were afraid of her. Nobody would dare marry her.

The king despaired. What could he do to help his daughter?

He consulted his wizards and magicians. One wizard told the king, "If your daughter touches one thing that does not melt in her hands, she will be cured."

The king was overjoyed and came up with a plan.

The next day, he held a competition. Any man who could bring his daughter an object that would not melt would marry her and inherit the king's wealth.

Three young princes took up the challenge.

The first brought a sword of the finest steel. But, alas, when the princess touched it, it melted.

The prince went away sadly.

The second prince brought diamonds. He thought since diamonds are the hardest substance in the world they would not melt. But, alas, once the princess touched them, they melted.

He, too, was sent away disappointed.

The third prince approached. He told the princess, "Put your hand in my pocket and feel what is in there." The princess did as she was told, though she turned red. She felt something hard. She held it in her hand. And it did not melt!

The king was overjoyed. Everybody in the kingdom was overjoyed.

And the third prince married the princess and they both lived happily ever after.

What was in the prince's pants? M&M's, of course. They melt in your mouth, not in your hand.

What were you thinking, you pervert?

•

A bored guy sat in the bar looking to strike up a conversation. He turned to the bartender and said, "Hey, about those Democrats in Congress . . ."

"*Stop*, pal—I don't allow talk about politics in my bar!" interrupted the bartender.

A few minutes later the guy tried again: "People say about the pope . . ."

"*No* religion talk, either," the bartender cut in.

One more try to break the boredom. "I thought the Yankees would . . ."

"*No* sports talk . . . That's how fights start in bars!" the barman said.

"Look, how about sex? Can I talk to you about sex?"

"Sure, that we can talk about," replied the barkeep.

"GREAT . . . GO F*** YOURSELF!"

•

A bus stops and two Italian men get on. They seat themselves, and engage in an animated conversation. The lady sitting behind them ignores their conversation at first, but her attention is galvanized when she hears one of the men say the following:

"Emma come first. Den I come. Two asses, they come together. I come again. Two asses, they come together again. I come again and pee twice. Then I come once-a more."

"You foulmouthed swine," says the lady indignantly. "In this country we don't talk about our sex lives in public!"

"Hey, coola down, lady," said the man. "Imma just tellun my friend to spella Mississippi."

•

A plane was taking off from Kennedy Airport. After it reached a comfortable cruising altitude, the captain made an announcement over the intercom. "Ladies and gentlemen, this is your captain speaking. Welcome to flight number 293, nonstop from New York to Los Angeles. The weather ahead is good and therefore we should have a smooth and uneventful flight. Now sit back and relax—OH MY GOD!"

Silence followed, and after a few minutes, the captain came back on the intercom and said, "Ladies and gentlemen, I am so sorry if I scared you earlier, but while I was talking, the flight attendant brought me a cup of coffee and spilled the hot coffee in my lap. You should see the front of my pants!"

A passenger in coach said, "That's nothing. He should see the back of mine!"

•

A woman passenger in a horse-drawn cab has offered the driver a large tip if he can deliver her to her destination in a hurry. However, she is horrified at the cruel whipping the driver is giving the horse to make him go faster.

"My good man, is there no other way you could urge the horse along?" she asks.

"Yessum," the cabdriver cheerfully replies, "but I've got to save his balls for the hill!"

•

A couple made a deal that whoever died first, they would come back and inform the other of the afterlife. The woman's biggest fear was that there was no heaven.

After a long life, the husband was the first to go; and true to his word, he made contact.

"Mary . . . Mary . . ."

"Is that you, Fred?"

"Yes, I have come back like we agreed."

"What is it like?"

"Well, I get up in the morning, I have sex, I have breakfast, I have sex, I bask in the sun, then I have sex—twice. I have lunch, then sex pretty much all afternoon—supper—then sex till late at night, sleep, then start all over again."

"Oh, Fred, you surely must be in heaven."

"Hell no, I'm a rabbit in Kansas."

This guy walks into a bar and sees a sign reading: IF YOU CAN MAKE THE OWNER'S HORSE LAUGH, YOU GET $1,000. The guy goes to the owner and accepts the deal, goes to the horse, comes back out in about a minute, the horse is crackin' up! The owner said, "Here is your one thousand dollars."

A few months later the same kind of deal is posted in the bar, only the guy sees that you have to make the horse cry. The guy goes back to the owner and accepts the challenge. Goes and sees the horse—comes back out and the horse is bawlin' like a baby. Finally the owner says, "Goddamnit! How did you do it?"

Guy says, "First time I went in, I told the horse I had a bigger dick than him. Second time, I actually showed him!"

●

## THE PERFECT ATTITUDE
## FOR THE PERFECT WOMAN . . .

1. I'll swallow it all . . . I love the taste.

2. Are you sure you've had enough to drink?

3. I'm bored. Let's shave my pussy!

4. Shouldn't you be down at the bar with your buddies?

5. That was a great fart! Do another one!

6. I've decided to stop wearing clothes around the house.

7. You're so sexy when you're hungover.

8. I'd rather watch football and drink beer with you than go shopping.

9. Let's subscribe to *Hustler*.

10. Would you like to watch me go down on my girl-friend?

11. Say, let's go down to the mall so you can check out women's asses.

12. I'll be out painting the house.

13. I love it when you play golf on Sundays, I just wish you had time to play on Saturday, too.

14. Honey . . . our new neighbor's daughter is sunbathing again. Come see!

15. I know it's a lot tighter back there, but would you please try again?

16. No, no. I'll take the car to have the oil changed.

17. Your mother is way better than mine.

18. Do me a favor, forget the stupid Valentine's Day thing and buy new clubs.

19. I understand fully . . . our anniversary comes every year. You go hunting with the guys—it's a wonderful stress reliever.

20. Oh, come on, what do ya say we get a good porno movie, a case of beer, a few joints, and have my friend Tammy over for a threesome!

21. Oh, come on, not the damn mall again, let's go to that new strip joint!

22. Listen, I make enough money for the both of us, why

don't you retire and get that nagging handicap down to 7 or 8?

23. You need your sleep, ya big silly, now stop getting up for the night feedings.

24. God . . . if I don't get to blow you soon, I swear I'm gonna bust!

25. I signed up for yoga so that I can get my ankles behind my head just for you.

•

Little Red Riding Hood is skipping down the road when she sees the Big Bad Wolf crouched down behind a log.

"My, what big eyes you have, Mr. Wolf," says Little Red Riding Hood. The surprised wolf jumps up and runs away!

Farther down the road, Little Red Riding Hood sees the wolf again; this time he is crouched behind a tree stump.

"My, what big ears you have, Mr. Wolf," says Little Red Riding Hood. Again the foiled wolf jumps up and runs away.

About two miles down the track, Little Red Riding Hood sees the wolf again, this time crouched down behind a road sign.

"My, what big teeth you have, Mr. Wolf," taunts Little Red Riding Hood.

With that, the Big Bad Wolf jumps up and screams, "Will you get lost! I'm trying to take a shit!"

•

An old Jewish man was riding on the subway in Brooklyn, and he sat down next to a younger man. He noticed that the young man had a strange kind of shirt collar—a priest's collar. Having never seen a priest before, he asked the man, "Excuse me, Sir, but why do you have your shirt collar on backward?"

The priest became a bit flustered but politely answered, "I wear this collar because I am a Father."

The Jew thought a second and responded, "Sir, I am also a father, but I wear my collar front-ways. So, *nu?* Why do you wear your collar so differently?"

The priest thought for a minute and said, "Sir, I am the father for many."

The Jewish man quickly answered, "I, too, am the father of many. *Kineahora,* I have four sons, four daughters, and too many grandchildren to count. But I wear my collar like everyone else. Why do you wear it your way?"

The priest, who was beginning to get exasperated, thought and then blurted out, "Sir, I am the father for hundreds and hundreds of people!"

The Jewish man was taken aback, and was silent for a long time. As he got up to leave the subway train, he leaned over to the priest and said, "Mister, maybe you should wear your pants backward!"

•

A group of second, third, and fourth graders, accompanied by two female teachers, went on a field trip to Churchill Downs, the local racetrack, to see and learn about Thoroughbred horses.

When it was time to take the children to the bathroom, it was decided that the girls would go with one teacher and the boys would go with the other.

The teacher assigned to the boys was waiting outside the men's room when one of the boys came out and told her that none of them could reach the urinal.

Having no choice, she went inside, helped the boys with their pants, and began hoisting the boys up, one by one, holding on to their "wee-wees" to direct the flow away from their clothes.

As she lifted one, she couldn't help but notice that he was unusually well-endowed. Trying not to show that she was staring, the teacher said, "You must be in the fourth grade."

"No, ma'am," he replied. "I'm riding Silver Arrow in the seventh race."

•

Sam decides to go on a safari in Africa. Three days into the jungle, something terrible happens—he's attacked by a savage lion! It's horrible. The lion takes out his eye, rips off his arm, and claws away his penis.

His native guides carry him to a small village nearby. But then, he undergoes a miracle. An old witch doctor does things no Western surgeon could possibly do.

He takes the eye from an eagle and puts it into Sam's empty socket. He removes the arm from a gorilla and attaches it to Sam's shoulder. But a replacement for Sam's penis—that presents a problem, until the amazing witch doctor finds a solution. He replaces Sam's penis with the trunk from a baby elephant!

Six months later, the fully recovered Sam is walking on Seventh Avenue, when he runs into Harry. "Sam, I heard the terrible thing that happened to you, are you all right?"

"All right? All right?" said Sam, "I'm better than ever! It was a *mitzvah*! A blessing in disguise. Let me tell you. Now, when I'm in my factory, and one of my nogoodnik workers is cutting on the bias, and he's on the other side of the shop, with my eagle eye I see him and I yell 'STOP.'

"And, when those union bums come up to bother me, I give them ONE punch from my gorilla arm, and those louses are out on the street.

"But, the best of all, THE BEAUTY PART. At cocktail receptions, when they pass around the peanuts, I'M THE LIFE OF THE PARTY!"

•

Miss Beatrice, the church organist, was in her eighties and had never been married. She was admired for her sweetness and kindness to all.

One afternoon, the pastor came to call on her and she showed him into her quaint sitting room. She invited him to have a seat while she prepared tea.

As he sat facing her old pump organ, the young minister noticed a cut-glass bowl sitting on top of it. The bowl was filled with water. In the water floated, of all things, a condom!

When she returned with tea and scones, they began to chat. The pastor tried to stifle his curiosity about the bowl of water and its strange floater, but soon it got the better of him and he could no longer resist.

"Miss Beatrice," he said. "I wonder if you would tell me about this?" He pointed to the bowl.

"Oh, yes," she replied, "isn't it wonderful? I was walking through the park a few months ago, and I found this little package on the ground. The directions said to place it on the organ, keep it wet, and that it would prevent the spread of diseases. Do you know I haven't had the flu all winter?"

•

Two old guys, one 80 and one 87, were sitting on their usual park bench one morning.

The eighty-seven-year-old had just finished his morning jog and wasn't even short of breath.

The eighty-year-old was amazed at his friend's stamina and asked him what he did to have so much energy.

The eighty-seven-year-old said, "Well, I eat Italian bread every day. It keeps your energy level high and you'll have great stamina with the ladies."

So, on the way home, the eighty-year-old stopped at the bakery.

As he was looking around, the lady asked if he needed any help.

He said, "Do you have any Italian bread?"

She said, "Yes, there's a whole shelf of it. Would you like some?"

He said, "I want five loaves."

She said, "My goodness, mister, five loaves . . . don't you think by the time you get to the fifth loaf, it'll be hard?"

He replied, "I can't believe it, everybody in the world knows about this Italian bread thing but me."

•

## FAIRY TALE FOR WOMEN OF THE 21ST CENTURY

Once upon a time, in a land far away, a beautiful, independent, self-assured princess happened upon a frog as she sat contemplating ecological issues on the shores of an unpolluted pond in a verdant meadow near her castle.

The frog hopped into the princess's lap and said: "Elegant Lady, I was once a handsome prince, until an evil witch cast a spell upon me. One kiss from you, however, and I will turn back into the dapper young prince that I am and then, my sweet, we can marry and set up housekeeping in your castle with my mother, where you can prepare my meals, clean my clothes, bear my children, and forever feel grateful and happy doing so."

That night, as the princess dined sumptuously on a repast of lightly sautéed frog legs covered in a white wine and onion cream sauce, she chuckled and thought to herself: "I don't f***ing think so!"

•

Three old black ladies were getting ready to take a plane across the ocean.

The first lady said, "I don't know 'bout y'all, but I'm gonna wear me some hot pink panties before I get on that plane."

"Why you gonna wear that?" the other two asked.

The first replied, " 'Cause, if that plane goes down and I'm out there laying butt-up in a corn field, they gonna find me first."

The second lady says, "Well, I'm gonna wear me some fluorescent orange panties."

"Why you gonna wear that?" the others asked.

The second lady answered. " 'Cause if this plane is goin' down and I'm floating butt-up in the ocean, they can see me first."

The third old lady says, "Well, I'm not going to wear any panties . . ."

"What? No panties?!" the others said in disbelief.

"That's right; you heard me. I'm not wearing any panties," the third lady said, " 'cause if this plane goes down, they always look for that black box first."

•

Question: What is the definition of a JAP (Jewish American Princess)?

Answer: A girl who thinks cooking and f\*\*\*ing are two cities in China.

•

One day, a man named Tony died. When he was sent to be judged, he was told that he had committed a sin, and that he could not go to heaven right away.

He asked what he did, and God told him that he cheated on his income taxes, and the only way he could get into heaven would be to sleep with a 500-pound, stupid, butt-ugly woman for the next five years and enjoy it. Tony decided that this was a small price to pay for an eternity in heaven. So off he went with this enormous woman, pretending to be happy.

As he was walking along, he saw his friend Carlos up ahead. Carlos was with an even bigger, uglier woman than he was. When he approached Carlos, Tony asked him what was going on. Carlos replied, "I cheated on my income taxes and scammed the government out of a lot of money . . . even more than you did." They both shook their heads and figured that, as long as they had to be with these women, they might as well hang out together to help pass the time.

Now Tony, Carlos, and their two beastly women were walking along one day minding their own business when Tony and Carlos could have sworn they saw their friend John up ahead—only this man was with an absolutely drop-dead-gorgeous supermodel-centerfold woman. Stunned, Tony and Carlos approached the man and, in fact, it *was* their friend John. They asked him how it was that he was with this unbelievable goddess, while they were stuck with these disgustingly awful women.

John replied, "I have no idea and I'm definitely not complaining. This has been positively the best time of my life (and I'm dead!) and I have five years of the best sex any man could hope for to look forward to. There is only one thing I can't seem to understand. Every time after we have sex, she rolls over and murmurs to herself 'Damn income taxes!'"

•

This good-looking man walked into an agent's office and said, "I want to be a movie star."

Tall, handsome, and with experience on Broadway, he had all the right credentials. The agent asked, "What's your name?"

The guy said, "My name is Penis Van Lesbian."

The agent said, "Sir, I hate to tell you, but in order to get into Hollywood, you are gonna have to change your name."

"I will *not* change my name!! The Van Lesbian name is centuries old, I will not disrespect my grandfather by changing my name. Not ever."

The agent said, "Sir, I have worked in Hollywood for years . . . you will *never* go far in Hollywood with a name like Penis Van Lesbian! I'm telling you, you will *have to* change your name, or I will not be able to represent you."

"So be it! I guess we will not do business together," the guy said and he left the agent's office.

FIVE YEARS LATER . . .

The agent opens an envelope sent to his office. Inside the envelope is a letter and a check for $50,000. The agent is awestruck . . . who would possibly send him $50,000? He reads the letter enclosed.

*Dear Sir,*

*Five years ago, I came into your office wanting to become an actor in Hollywood. You told me I needed to change my name.*

*Determined to make it with my God-given birth name, I refused. You told me I would never make it in Hollywood with a name like Penis Van Lesbian.*

*After I left your office, I thought about what you said. I decided you were right. I had to change my name. I had too much pride to return to your office, so I signed with another agent. I would never have made it without changing my name, so the enclosed check is a token of my appreciation.*

*Thank you for your advice.*

*Sincerely,*

*Dick Van Dyke*

•

A bald man with a wooden leg gets invited to a Halloween party. He doesn't know what costume to wear to hide his head and his leg so he writes to a costume company to explain his problem. A few days later he received a parcel with the following note:

> Dear Sir,
>
> Please find enclosed a pirate's outfit. The spotted handkerchief will cover your bald head and, with your wooden leg, you will be just right as a pirate.
>
> Very truly yours,
>
> Acme Costume Co.

The man thinks this is terrible because they have emphasized his wooden leg and so he writes a letter of complaint. A week goes by and he receives another parcel and a note, which says:

> Dear Sir,
>
> Please find enclosed a monk's habit. The long robe will cover your wooden leg and, with your bald head, you will really look the part.
>
> Very truly yours,
>
> Acme Costume Co.

Now the man is really upset since they have gone from emphasizing his wooden leg to emphasizing his bald head, so again he writes the company another nasty letter of complaint. The next day he gets a small parcel and a note, which reads:

> Dear Sir,
>
> Please find the enclosed bottle of molasses. Pour the molasses over your bald head, stick your wooden leg up your ass, and go as a caramel apple.
>
> Very truly yours,
>
> Acme Costume Co.

•

The famous Yiddish actor Boris Tomashefsky was celebrated for his bedroom exploits as well as his stage virtuosity. After a sexual bout with a local whore, he presented her with a pair of tickets to the evening performance of his play.

The lady looked with skepticism at the tickets. "With these you can buy bread?" she asked.

"If you're looking for bread," the actor said, "f*** a baker."

•

Watch out for the new scam that is happening at the local mall.

Two good-looking eighteen-year-old women come to your car as you are parking it. One starts wiping your windshield with a rag and Windex, the other comes to your window saying "Hi" while bending over with her breasts almost coming out of her blouse, impossible not to look. When you thank them and offer them a tip, they say no and beg you for a ride. You agree and tell them to sit in the back. On the way they start having sex in the backseat. Then one of them performs oral sex on you, while the other one steals your wallet. I was assaulted last Tuesday, Wednesday, Thursday, Friday, but I couldn't find them Saturday or Sunday. Be careful.

•

Nowadays 80 percent of women have decided against marriage.

They have realized that for 4 ounces of sausage, it's not worth marrying the whole pig!

•

Question: If a man has a ten-inch cock growing out of the top of his head, how much of it can he see?
Answer: He can't see any of it because his two balls are hanging in his eyes.

•

Question: Why do farts smell?
Answer: The Lord put a smell in them so the deaf could enjoy them, too.

•

I walked up to a really pretty girl at the bar the other night and said, "Hey, babe, can I buy you a drink?"

She said, "Do you like sex?"

I said, "Of course I like sex."

She said, "Do you like to travel?"

I said, "Yeah, I love to travel."

She said, "Then f*** off."

•

This guy was walking down the street and this hooker says, "Say, want to have a good time?" as she looks him up and down seductively.

"Sure," he says, and they are off to the nearest motel. As she takes off her clothes, he keeps staring at her.

She says, "Is this the first pussy you've seen since you crawled out of one?"

The guy says, "Nope, just the first one I've seen big enough to crawl back into."

•

A crowded flight was canceled. A single agent was assigned to rebook the long line of inconvenienced travelers. She was doing her best when suddenly an angry customer pushed his way to her desk. He slapped his ticket down on the counter and shouted:

"I don't want to stand in line. I HAVE to be on that flight and it has to be FIRST CLASS and RIGHT NOW!"

The young agent replied, "I'm sorry, sir. I'll try to help you, but I've got to help these folks first. I'm sure we'll be able to work things out for you."

The passenger was unimpressed and unrelenting. He asked loudly, so that all the passengers could hear, "I don't want to stand in line! Do you have any idea who I am?"

Without hesitation, the agent smiled and grabbed her microphone. "May I have your attention, please," her voice bellowed through the terminal. "We have a passenger here WHO DOES NOT KNOW WHO HE IS. If anyone can help him identify himself, please come to the gate."

With the crowd laughing hysterically, he glared at her and swore, "F*** you!"

Without flinching she smiled and said, "I'm sorry, sir, but you'll have to stand in line for that, too!"

•

One fine morning in Eden, God was looking for Adam and Eve, but couldn't find them. Later in the day, God saw Adam and asked where he and Eve were earlier. Adam said, "This morning Eve and I made love for the first time."

God said, "Adam, you have sinned. I knew this would happen. Where is Eve now?"

Adam replied, "She's down at the river, washing herself out."

"Damn," says God, "now all the fish will smell funny."

•

What's the difference between erotic and kinky?

Erotic is when you use a feather, kinky is when you use the whole chicken!

•

The famous stage magician had a thundering climax to his act. He would fill a large bowl with shit and proceed to slurp it noisily, to the amazement and delight of the audience.

One evening he had just begun the wow finish of the act when he stopped in his tracks.

"Go ahead," murmured the stage manager. "Eat the shit. Eat it!"

"Can't do it," said the magician. "There's a hair in it!"

•

Mary O'Malley is home making dinner, as usual, when Patrick Finnegan arrives at her door.

"Mary, may I come in?" he asks. "I've sometin' to tell ya."

"Of course you can come in, you're always welcome, Patrick. But where's me husband?"

"That's what I'm here to be tellin' ya, Mary. There was an accident down at the Guinness brewery . . ."

"Oh God, no!" cries Mary. "Please don't tell me . . ."

"I must, Mary. Your husband Shamus is dead and gone. I'm sorry."

Finally, she looked up at Patrick. "How did it happen, Patrick?"

"It was terrible, Mary. He fell into a vat of Guinness Stout and drowned."

"Oh, dear Jesus! But you must tell me true, Patrick. Did he go quickly?"

"Well, I'm afraid not, Mary . . . they say he got out three times to pee."

•

Maria is sitting on her stoop eating a slice of pizza.

Two of her girlfriends walk by and notice that she's not wearing any underwear.

"Hey, Maria," one of them calls out, "did you take off your panties to keep yourself cool?"

"I don't know about keeping cool," she said, "but it sure keeps the flies away from my pizza!"

•

As Adam wandered about the Garden of Eden, he noticed two birds up in a tree. They were snuggled up together, billing and cooing.

Adam called to the Lord, "What are the two birds doing in the trees?"

The Lord said, "They are making love, Adam."

A little while later he wandered into the fields and saw a bull and a cow going at it hot and heavy. He called to the Lord, "Lord, what's going on with that bull and cow?"

And the Lord said, "They're making love, Adam."

Adam said, "How come I don't have anyone to make love with?"

So the Lord said, "We'll change that. When you awake tomorrow morning, things will be different."

So Adam lay down beneath the olive tree and fell asleep. When he awoke, there was Eve next to him.

Adam jumped up, grabbed her hand, and said, "Come with me. Let's go into the bushes." And so they went.

But a few moments later, Adam stumbled out, looking very dejected, and called to the Lord, "Lord, what's a headache?"

•

A retired corporate executive decides to take a vacation. He books himself on a Caribbean cruise and proceeds to have the time of his life . . . until the boat sinks! He finds himself on an island with no other people, no supplies, nothing, only bananas and coconuts.

After about four months, he is lying on the beach one day when the most gorgeous woman he has ever seen rows up to the shore. In disbelief, he asks her, "Where did you come from? How did you get here?"

She replies, "I rowed from the other side of the island. I landed here when my cruise ship sank."

"Amazing," he says. "You were really lucky to have a row-boat wash up with you."

"Oh, this?" replies the woman. "I made the boat out of raw material I found on the island. The oars were whittled from gum tree branches. I wove the bottom from palm branches and the sides and stern came from the tree trunks."

"But where did you get the tools?"

"Oh, that was no problem," replies the woman. "A very unusual stratum of alluvial rock is exposed on the south side of the island. I found if I fired it to a certain temperature in my kiln, it melted into forgeable, ductile iron. I used that for tools and used the tools to make the hardware."

The guy is stunned.

"Let's row over to my place," she says. After a few hours of rowing, she docks the boat at a small wharf. As the man looks to shore, he nearly falls out of the boat. Before him is a stone walk leading to an exquisite bungalow painted in blue and white. While the woman ties up the rowboat with an expertly woven hemp rope, the man can only stare ahead, dumbstruck.

As they walk into the house, she says casually, "It's not much, but I call it home. Sit down, please. Would you like a drink?"

"No. No, thank you," he says, still dazed. "Can't take any more coconut juice."

"It's not coconut juice," the woman replies. "I have a still. How about a piña colada?"

Trying to hide his continued amazement, the man accepts, and they sit down on her couch to talk. After they have exchanged their stories, the woman announces, "I'm going to slip into something more comfortable. Would you like to take a shower and shave? There is a razor upstairs in the bathroom cabinet."

No longer questioning anything, the man goes into the bathroom. There, in the cabinet, is a razor made from a bone handle with two shells honed to a sharp edge fastened to its end inside a swivel mechanism.

"This woman is amazing," he muses. "What next?"

When he returns, she greets him wearing nothing but strategically positioned vines and flowers, and smelling of gardenias. She beckons for him to sit down next to her.

"Tell me," she begins suggestively, slithering closer to him, "we've been out here for a really long time. You've been lonely. There's something I'm sure you really feel like doing right now, something you've been longing for all these months?" She stares into his eyes and takes his hand in hers.

He can't believe what he's hearing. He swallows excitedly, tears start to form in his eyes, and he says, "You mean . . . I can check my e-mail from here?"

•

### THE 4 ANSWERS
### WE HAVE ALL BEEN WAITING FOR:

Q: What are the small bumps around a woman's nipples for?
A: It's Braille for "suck here."

Q: What is an Australian kiss?
A: It's the same as a French kiss, but only "down under."

Q: What do you do with 365 used condoms?
A: Melt them down, make a tire, and call it a Goodyear.

Q: Why are hurricanes normally named after women?
A: Because when they come, they're wild and wet. But when they go, they take your house and car with them.

•

A bosomy blonde was trying on an extremely low-cut dress. As she studied herself in the mirror, she asked the saleswoman if she thought it was too low-cut.

"Do you have hair on your chest?" the saleswoman asked.
"No!"
"Then," the saleswoman said, "it's too low-cut!"

•

This guy walked into a bar and said to the bartender, "I'll have a scotch and soda . . . and get that douche-bag whatever she'd like, on me." He motioned at a young woman sitting at the far end of the bar.

"Listen, buddy," said the bartender, "this is a family place, and I'll thank you not to use that sort of language in here."

"Right, right," said the customer. "Just get me that scotch and soda and get the douche-bag a drink."

"Now see here," sputtered the bartender, "that's a perfectly nice girl, and—"

"I'm getting thirsty," interrupted the guy, "and hurry up with the douche-bag's order, too."

Giving up, the bartender walked over to the young woman and rather shamefacedly said, "The gentleman over there would like to offer you a drink—what'll you have?"

She looked up with a smile and answered, "Vinegar and water, please."

•

### I, the Penis, hereby request a raise in salary for the following reasons:

1. I do physical labor.
2. I work at great depths.
3. I plunge headfirst into everything I do.
4. I do not get weekends or public holidays off.
5. I work in a damp environment.
6. I work in a dark area that has poor ventilation.
7. I work in high temperatures.
8. My work exposes me to diseases.

*Dear Penis,*

*After assessing your request, and considering the arguments you have raised, the management denies your request for the following reasons:*

1. *You do not work eight hours straight.*
2. *You work in short spurts and fall asleep after each brief work period.*
3. *You do not always follow the orders of the management team.*
4. *You do not stay in your designated area, and are often seen visiting other locations.*
5. *You do not take initiative—you need to be pressured and stimulated in order to start working.*
6. *You leave the workplace rather messy at the end of your shift.*
7. *You don't always observe necessary safety regulations, such as wearing the correct protective clothing.*
8. *You will retire long before you are sixty-five.*
9. *You are unable to work double shifts.*
10. *You sometimes leave your designated work area before you have completed the assigned task.*
11. *And if that were not all, you have constantly been seen entering and exiting the workplace carrying two suspicious-looking bags.*

*Sincerely,*
*The Management*

•

"Mom, I'm pregnant," announced the sixteen-year-old one morning in a belligerent tone.

Her mother paled.

"And it's all your fault," continued the girl.

"My fault?" gasped her mother, startled. "I bought you books, showed you pictures . . . I told you all about the facts of life."

"Yeah, yeah—but you never taught me how to give a decent blow job."

•

The young lawyer was thrilled to make partner at long last, but disappointed that it didn't immediately make his life easier and more prosperous. In fact, business was hurt by the recession and soon he was bringing home less money than ever. His wife, however, had grown accustomed to a grander vision of their future, and was spending like there was no tomorrow.

Finally he sat down with her to discuss the need to trim their budget a bit. "For starters," he suggested rather snidely, "if you could learn to make something for dinner besides reservations, we could fire the cook."

"That's a thought," she conceded graciously. "And if you'd just learn to f***, we could fire the gardener."

•

A cowboy traveling in the desert came across a lovely woman, naked and battered, her limbs tied to four stakes in the ground.

"Thank God you've come!" she cried. "I was on my way to San Francisco when a whole tribe of Indians attacked our wagon train. They stole our food, kidnapped our children, torched our wagons . . . and raped me over and over."

"Lady," said the cowboy as he unbuckled his belt, "today just ain't your day."

•

The town gossip came over to the editor of the newspaper and whispered, "Mr. Smith, I do believe I saw Mrs. Smith engaged in carnal relations with someone other than yourself. This was just the other day, underneath that big pine tree in your backyard, you know the one?"

The editor appeared unfazed. "Was the man bald?"

"As a matter of fact, he was."

"With a black mustache?"

"I do believe so." The busybody was all atwitter with excitement.

"That's just my chauffeur," said the man with a shrug. "He'll f*** anything."

•

My neighbor found out her dog could hardly hear, so she took it to the veterinarian. He found the problem was hair in its ears; once he got rid of the hair, the dog could hear fine.

The vet told the lady if she wanted to keep this from reoccurring, she should go to the store and get some Nair hair remover and rub it in the dog's ears once a month.

The lady went to the drugstore to get some Nair. At the register, the druggist told her, "If you're going to use this under your arms, don't use deodorant for a few days."

The lady said, "I'm not using it under my arms."

The druggist said, "If you're using it on your legs, don't shave for a couple of days."

The lady said, "I'm not using it on my legs either; if you must know, I'm using it on my schnauzer."

The druggist said, "Stay off your bicycle for a week."

•

A nymphomaniac goes to the supermarket and gets all hot and bothered eyeing the carrots and cucumbers. By the time she gets to the checkout line she can't hold out much longer, so she asks one of the supermarket baggers to carry her groceries out to the car for her. They're halfway across the lot when the nympho slips her hand down his pants and whispers, "You know, I've got an itchy pussy."

"Sorry, lady," says the bagger, "but I can't tell one of those Japanese cars from another."

•

"Say," said Lucille one day over lunch, "weren't you going to go out with that guy who played the French horn?"

"Yeah," said Diane, stirring her iced tea. "He was a pretty nice guy. But there was one real problem . . ."

"Oh, really?"

"Every time he kissed me, he wanted to shove his fist up my ass."

•

God has just spent six days creating the heavens and the Earth. Now, since it's the seventh day, He and Gabriel are sitting back and admiring His handiwork.

"You know, God," says Gabriel, "you've done one hell of a job—pardon my language. Those snowy peaks are unbelievably majestic, and those woods, with their little sunny dells and meadows . . . masterful. Not to mention the oceans: those fantastic coral reefs, and all the sea creatures, and the waves crashing on the pristine beaches. And all the animals, from fleas to elephants, what vision! Not to mention the heavens; how could I leave them out? What a touch, that Milky Way."

God beams.

"If you'll excuse my presumption," Gabriel goes on, "I have just the teeniest question. You know those sample humans you put down in the Garden of Eden?"

God nods, a frown furrowing His divine brow.

"Well, I was just wondering whether, for the obvious reasons, they shouldn't have differing sets of genitalia, the way all the other animals do?"

After God reflects on the matter for a minute or two, a big smile crosses His face. "You're absolutely right," He agrees. "Give the dumb one a cunt!"

•

Because over the past few years more money has been spent on breast implants and Viagra than on Alzheimer's disease research, it is believed that by the year 2030 there will be a large number of people wandering around with huge breasts and erections . . . who can't remember what to do with them.

•

Men and women are different in the morning. We men wake up aroused in the morning. We can't help it. We just wake up and we want you. And the women are thinking, "How can he want me the way I look in the morning?" It's because we can't see you. We have no blood anywhere near our optic nerves.

•

Pinocchio had a human girlfriend who would sometimes complain about splinters when they were having sex. Pinocchio, therefore, went to visit Gepetto to see if he could help.

Gepetto suggested he try a little sandpaper wherever indicated and Pinocchio skipped away enlightened.

A couple weeks later, Gepetto saw Pinocchio bouncing happily through town and asked him, "How's the girlfriend?"

Pinocchio replied, "Who needs a girlfriend?"

•

Little Red Riding Hood was walking through the woods when suddenly the Big Bad Wolf jumped out from behind a tree and, holding a sword to her throat, said, "Red, I'm going to screw your brains out!"

To that, Little Red Riding Hood calmly reached into her picnic basket and pulled out a .44 Magnum and pointed it at him and said, "No, you're not. You're going to eat me, just like it says in the book."

•

Mickey Mouse and Minnie Mouse were in divorce court and the judge said to Mickey, "You say here that your wife is crazy."

Mickey replied, "I didn't say she was crazy, I said she's f***ing Goofy."

•

Snow White saw Pinocchio walking through the woods so she ran up to him, knocked him flat on his back, and then sat on his face crying, "Lie to me! Lie to me!"

•

Typical macho man married typical good-looking lady and after the wedding, he laid down the following rules:

"I'll be home when I want, if I want, and at what time I want, and I don't expect any hassle from you. I expect a great dinner to be on the table unless I tell you that I won't be home for dinner. I'll go hunting, fishing, boozing, and card-playing when I want with my old buddies and don't you give me a hard time about it. Those are my rules. Any comments?"

His new bride said, "No, that's fine with me. Just understand that there will be sex here at seven o'clock every night . . . whether you're here or not."

•

A little old lady from North Carolina had worked in and around her family dairy farms since she was old enough to walk, with hours of hard work and little compensation. When canned Carnation Milk became available in grocery stores, she read an advertisement offering $5,000 for the best slogan/rhyme beginning with "Carnation Milk is best of all. . . ."

She said to herself, "I know all about milk and dairy farms . . . I can do this!"

She sent in her entry, and about a week later, a black limo drove up in front of her house. A man got out and said, "Carnation *loved* your entry so much, we are here to award you one thousand dollars, even though we will not be able to use it. . . ."

Here is her entry:
*Carnation milk is best of all,*
*no tits to pull, no hay to haul,*

*no buckets to wash, no shit to pitch,*
*just poke a hole in the son-of-a-bitch!*

•

Three guys go to a ski lodge. There aren't enough rooms, so they have to share a bed.

In the middle of the night, the guy on the right wakes up and says, "I had this wild, vivid dream last night that someone had their hand in my pants and was playing with me!"

The guy on the left wakes up and unbelievably, he's had the same dream, too.

Then the guy in the middle wakes up and exclaims, "That's funny, I dreamed that I was skiing!"

•

Two friends decided they would beat the draft by having all their teeth pulled. They knew the army would not take them if they were toothless.

Finally, the day came when they were to report to the draft board. As they lined up, they were separated by a big truck driver who obviously had not bathed for weeks. When the first friend stood before the sergeant for a physical examination, he told the sergeant that he had no teeth. The sergeant ran his fingers around the man's gums and said, "All right, you have no teeth—you're 4F."

Next came the big, smelly truck driver. The sergeant said, "What's wrong with you?"

The truck driver replied, "I have a terrible case of piles."

The sergeant inserted his fingers in the truck driver's ass, felt around, and said, "Yes, indeed you do; you're 4F."

Next came the second friend, and the sergeant said, "What's wrong with you?"

The recruit stared at the sergeant's finger. "Nothing, Sergeant," he said. "Nothing at all."

•

The American tourist stood staring at the highland sentry standing guard outside Edinburgh Castle.

After a few minutes she went up to the sentry and asked, "I've always wanted to find out what's worn under the kilt."

The sentry replied: 'There is nothing worn, ma'am, it's all in perfect working order."

•

If Dr. Seuss were a woman, she'd write:

*I'm glad I'm a woman—yes I am, yes I am. I don't live on Budweiser, beer nuts, and Spam.*

*I don't brag to my buddies about my erections; I won't drive to hell before asking directions.*

*I act nice at parties; don't act like a clown. And I know how to put the damn toilet seat down.*

*I won't grab your boobies; I won't pinch your butt.*

*My belt is not hidden beneath my beer gut.*

*I don't go around readjusting my crotch; or make sure my headboard bears each hard-earned notch.*

*I don't belch in public; don't scratch my behind. I'm a woman, you see—I'm just not that kind!*

*I'm glad I'm a woman, so glad I could sing—and thrilled I'm not covered in shag carpeting.*

*Hair won't grow from my ears, or cover my back.*

*And when I bend over, you can't see my crack.*

*I'm a woman, alas—and I'm proud, don't you see?*

*I'm blessed to have two boobs and squat when I pee.*

*I don't live for golf, or shoot basketball.*

*I don't swagger and spit like a Neanderthal.*

*I don't need male bonding;*

*I don't cruise for a chick.*

*I'll never join "Hair Club," or think with my dick.*

*I'm a woman, by chance, and thankful I am!*

*I'm so glad I'm a woman, not a man, yes I am!*

•

According to a new article in *Cosmopolitan* magazine, they say the position you sleep in says a lot about you.

They say women who sleep on their sides are sensitive, women who sleep on their stomachs are competent, and women who sleep on their backs with their ankles behind their ears are very popular.

•

A bakery owner hires a young female clerk who likes to wear very short skirts and thongs. One day a young man enters the store, glances at the clerk, then glances at the loaves of bread behind the counter.

Noticing the length of her skirt (or lack thereof), and the location of the raisin bread, he has a brilliant idea.

"I'd like some raisin bread, please," the man says politely.

The female clerk nods and climbs up a ladder to reach the raisin bread, which is located on the very top shelf.

The young man, standing almost directly beneath her, is provided with an excellent view, just as he surmised he would. Once she descends the ladder he muses that he really should get two loaves, as he is having company for dinner. As the clerk retrieves the second loaf of bread, one of the other male customers notices what is going on. Thinking quickly, he requests his own loaf of raisin bread so he can enjoy the view also.

With each trip up the ladder, the young lady seems to catch the eye of another male customer. Pretty soon, each male customer is asking for raisin bread, just to see the clerk climb up and down.

After many trips she is tired, irritated, and thinking that she is really going to have to try the bread herself. Finally, once again atop the ladder, she stops and fumes, glaring at the men standing below.

She notices an elderly man standing amongst the crowd, staring up at her.

Thinking to save herself a trip, she yells at the elderly man, "Is it raisin for you, too?"

"No," stammers the old man, "but it's a-quiverin'."

•

One hot July day we found an old straggly cat at our door. She was a sorry sight. Starving, dirty, smelled terrible, skinny, and hair all matted down. We felt sorry for her, put her in a carrier, and took her to the vet. We didn't know what to call her, so we named her "Pussycat."

The vet decided to keep her for a day or so. He said he would let us know when we could come and get her. My husband (the complainer) said, "OK, but don't forget to wash her, she stinks." He reminded the vet that it was his *wife* who wanted the dirty cat, not him.

My husband and my vet don't see eye to eye. He calls my husband "El Cheap-O," my husband calls him "El Take-O." They love to hate each other and constantly snipe at each other, with my husband getting in the last word on this occasion.

The next day my husband had an appointment with his doctor, who is located next door to the vet. The doctor's office was full of people waiting to see him.

A side door opened and in leaned the vet; he had obviously seen my husband arrive. He looked straight at my husband and in a loud voice said, "Your wife's pussy is finally clean and shaved and she now smells like a rose. Oh, and by the way, I think she's pregnant. God knows who the father is!" And he closed the door.

•

In a tiny village on the Irish coast lived an old lady, a virgin and very proud of it. Sensing that her final days were rapidly approaching, and desiring to make sure everything was in proper order when she died, she went to the town's undertaker (who also happened to be the local postal clerk) to make the proper final arrangements. As a last wish, she informed the undertaker that she wanted the following inscription engraved on her tombstone:

BORN A VIRGIN, LIVED AS A VIRGIN, DIED A VIRGIN

Not long after, the old maid died peacefully. A few days after the funeral, as the undertaker/postal clerk went to prepare the tombstone that the lady had requested, it became quite apparent that the tombstone that she had selected was much too small for the wording that she had chosen. He thought long and hard about how he could fulfill the old maid's final request, considering the very limited space available on the small piece of stone. For days, he agonized over the dilemma. But finally, his experience as a postal worker allowed him to come up with what he thought was the appropriate solution to the problem.

The virgin's tombstone was finally completed and duly engraved, and it read as follows:

RETURNED UNOPENED

•

Question: Why is life like a penis?
Answer: Because when it's soft it's hard to beat, but when it's hard you get screwed.

•

A man was strolling on the beach one day when he came across a lamp lying in the sand. He picked it up and rubbed it. Sure enough, a genie popped out. "I will grant you your one true desire," boomed the huge genie.

"Wow, that's fantastic!" exclaimed the man. "All my life I wanted a cock so big that it would touch the ground."

So, poof, the genie cut the man's legs off.

•

A recent news story detailed a medical implant that offers women the chance to experience orgasms with the press of a button. Tiny electrodes are implanted into the spine and a small signal generator in the skin close to the groin. The patient then controls the sensation with a handheld remote.

### Side effects of the new orgasm implant:

* *Dramatic increase in the number of women seen hanging out at Radio Shack.*

* Cosmopolitan *magazine folds due to a drastic shortage of orgasm-related headlines.*

* *Dad: now surfs with two remotes. Mom: never complains.*

* *She never wants to cuddle anymore—it's click, click, click, and she's out the door.*

* *Thanks to a malfunctioning garage door opener, you're looking at $600 to fix the hole your wife kicked in the dashboard of your SUV.*

* *The Energizer Bunny keeps coming and coming . . .*

* *"Not tonight, honey. I have a thumbache."*

* *Finally, size really doesn't matter.*

* *"I'm sorry, could you repeat that? I wasn't paying attention . . . I'm sorry, could you repeat that? I wasn't paying attention . . . I'm sorry . . ."*

* *Every time your cell phone rings, you feel the uncontrollable urge to shout your surgeon's name.*

* *Side effects? Who cares about . . . oh . . . oh . . . OH, GOD! YESSSSSS!!!!*

* *In addition to "Mute" and "Favorite," the wildly popular Ultimate Universal Remote now has a new button: "Big O."*

•

A Russian wrestler and an American wrestler were set to square off for the Olympic gold medal. Before the final match, the American wrestler's trainer came to him and said, "Now, don't forget all the research we've done on this Russian. He's never lost a match because of this 'pretzel' hold he has . . . whatever you do, don't let him get you in this hold! If he does, you're finished!" The wrestler nodded in acknowledgment.

As the match started, the American and the Russian circled each other several times, looking for an opening. All of a sudden, the Russian lunged forward, grabbing the American and wrapping him up in the dreaded pretzel hold. A sigh of disappointment arose from the crowd and the trainer buried his face in his hands, for he knew all was lost. He couldn't watch the inevitable happen. Suddenly, there was a scream, then a cheer from the crowd, and the trainer raised his eyes just in time to watch the Russian go flying up in the air. His back hit the mat with a thud and the American collapsed on top of him; making the pin and winning the match!

The trainer was astounded. When he finally got the American wrestler alone, he asked, "How did you ever get out of that hold? No one has ever done it before!"

The wrestler answered, "Well, I was ready to give up when he got me in that hold but at the last moment, I opened my eyes and saw this pair of testicles right in front of my face. I had nothing to lose, so with my last ounce of strength I stretched out my neck and bit those babies just as hard as I could."

"So," the trainer exclaimed, "that's what finished him off?!"

"Not really," came his reply. "But you'd be amazed how strong you get when you bite your own balls."

•

Mike and Maureen landed on Mars. They met a Martian couple and were talking about all sorts of things. Finally Maureen brought up the subject of sex.

"Just how do you guys do it?" asked Maureen.

The male Martian responded, "Pretty much the way you do." A discussion ensued and finally the couples decided to swap partners for the night.

Maureen and the male Martian went off to a bedroom, where the Martian stripped. Maureen was disappointed to find that he had a very small member, no more than half an inch long and just a quarter-inch thick.

"I don't think this is going to work," said Maureen.

"Why?" he asked. "What's the matter?"

"Well," she replied, "it's just not long enough to reach me!"

"No problem," he said and proceeded to slap his forehead with his palm. With each slap, his member grew until it was impressively long.

"Well," she said. "That's quite impressive, but it's still pretty narrow."

"No problem," he said and started pulling his ears. With each pull his member grew wider and wider.

"Wow!" she exclaimed.

They fell into bed and made mad passionate love. The next day the couples joined their normal partners. As they walked along, Mike asked, "Well, was it any good?"

"I hate to say it," said Maureen, "but it was pretty wonderful. How about you?"

"It was horrible," he replied. "All I got was a headache. She kept slapping my forehead and pulling my ears!"

•

## Correct use of the "F "word

*There have been only thirteen times in history when the "F"*
*word was considered acceptable for use. They are as follows:*

13. "What the f*** do you mean, we are sinking?"—Capt. E. J. Smith of RMS *Titanic*, 1912

12. "What the f*** was that?"—Mayor of Hiroshima, 1945

11. "Where did all those f***ing Indians come from?"
—General George Custer, 1877

10. "Any f***ing idiot could understand that."—Albert Einstein, 1938

9. "It does so f***ing look like her!"—Pablo Picasso, 1926

8. "How the f*** did you work that out?"—Pythagoras, 126 BC

7. "You want WHAT on the f***ing ceiling?"—Michelangelo, 1566

6. "Where the f*** are we?"—Amelia Earhart, 1937

5. "Scattered f***ing showers, my ass!"—Noah, 4314 BC

4. "Aw, c'mon. Who the f*** is going to find out?"—Bill Clinton, 1998

3. "What do you mean there is no f***ing key to my ankle bracelet?"—Martha Stewart, 2005

2. "Jeez, I didn't think they'd get this f***ing mad."
—Saddam Hussein, 2003

*and a drum roll please . . . !*

1. "How did he get in my f***ing way?"—Vice President Dick Cheney, 2006

•

A white guy is walking along a beach when he comes across a lamp partially buried in the sand. He picks up the lamp and gives it a rub. Two blond genies appear, and they tell him he has been granted three wishes. The guy makes his three wishes and the blond genies disappear.

The next thing the guy knows, he's in a bedroom in a mansion, surrounded by fifty beautiful women. He makes love to all of them and begins to explore the house. Suddenly he feels something soft under his feet. He looks down and the floor is covered in $100 bills. Then, there's a knock at the door . . .

He answers it and standing there are two people dressed in Ku Klux Klan outfits. They drag him outside to the nearest tree, throw a rope over a limb, and hang him by the neck until he's dead.

As the Klansmen are walking away, they remove their hoods; it's the two blond genies. One blond genie says to the other one, "I can understand the first wish, having all these beautiful women in a big mansion to make love to. I can also understand him wanting to be a millionaire . . . but why he wanted to be hung like a black man is beyond me."

•

Two men are occupying booths in a public restroom, when one calls to the other, "There is no toilet paper over here—do you have any over there?"

The second man replies, "No, sorry, I don't seem to have any, either."

The first man then asks, "Well, do you have a magazine or newspaper?"

The second man says, "No, sorry!"

The first man pauses, then inquires, "Do you have change for a twenty?"

•

An Englishman, a Scotsman, and an Irishman are all to give speeches to the Deaf Society. All are keen to make an impression on their audience.

The Englishman goes first and, to the surprise of his colleagues, starts by rubbing first his chest and then his groin. When he finishes, the Scotsman and Irishman ask him what he was doing.

"Well," he explained, "by rubbing my chest I indicated breasts and thus ladies, and by rubbing my groin I indicated balls and thus gentlemen. So my speech started: Ladies and gentlemen."

On his way up to the podium the Scotsman thought to himself, "I'll go one better than that English bastard," and started his speech by making an antler symbol with his fingers above his head before also rubbing his chest and his groin.

When he finished, his colleagues asked what he was doing. "Well," he explained, "by imitating antlers and then rubbing my chest and groin I was starting my speech by saying: Dear ladies and gentlemen."

On his way up to the podium, the Irishman thought to himself, "I'll go one further than those mainland bastards," and started his speech by making an antler symbol above his head, rubbing his chest, and then his groin, and then masturbating furiously.

When he finished, his colleagues asked him what he was doing. "Well," he explained, "by imitating antlers, rubbing my chest and then my groin, and then masturbating, I was starting my speech by saying: Dear ladies and gentlemen, it gives me great pleasure . . ."

•

One day, this fellow noticed that a new couple had moved into the house next door. He was also quick to notice that the woman liked to sunbathe in the backyard, usually in a skimpy bikini that showed off a magnificent pair of breasts. He made it a point to water and trim his lawn as much as possible, hoping for yet another look. Finally, he could stand it no more. Walking to the front door of the new neighbor's house, he knocked and waited. The husband, a large, burly man, opened the door.

"Excuse me," our man stammered, "but I couldn't help noticing how beautiful your wife is."

"Yeah? So?" his hulking neighbor replied.

"Well, in particular, I am really struck by how beautiful her breasts are. I would gladly pay you ten thousand dollars if I could kiss those breasts."

The burly gorilla was about to deck our poor guy when his wife appeared and stopped him. She pulled him inside and they discussed the offer for a few moments. Finally, they returned and asked our friend to step inside.

"OK," the husband said gruffly, "for ten thousand dollars you can kiss my wife's tits."

At this the wife unbuttoned her blouse, and the twin objects of desire hung free at last. Our man took one in each hand, and proceeded to rub his face against them in total ecstasy. This went on for several minutes, until the husband got annoyed. "Well, come on already, kiss 'em!" he growled.

"I can't," replied our awestruck hero, still nuzzling away.

"Why not?" demanded the husband, getting really angry.

The neighbor replied, "I don't have ten thousand dollars!"

•

Explaining to his doctor that his sex life wasn't all it could be, Joe asked for a pill that would enable him to get it up for his wife. It so happened that the doctor had just the right medication, so the man took a pill and drove home. But when he got to the apartment, his wife wasn't at home, and after waiting for an hour or so in growing discomfort, he finally had to jerk off.

When the doctor called to check in the next day, Joe explained what had happened. "Well, gee, Joe, you didn't have to do for yourself," pointed out the doctor. "There are other women in the building."

"Doctor," said Joe, "for other women I don't need a pill."

•

A young man wanted to buy a gift for his girlfriend's birthday. They had not been together very long, so he thought long and hard before remembering that on their last date she had complained that her hands were cold. So he decided on a pair of gloves, not too personal at this stage of their relationship, but thoughtful nonetheless.

Accompanied by his girlfriend's sister, he went to Macy's and bought a stylish pair of dainty white gloves. At the same time the sister bought a pair of panties for herself and they both asked for them to be gift-wrapped.

Unfortunately, the shop assistant mixed the items up and the guy left with his girlfriend's sister's purchase and the girlfriend's sister left with the gloves.

The boyfriend, obviously none the wiser, decided to deliver his present in person. When he arrived at his girlfriend's house, she wasn't in. So instead he left the following thoughtful note along with the present at her front door:

> *I hope you like your present. I chose these because I noticed that you are not in the habit of wearing any when we go out in the evenings. Had it not been for your sister I would have chosen some long ones with white buttons, but she wears short ones and they are easier to pull off.*
>
> *These are a delicate shade and the shop assistant showed me the pair she has been wearing for the past three weeks and they are hardly soiled at all. I had her try on yours and, although a little tight, they looked really smart. She told me that the material helps keep her ring clean and in fact she hasn't had to wash it since wearing them.*
>
> *I wish you had been here so that I could have put them on for you as no doubt many hands will touch them before I have the chance to see you again. When you take them off, remember to blow into them as they will be a little damp from wearing.*
>
> *Just think how many times I will be holding them in my*

*hand over the coming year. I hope that you will wear them for
me on Friday night.*

*All my love,*

*Adam.*

*P.S. The latest style is to wear them folded down with a
little fur showing.*

•

A woman walks into a tattoo parlor.

"Do you do custom work?" she asks the artist.

"Why, of course!"

"Good. I'd like a portrait of Robert Redford on the inside of
my right thigh, and a portrait of Paul Newman on the inside
of my left thigh. And I want them both looking at my pussy."

"No problem," says the artist. "Strip from the waist down
and get up on the table."

After two hours of hard work, the artist finishes. The
woman sits up and examines the tattoos. "That doesn't look
like them!" she complains loudly.

"Oh, yes it does," the artist says indignantly, "and I can
prove it."

With that, he runs out of the shop and grabs the first man
off the street he can find; it happens to be the town drunk.

"Well, what do you think?" the woman asks, spreading her
legs apart. "Do you know who these men are?"

The drunk studies the tattoos for a couple of minutes and
says, "I'm not sure who the guys on either side are, but the
fellow in the middle is definitely Willie Nelson!"

•

The young man had invited his parents to meet his fiancée
over cocktails at the Plaza Hotel in New York. After his family
had departed, the girl wanted to know what kind of impression she'd made.

"I'm sorry to tell you this, dear," the young man said. "But while you were in the ladies' room, my mother told me that she considered you rather uncouth."

"Did you tell them I graduated from finishing school and from Bennington?"

"Yes."

"Did you tell them my family enjoys the highest social standing in Southampton?"

"I certainly did, dear."

"Then what the f*** is all this uncouth shit about?" the girl demanded to know.

•

A nun went to her mother superior to complain about the language the construction workers working next to the convent were using. Sister Margaret was Polish, so the mother superior was used to breaking things down and making the simplest of explanations to her.

"Sister Margaret, don't get so upset by their bad language. Those men are just people of the earth. They call a spade a spade," the mother superior explained patiently.

Still agitated, Sister Margaret replied, "Oh no they don't, Mother. They call it a f***in' shovel!"

•

A salesman who is on the road is staying in a futuristic motel. He has an important sales call the next morning and, realizing he needs a trim, he calls the desk clerk to inquire whether there was a barber on the premises. "I'm afraid not, sir," the clerk says, "but down the hall there is a bank of vending machines and one will give you a haircut." Thoroughly intrigued, the salesman finds the machine, inserts fifty cents, and sticks his head in the opening. The machine starts buzzing and whirring. Fifteen seconds later, he pulls out his head and discovers he's just gotten the best haircut he has ever received. Two feet away is another machine that says MANICURES

50 CENTS, and the salesman thinks, "Why not?" So he pays the money, inserts his hands into the slot, and out they come with a terrific manicure.

The next machine has a big sign: THIS MACHINE DOES WHAT MEN NEED MOST WHEN AWAY FROM THEIR WIVES. The salesman looks both ways, unzips his fly, inserts his cock, and puts in the fifty cents. The machine buzzes away as the guy screams in excruciating pain. Fifteen seconds later, it stops. He pulls out his cock with trembling hands, and stares at the button sewn to the tip.

•

Q: What's the difference between a young whore and an old whore?
A: A young whore uses Vaseline and an old whore uses Poli-Grip.

•

Q: How many animals can you find in a pair of panty hose?
A: Two calves; ten little piggies; one ass; one pussy; one thousand hares; maybe some crabs; and a dead fish nobody can find.

•

A man who was obviously the victim of a nasty accident comes staggering into the pub with both arms in plaster casts.

"I'll have a beer, thanks mate," he says to the barman. "And could you hold it up to my lips for me?"

"No worries," says the barman.

"Couldn't light a ciggie for me, too, could you?" asks the man.

"Not a problem," says the barman.

"Thanks, mate," says the man. "My wallet's in me back pocket, if you'd like to get it out for me."

"There you go," says the barman.

"Thanks," says the man. "By the way, where's the toilet?"

And without a moment's hesitation, the barman says, "Go two blocks up the street, turn right, and it's the second building on the left."

•

The gynecologist stuck up his head after completing his examination. "Removing that vibrator's going to be tricky, but I'm pretty sure I can manage it."

"Don't knock yourself out," said the woman cheerfully. "Why don't you just replace the batteries?"

•

A woman went into surgery for a routine breast biopsy, and when she came to, she found the doctor standing by her bed.

"I've got some bad news and some good news," he said, taking her hand comfortingly in his. "I'm afraid we found malignant tumors in both breasts, and had to remove both of them completely."

"Oh, my God," said the poor woman, bursting into tears.

"There, there, don't forget the good news," the surgeon reminded her.

"What could that be?" she sobbed.

"The transvestite in the next bed wants to buy all your old bras."

•

A veterinarian had a tough day. However, when he got home his wife was ready with a long cool drink and a romantic candlelit dinner. Then they had a few more drinks and went to bed. Then the phone rang . . .

"Is this the vet?" asked an elderly lady's voice.

"Yes, it is," replied the vet. "Is this an emergency?"

"Well, yes," said the lady, "there's a whole bunch of cats on the roof outside making a terrible noise mating and I can't get to sleep. What can I do about it?"

The vet drew a long breath, and replied, "Open the window and tell them they're wanted on the phone."

"Really?" said the elderly lady. "Will that stop them?"

"Well," said the vet, "it stopped me!"

•

A man goes into a bar with his dog and asks for a drink. The bartender says, "You can't bring that dog in here!"

The man, without missing a beat, says, "This is my seeing-eye dog."

"Oh man, I'm sorry," the bartender says, "I didn't realize you were blind. Here, the first drink's on me." The man takes his drink and goes to a table near the door.

Another guy walks in the bar with a chihuahua. The first man sees him, stops him, and says, "They don't allow dogs in here, so you won't get a drink unless you tell him it's a seeing-eye dog."

The second man graciously thanks the first man and continues to the bar. He asks for a drink. The bartender says, "Sorry, you can't bring that dog in here!"

The second man replies, "This is my seeing-eye dog."

The bartender peers over the edge and says, "No, I don't think so. They do not have chihuahuas as seeing-eye dogs."

The man pauses for a half-second and replies, "What?! They gave me a f***ing chihuahua?"

•

An infamous stud with a long list of conquests walked into his neighborhood bar and ordered a drink.

The bartender thought he looked worried and asked him if anything was wrong.

"I'm scared out of my mind," the stud replied. "Some pissed-off husband wrote to me and said he'd kill me if I didn't stop f***ing his wife."

"So stop," the barkeep said.

"I can't," the womanizer replied, taking a long swill. "The prick didn't sign his name!"

•

A very unattractive, mean-actin' woman walks into Wal-Mart with her two kids.

The Wal-Mart greeter, asks, "Are they twins?"

The ugly woman says, "No, the older one, he's nine, and the younger one, she's seven. Why? Do you think they really look alike?"

"No," replies the greeter, "I just couldn't believe you got laid twice!"

•

A man goes to the doctor and says, "Doc, you have to help me!"

The doctor asks, "What's your problem?"

The guy says, "Every morning I wake up with my 'morning flagpole,' give the wife a quick one, and then go to work. I carpool with the next-door neighbor's wife who gives me a blow job during the ride. Once I get there, I do some work and then at morning tea time, I go into the photocopy room and crank one out with one of the young office girls. At lunch, I take my secretary out to a hotel and give her a good boning. For afternoon tea, I give the boss's wife a good servicing. Then, I go home and slip the maid a few inches. Then at night, I give the wife another screw."

"So . . . ?" asks the doctor. "What's your problem?"

The guy says, "Well, it hurts when I jerk off."

•

At the cinema a man noticed a young woman sitting all by herself. He was excited to see she had both hands under her skirt and was fingering herself furiously. He moved to the seat next to her and offered his help. She welcomed his help, and so the man started fingering her like crazy. When he tired and withdrew his hand, he was surprised to see her go back to work on herself with both hands.

"Wasn't I good enough?" he asked sheepishly.

"Great," she said, "but these crabs are still itching!"

•

A man is at the dentist's for a checkup. As the dentist leans over, he asks, "Well . . . so you had oral sex this morning?"

"How did you know?" asks the man, embarrassed but also amazed at his dentist's perception. "Was it the smell on my breath?"

"No," says the dentist.

"Well, did you see a pubic hair caught in my teeth?" asks the man.

"No," says the dentist.

"Well, what then? How did you know?" asks the man, losing patience.

The dentist says, "There's a little bit of shit on the end of your nose."

•

A guy goes into a bar and says to the bartender, "Man, I'm dying to have sex in the worst way."

So the bartender says, "Well, the worst way I know of is standing up in a hammock."

•

I've never gone to bed with an ugly woman, but I've woken up with a few.

•

A group of prisoners are in their rehabilitation meeting. Their task for today is to each stand up in turn, speak their name, and admit to their fellow inmates what crime they committed. The first prisoner stands and says, "My name is Daniel and I'm in for murder." Everyone gives him approving looks and pats him on the back for admitting his wrongdoing.

The next guy stands up and says, "My name is Mike and I'm in for armed robbery." Again, there is a round of approving looks.

This goes around the circle until it gets to the last guy. He stands up and says, "My name is Luke, but I'm not telling you what I'm in for."

The group leader says, "Now, come on, Luke, you have to admit it to us to make any progress. Tell us what you did."

"OK, then. I'm in for f***ing dogs."

Everyone is disgusted! They all shout "What??!! How LOW can you get!"

"Well . . . I did manage to do a dachshund one time, but I had to lift her back legs up a little," Luke replies.

•

On the first day of college, the dean addressed the students, pointing out some of the rules, saying, "The female dormitory will be out-of-bounds for all male students, and the male dormitory to the female students. Anyone caught breaking this rule once will be fined fifty dollars."

He continued, "Anyone caught breaking this rule a second time will be fined one hundred fifty dollars. Being caught a third time will incur a hefty fine of four hundred dollars. Are there any questions?"

At this point, a male student in the crowd inquired, "How much for a season pass?"

•

Two marines were sitting around talking one day. The first marine asked the second marine, "If they were to drop a bomb right now, what would be the first thing you would do?"

The second marine said, "I would screw the first thing that moved. What would you do?"

The first marine replied, "I would stand very still for half an hour."

•

Two young guys were picked up by the cops for smoking dope and appeared in court on Friday before the judge. The judge said, "You seem like nice young men, and I'd like to give you a second chance rather than jail time. I want you to go out this weekend and try to show others the evils of drug use and get them to give up drugs forever. I'll see you back in court Monday."

Monday, the two guys were in court, and the judge asked the first one, "How did you do over the weekend?"

"Well, Your Honor," he replied, "I persuaded seventeen people to give up drugs forever."

"Seventeen people? That's wonderful. What did you tell them?"

"I used a diagram, Your Honor. I drew two circles and told them the big circle is your brain before drugs, and the small circle is your brain after drugs."

"That's admirable," said the judge. "And you, how did you do?" he asked the second boy.

"Well, Your Honor, I persuaded one hundred fifty-six people to give up drugs forever."

"One hundred fifty-six people! That's amazing! How did you manage to do that?"

"Well, I used a similar approach," he answered. "I drew a large and a small circle. Pointing to the small circle, I said, this is your asshole before you go to prison . . ."

•

There are these three girls and their boyfriends all have the same name. So, in order to keep them from getting confused, they decided to give their boyfriends nicknames. So, they asked the first girl what she called her boyfriend. And she says, "I call my man 7-Up."

They ask her, "Why do you call your man that?"

And she says, "Because he's seven inches long and is always up."

They ask the second girl what she calls her man. She says, "I call my man Mountain Dew."

They ask, "Why do you call your man that?" She says, "Because he likes to mount me and to do me."

They ask the third girl the same thing and she says, "I like to call my man Jack Daniel's."

They look at her, puzzled, and say, "Why do you call your man that? Jack Daniel's is a hard liquor." She says, "Exactly."

The limousine was taking the beautiful, raven-haired model to the airport. Halfway there, the front tire went flat. The model said, "Driver, I don't have time to wait for road service. Can you change it yourself?"

The driver said, "Sure." He got out of the car and proceeded to change the tire, but couldn't get the hubcap off.

The model saw him struggling and asked, "Do you want a screwdriver?"

He said, "Sure! But first I have to change this tire."

•

A young kid's in a shipwreck and he winds up stranded on a tropical island. For twenty years he never sees another human being. Then one day a beautiful girl with long blond hair, her clothes half ripped off, washes up on a piece of driftwood. He explains to her how he existed for twenty years, digging for clams and eating fruits and berries. She says, "Well, what did you do for love?"

He says, "Love? What's that?"

She says, "I'll show you." She shows him. Then she shows

him again. Then she shows him one more time. When they're finally done, she says, "Well, how do you like love?"

He says, "It's great. But look what you did to my clam digger."

•

In the backwoods of Scotland, Ian's wife went into labor in the middle of the night, and the doctor was called out to assist in the delivery.

To keep the nervous father-to-be busy, the doctor handed him a lantern and said, "Here, you hold this high so I can see what I'm doing." Soon, a wee baby boy was brought into the world.

"Whoa there, Ian!" said the doctor. "Don't be in a rush to put the lantern down . . . I think there's yet another wee one to come yet."

Sure enough, within minutes he had delivered a bonnie lass.

"No, no, don't be in a great hurry to be putting down that lantern, lad . . . It seems there's yet another one besides!" cried the doctor.

Then Ian scratched his head in bewilderment, and asked the doctor, "Do ye think it's the light that's attractin' them?"

•

Mr. Smith is checking out of a hotel when suddenly he has to take a shit real bad. The toilet in his room isn't working, so he bolts down to use the lobby men's room, but all of the stalls are occupied, so he runs back up to his room, and in desperation, he drops his pants, uproots a plant, and takes a shit in the pot. Then he puts the plant back in the pot and leaves. Two weeks later, he gets a postcard from the hotel that says, "Dear Mr. Smith . . . All is forgiven. Just tell us . . . where is it?"

•

This guy decides to join the navy. On his first day of service, he gets aquainted with all the facilities around the ship he will be serving on. The guy asks the sailor showing him around, "What do you guys do around here when you get really horny after months of being out at sea?"

To which the other replies, "Well, there is this barrel on the upper deck, just pump your cock in the side with the hole."

Weeks pass, and the new guy is getting real horny and remembers the barrel. He climbs to the upper deck and sees the barrel. He flings his schlong out and starts f***ing the barrel. It's simply the best feeling he has ever experienced, it is truly a success!

After he's done, zipped up, and merrily walking along, the guy who originally told him about the barrel walks by. "That barrel really was great! I could do it every day!"

To which the other crew member replies, "Yeah, you can every day except Thursday."

Confused, the new guy asks why, to which the other guy replies, "Because it's your turn in the barrel on Thursday."

•

Two women walked into a department store, stopped at the perfume counter, and picked up a sample bottle. One sprayed the perfume on her wrist and smelled it. "That's nice, isn't it?" Sharon said, waving her arm under her friend's nose.

"Yeah. What's it called?"

"*Viens a moi.*"

"*Viens a moi*? What's that mean?"

A clerk offered some help. "*Viens a moi*, ladies, is French for 'come to me.'"

Sharon took another sniff. "That doesn't smell like come to me," she said, offering her arm to her friend again. "Does that smell like come to you?"

•

A mother walks into her daughter's room holding a condom in her hand. "I found this while cleaning your room today. . . . Are you sexually active?"

To which the daughter replies, "No, I just lie there."

•

There's a tour bus in Egypt that stops in the middle of a town square. The tourists are all shopping at the little stands surrounding the square. One tourist looks at his watch, but it is broken, so he leans over to a local who is squatting down next to his camel. "What time is it, sir?"

The local reaches out and softly cups the camel's genitals in his hand, and raises them up and down. "It's about two," he says. The tourist can't believe what he just saw.

He runs back to the bus, and sure enough, it is 2 P.M. He tells a few of the fellow tourists his story. "The man can tell the time by the weight of the camel's genitals!!" One of the doubting tourists walks back to the local and asks him the time, and the same thing happens! It is 2:05 P.M. He runs back to tell the story.

Finally, the bus driver wants to know how it is done. He walks over and asks the local how he knows the time from the camel's genitals. The local says, "Sit down here and grab the camel's genitals. Now, lift them up in the air. Now, look underneath them to the other side of the courtyard, where that clock is hanging on the wall."

•

The racing-car driver picked up a girl after a race, went home with her, and took her to bed. He fell asleep only to be awakened suddenly when she smacked him in the face. "What's the matter?!? Didn't I satisfy you when we screwed?" he asked.

"It was after you fell asleep that got you into trouble," said the angry woman. "In your sleep, you felt my tits and mumbled, 'What perfect headlights.' Then you felt my thighs and murmured, 'What a smooth finish.' "

"What's wrong with that?" asked the driver.

"Nothing, but then you felt my pussy and yelled, 'Who the hell left the garage door open?' "

•

There were three prostitutes living together—a mother, daughter, and grandmother. One night, the daughter came home looking very down. "How did you get on tonight, dear?" asked her mother.

"Not too good," replied the daughter. "I only got twenty dollars for a blow job."

"Wow!" said the mother. "In my day we gave a blow job for fifty cents!"

"Good God!" said the grandmother. "In my day we were just glad to get something warm in our stomachs!"

•

A farmer and his wife were lying in bed one evening; she was knitting, and he was reading the latest issue of *Animal Husbandry*. He looked up from the page and said to her, "Did you know that humans are the only species in which the female achieves orgasm?"

She looked at him wistfully, smiled, and replied, "Oh, yeah? Prove it."

He frowned for a moment, then said, "Okay." He got up and walked out, leaving his wife with a confused look on her face. About a half hour later, he returned all tired and sweaty and proclaimed, "Well, I'm sure the cow and sheep didn't, but the way that pig is always squealing, how can I tell?"

•

A guy is driving out in the middle of nowhere, very lost. Finally, he spots two houses, so he goes up to the first house and looks in the doorway. He sees an old lady yanking on her boobs and an old man jerking off. He is so freaked out that he goes to the next house and says, "What's up with your neighbors?"

And the owner of the house says, "Oh, that's the Robinsons, they're both deaf. She's telling him to go milk the cow and he's telling her to go f*** herself!"

•

A young girl was having a heart-to-heart talk with her mother on her first visit home since starting university. "Mom, I have to tell you," the girl confessed. "I lost my virginity last weekend."

"I'm not surprised," said her mother. "It was bound to happen sooner or later. I just hope it was a romantic and pleasurable experience."

"Well, yes and no," the pretty student remarked. "The first eight guys felt great, but after them my pussy got really sore."

•

A young guy was lying on his back on a massage table, wearing only a towel over his groin. A young, very attractive Swedish girl was massaging his shoulders, then his chest, and gradually worked her way down his torso. The guy was getting sexually excited as the masseuse approached the towel. The towel began to lift and the Swedish girl arched her eyebrows. "You wanna wank?" she asked.

"You bet," came the excited reply.

"OK," she said. "I come back in ten minutes."

•

There're a few guys who always get together on Fridays after work for a drink. One Friday, Jeff showed up late, sat down at the bar, and kicked back his entire first beer in one gulp. Then he turned to Bob and said, "Times are getting tough, my friend. I mean, just today my wife told me that she's going to cut me back to only two times a week . . . I can't believe it."

At which point Bob put his hand on Jeff's shoulder and said reassuringly, "You think you've got it bad, she's cut some guys out altogether."

•

A guy goes to a doctor and says, "Doc, you've got to help me. My penis is orange." The doctor pauses to think and asks the guy to drop his pants so he can check. Damned if the guy's penis isn't orange.

Doc tells the guy, "This is very strange. Sometimes things like this are caused by a lot of stress in a person's life."

Probing as to the causes of possible stress, the doc asks the guy, "How are things going at work?" The guy responds that he was fired about six weeks ago. The doctor tells him that this must be the cause of the stress. Guy responds, "No. The boss was a real asshole, I had to work twenty to thirty hours of overtime every week, and I had no say in anything that was happening. I found a new job a couple of weeks ago where I can set my own hours, I'm getting paid double what I got on the old job, and the boss is a really great guy." So the doc figures this isn't the reason.

He asks the guy, "How's your home life?"

The guy says, "Well, I got divorced about eight months ago." The doc figures that this has got to be the reason for all of the guy's stress. Guy says, "No. For years, all I listened to was nag, nag, nag. God, am I glad to be rid of that old bitch." So the doc takes a few minutes to think a little longer.

He inquires, "Do you have any hobbies or a social life?"

The guy replies, "No, not really. Most nights I sit home, watch some porno flicks, and munch on Cheetos."

•

A young couple went to the doctor for their annual physical exams. Afterward, the doctor called the young man into his office and told him that he had some good news and some bad news. "The good news," he explained, "is that your fian-cée has a particular strain of gonorrhea that I have only heard of once before."

The guy paled. "If that's the good news, then what the hell is the bad news?"

"Well," the doctor elaborated, "the bad news is that I heard about this nasty strain just last week from my dog's vet."

•

This nun was going to Chicago. She went to the airport and sat down waiting for her flight. When she looked over in the corner, she saw one of those weight machines that tells your fortune. She thought to herself, "I'll give it a try just to see what it tells me." So she went over to the machine and she put her nickel in and a card came out and it said, "You are a nun, you weigh 128 lbs., and you are going to Chicago, Illinois." So she sat back down and thought to herself, "It probably tells everyone the same thing, I'm going to try it again."

So she went over to the machine again and put her nickel in it, and a card came out that said, "You are a nun, you weigh 128 lbs., you are going to Chicago, Illinois, and you are going to play a fiddle." She said to herself, "I know that's wrong, I have never played a musical instrument a day in my life." She sat back down and this cowboy came over and set his fiddle case down. She picked up the fiddle and just started playing beautiful music. She looked back at the machine and said, "This is incredible! I've got to try it again."

So she went back to the machine, put her nickel in, and another card came out. It said, "You are a nun, you weigh 128 lbs., you are going to Chicago, Illinois, and you are going to break wind." She thinks, "I know it's wrong now. I've never broke wind in public a day in my life." Well, she tripped and fell off the scales and farted like a bay mule. So she sat back down and looked at the machine once again. She said to herself, "This is truly unbelievable, I've got to try it again."

She went back to the machine, put her nickel in, and a card came out: "You are a nun, you weigh 128 lbs., you are going to Chicago, Illinois, and you are going to have sex." She said, "Aha, that does it. I know for sure it's wrong now. I'm a nun, ain't ever had none, and ain't ever gonna get none." Well, a huge electrical storm came through and the electricity went off and she got raped. She sat back down and thought about it for a few minutes, and then said, "This is truly, truly incredible. But one thing is for certain, I've got to try it again just to see what is gonna happen to me before I leave this airport."

She went over to the machine, put her nickel in, and a card came out. And it said, "You are a nun, you weigh 128 lbs., you have fiddled, farted, f***ed around, and missed your flight to Chicago!"

•

A little boy and his grandfather are raking leaves in the yard. The little boy sees an earthworm trying to get back into its hole. He says, "Grandpa, I bet I can put that worm back in that hole."

The grandfather replies, "I'll bet you five dollars you can't. It's too wiggly and limp to put back in that little hole."

The little boy runs into the house and comes back out with a can of hair spray. He sprays the worm until it is straight and stiff as a board. The boy then proceeds to put the worm back into the hole. The grandfather hands the little boy five dollars, grabs the hair spray, and runs into the house.

Thirty minutes later the grandfather comes back out and hands the boy another five dollars. The little boy says, "Grandpa, you already gave me five dollars."

The grandfather replies, "I know. That's from your grandma."

•

There was a guy who was struggling to decide what to wear to go to a fancy costume party. Then he had a bright idea. When the host answered the door, he found the guy standing there with no shirt and no socks on. "What the hell are you supposed to be?" asked the host.

"A premature ejaculation," said the man. "I just came in my pants!"

•

One Christmas Eve, Santa Claus comes down the chimney and is startled by a beautiful nineteen-year-old blonde. She says, "Santa, will you stay with me?"

Santa replies, "Ho, ho, ho, gotta go, gotta go, gotta deliver these toys to good girls and boys."

So she takes off her nightgown. Wearing only a bra and panties, she asks, "Santa, now will you stay with me?"

"Ho, ho, ho, gotta go, gotta go, gotta deliver these toys to good girls and boys."

She takes off everything and says, "Santa, now will you stay with me?"

Santa replies, "Gotta stay, gotta stay, can't get up the chimney with my dick this way!"

•

The first fellow says, "My wife's so cold I can put a glass of water in bed with her and the next morning it's turned to ice."

The second fellow says, "Hell, every time my old lady spreads her legs the furnace kicks in!"

•

A construction worker on the fifth floor of a building needs a handsaw. So he spots another worker on the ground floor and yells down to him, but he can't hear him. So the worker on the fifth floor tries sign language.

He points to his eye meaning "I," points to his knee meaning "need," then moved his hand back and forth in a handsaw motion. The man on the ground floor nods his head, pulls down his pants, whips out his chop, and starts masturbating.

The worker on the fifth floor gets so pissed off he runs down to the ground floor and says, "What the f*** is your problem!!! I said I needed a handsaw!"

The other guy says, "I knew that! I was just trying to tell you—I'm coming!"

•

Husband and wife are getting all snuggly in bed. The passion is heating up. But then the wife stops and says, "I don't feel like it, I just want you to hold me."

The husband says, "WHAT??"

The wife explains that he must not be in tune with her emotional needs as a woman. The husband realizes that nothing is going to happen tonight, and he might as well deal with it. So the next day the husband takes her shopping at a big department store. He walks around and has her try on three very expensive outfits. And then he tells his wife, "We'll take all three of them." Then he goes over and gets matching shoes worth $200 each. And then goes to the jewelry department and gets a set of diamond earrings. The wife is so excited (she thinks her husband has flipped out, but she does not care), she goes for the tennis bracelet. The husband says, "You don't even play tennis, but OK, if you like it, then let's get it."

The wife is jumping up and down, so excited she cannot even believe what is going on. She says, "I am ready to go, let's go to the cash register."

The husband says, "No, no, no. Honey, we're not going to buy all this stuff." The wife's face goes blank. "No, honey—I just want you to *hold* this stuff for a while." Her face gets really red and she is about to explode and then the husband says, "You must not be in tune with my financial needs as a man!"

•

A cop saw a car weaving all over the road and pulled it over. He walked up to the car and saw a nice-looking woman behind the wheel. There was a strong smell of liquor on her breath.

He said, "I'm going to give you a Breathalyzer test to determine if you are under the influence of alcohol." She blew up the balloon and he walked it back to the police car. After a couple of minutes, he returned to her car and said, "It looks like you've had a couple of stiff ones."

She replied, "You mean it shows that, too?"

•

Two girls were discussing their heavy smoking habits. "I get such a yen for a cigarette," said one, "that the only effective countermeasure is to pop a Life Savers into my mouth and suck hard."

"That's fine for you," huffed her friend, "but I don't happen to live in a house that's right on the beach!"

•

A man got a job in the sales promotion department of a cola company. When he asked about his duties, the manager explained, "Oh! It's an easy job! All you have to do is call on ten women buyers every day, and knock 7-Up!"

•

A Southern belle has just returned from her big trip to New York City and is having refreshments on the front porch of her daddy's mansion with her Southern belle friends. She tells them the stories of her trip as they stare, spellbound. "You just wouldn't believe what they have there in New York City," says Miss Annabell. "They have men there who kiss other men on the lips."

Miss Annabell's friends fan themselves and say, "Oh my! Oh my!"

"They call them homosexuals," proclaims Miss Annabell.

"Oh my! Oh my," proclaim the girls as they fan themselves.

"They also have women there in New York City who kiss other women on the lips!"

"Oh my! Oh my," exclaim the girls. "What do they call them?" they ask.

"They call them lesbians," says Miss Annabell. "They also have men who kiss women between the legs, there in New York City," sighs Miss Annabell.

"Oh my! Oh my! Oh my," exclaim the girls as they sit on the edge of their chairs and fan themselves even faster. "What do they call them?" they ask in unison.

Annabell leans forward and says in a hushed voice, "Why, when I caught my breath, I called him Precious."

•

A little old lady goes into the store to do some shopping. She is bewildered over the large selection of toilet paper. "Pardon me, sir," she says to the store manager, "but can you explain the differences in all these toilet papers?"

"Well," he replies, pointing out one brand, "this is as soft as a baby's bottom. It's a dollar fifty per roll."

He grabs another and says, "This is nice and soft, strong but gentle, and it's one dollar a roll." Pointing to the bottom shelf he tells her, "We call that our No Name brand, and it's twenty cents per roll."

"Give me the No Name," she says. She comes back about a week later, seeks out the manager, and says, "Hey! I've got a name for your No Name toilet paper. I call it John Wayne."

"Why?" he asks.

"Because it's rough, it's tough, and it don't take crap from anybody!"

•

A little dwarf lady goes into her doctor's office complaining of an irritated crotch. After an examination, the doctor sighs. "I don't seem to see any problem. Does it get better or worse at any time?"

"Yeah, it's really bad whenever it rains," she replies.

"Well, then," says the doc, "next time it rains, get in here at once, and we'll take another look at it."

Two weeks later, it's raining really hard, and the little lady shows up at the doctor's office. "Doctor, it's really bad today. Please, you have to help me!!"

"Well, let's have a look," he says, as he lifts her up onto the table. "Oh, yes, I think I see the problem. Nurse, bring me a surgical kit. Don't worry, ma'am, this won't hurt a bit."

The dwarf lady closes her eyes in painful anticipation. The doctor begins snipping away and finishes a few minutes later. "There you go, ma'am, try that." She walks back and forth around the office and exclaims, "That's great, Doc, what did you do?"

"I just took a couple of inches off the top of your rain boots."

•

Two pedophiles were walking down the street one day when they came across a pair of small lacy panties on the ground. The first one picks them up, smells them, and goes, "Aahhh . . . A seven-year-old girl."

The other grabs them from him and also takes a smell and goes, "No, no . . . Definitely an eight-year-old girl!" The two of them are then smelling them in turns and arguing.

"An eight-year-old!"

"No, a seven-year-old!"

"Definitely an eight-year-old!" . . . and so on.

The local priest is walking past as the two men argue, and can't help but ask them what the commotion is all about.

The first pedophile tells the priest and asks him if he could sort out the argument, so the priest takes the panties, has a good long sniff, and after pondering for a few moments he looks at the two men and says: "Definitely an eight-year-old girl! But not from my parish!"

•

During his monthly visit to the corner barbershop, this fellow asked his barber for suggestions on how to treat his increasing baldness. After a brief pause, the barber leaned over and confided that the best thing he'd come across was, er, female juices. "But you're balder than I am," protested the customer.

"True," admitted the barber, "but you've gotta admit I've got one hell of a mustache!"

•

Three women were sitting around throwing back a few drinks and talking about their sex lives. Karen said, "I call my husband the dentist because nobody can drill like he does."

Joanne giggled and confessed, "I call my husband the miner because of his incredible shaft."

Kathy quietly sipped her whiskey until Joanne finally asked, "Well, what do you call your boyfriend?" Kathy frowned and said, "The postman."

"Why the postman?" asked Joanne.

"Because he always delivers late and half the time it's in the wrong box."

•

In pharmacology, all drugs have a generic name. Tylenol is acetaminophen, Advil is ibuprofen, and so on. The FDA has been looking for a generic name for Viagra, and announced today that they have settled on mycoxafloppin.

•

Five people are on a plane, four guys and one girl. Suddenly, the engine stalls and they crash. Miraculously, all five of them survive the crash but are stranded on a small deserted island. Since these four guys will need to have their natural urges satisfied, they decide to make up a schedule. Each guy will get a week to f*** the woman as much as possible, the next week another guy, and so on. This arrangement works out great for years, satisfying both the guys and the nymphomaniac woman until she suddenly dies. The first month goes by and it's really awful; second month is really bad; third month is almost unbearable; fourth month rolls around and the guys can't handle it anymore—so they bury her.

•

There is this guy who has a twenty-five-inch dick. He goes to a witch in the woods and asks her if she can make his dick smaller because he just can't please the ladies, it is just too big. He hasn't found a lady yet who likes it, and he can't get any pleasure.

She tells him to go into the woods and he will find a frog. When he finds the frog, he is to ask it to marry him. If the frog says no, his cock will shrink five inches.

He goes into the woods and finds this frog. He asks, "Frog, will you marry me?"

The frog says, "No." And his prick shrinks five inches. The guys thinks to himself, "Wow, that was pretty cool. But it's still too big." So he goes back to the frog and again asks: "Frog, will you marry me?"

Frog: "No, I won't marry you."

The guy's dick shrinks another five inches. But that's still fifteen inches, and he thinks his chop is still just a little bit too big. He thinks that ten inches would be just great. He goes back to the frog and asks: "Frog, will you marry me?"

Frog: "How many times do I have to tell you? NO, NO, NO!!!"

•

Two sweethearts who went out together for all four years of high school enjoyed losing their virginity to each other in tenth grade. When they graduated, they wanted to both go to the same college, but the girl was accepted to a college on the East Coast, and the guy went to the West Coast. They agreed to be faithful to each other and spend any time they could together.

As time went on, the guy would call the girl and she would never be home, and when he wrote, she would take weeks to answer the letters. Even when he e-mailed her, she took days to return his messages.

Finally, she confessed to him she wanted to date around. He didn't take this very well, and increased his calls, letters, and e-mails trying to win back her love. Because she became annoyed, and now had a new boyfriend, she wanted to get him off her back.

So, what she did was this: She took a Polaroid picture of herself sucking her new boyfriend's cock and sent it to her old boyfriend with a note reading, "I found a new boyfriend, leave me alone." Well, needless to say, this guy was heartbroken but, even more so, was pissed. So, what he did next was awesome.

He wrote on the back of the photo: "Dear Mom and Dad, having a great time at college, please send more money!" and mailed the picture to her parents.

•

This little girl walks over to her grandmother and asks, "Granny, can you show me a magic trick?"

"No, dear, but I think your grandfather knows one."

So the little girl walks over to her grandpa and asks, "Grandpa, Granny says you know some magic tricks, could you show me one?"

The grandfather looks at her. "Sure, just hop on my lap!" So the little girl jumps on his lap. "Now, can you feel a finger poking up your ass?" asks the grandpa.

"Yeah," replies the girl.

"Well, look, no hands!"

•

A guy comes home from work, walks into his bedroom, and finds a stranger f***ing his wife. He says, "What the hell are you two doing?"

His wife turns to the stranger and says, "I told you he was stupid."

•

A pianist was hired to play background music for a movie. When it was completed, he asked when and where he could see the picture. The producer sheepishly confessed that it was actually a porno film and it was due out in a month. A month later, the musician went to a porno theatre to see it. With his collar up and dark glasses on, he took a seat in the back row, next to a couple who also seemed to be in disguise.

The movie was even raunchier than he had feared, featuring group sex, S&M, and even a dog. After a while, the embarrassed pianist turned to the couple and said, "I'm only here to listen to the music."

"Yeah?" replied the man. "We're only here to see our dog."

•

A tourist arrived in Australia, hired a car, and set off for the outback. On his way he saw a man having sex with a sheep. Deeply horrified, he pulled up at the nearest pub and ordered a straight scotch. Just as he was about to throw it back, he saw a guy with one leg masturbating furiously at the bar. "For f***'s sake!" he cried. "What the hell's going on here? I've been here one hour and I've seen a man shagging a sheep, and now some guy's wanking himself off in the bar!"

"Fair dinkum, mate," the bartender told him. "You can't expect a man with only one leg to catch a sheep."

•

Between the ages of 16 and 18, she is like Africa—virgin and unexplored. Between the ages of 19 and 35, she is like Asia— hot and exotic. Between the ages of 36 and 45, she is like America—fully explored, breathtakingly beautiful, and free with her resources. Between the ages of 46 and 56, she is like Europe—exhausted but still has points of interest. After 56, she is like Australia—everybody knows it's down there, but who gives a damn.

•

Jack was returning to work Monday morning with two black eyes. His workmates were understandably curious: "Jack, what happened to you?!?"

"It was the darndest thing! I was at church yesterday, and this fat lady stood up in front of me. You know how a dress can get stuck in the crack of the butt of a fat lady? It looked funny. I figured she wouldn't like that, so I just reached over and pulled it out with a little tug. Next thing I know, she spins around and socks me one!"

"Jeez, you got *two* black eyes in one blow?"

"Naw. After she turned back around, I figured she was angry that I pulled the dress out of her crack, so I tried to poke it back in . . ."

•

One dismal rainy night, a taxi driver spotted an arm waving from the shadows of an alley halfway down the block. Even before he rolled to a stop at the curb, a figure leaped into the cab and slammed the door. Checking his rearview mirror as he pulled away, he was startled to see a dripping wet, naked woman sitting in the backseat. "Where to?" he stammered.

"Union Station," answered the woman.

"You got it," he said, taking another long glance in the mirror.

The woman caught him staring at her and asked, "Just what the hell are you looking at, driver?"

The driver replies, "Well, ma'am, I noticed that you're completely naked, and I was just wondering how you'll pay your fare."

The woman spread her legs, put her feet up on the front seat, smiled at the driver, and said, "Does this answer your question?"

Still looking in the mirror, the cabbie asked, "Got anything smaller?"

•

A husband and wife are traveling by car from Louisiana to New York. After almost twenty-four hours on the road, they decide to stop at a nice hotel and take a room. They only plan to sleep for four hours and then get back on the road. When they check out four hours later, the desk clerk hands them a bill for $350. The man explodes and demands to know why the charge is so high. He tells the clerk although it's a nice hotel, the rooms certainly aren't worth $350. When the clerk explains that $350 is the standard rate, the man insists on speaking to the manager.

The manager enters the conversation and explains that the hotel has an Olympic-size pool and a huge conference center that were available for the husband and wife to use.

He also explains that they could have taken in one of the shows that the hotel is famous for: "The best entertainers from New York, Hollywood, and Las Vegas perform here."

No matter what facility the manager mentions, the man replies, "But we didn't use it!"

The manager is unmoved. Eventually the man gives up and agrees to pay. He writes a check and hands it to the manager. "But sir," the manager says, "this check is only made out for one hundred dollars."

"That's right," replies the man. "I charged you two hundred fifty dollars for sleeping with my wife."

"What! I didn't sleep with your wife!" exclaims the manager.

"Well," the man replies, "she was here, and you could have."

•

There was this geriatric woman who thought she needed some toughening to cope with today's world, so she decided to join a gang. She rocked up to the Hell's Angels biker club and tapped on the door. "Excuse me, sirs, I'd like to join your club if you please," she croaked in her feeble voice.

A grunt came from inside. "Ha! You got no chance, woman. We only take the toughest into our club. You can only join if you drink!"

"Oh boy, do I drink! I slam a few down every night after playing pool with the boys," she croaked back.

"Oh, umm, well . . . you can only join if you smoke," he lied, trying to brush her off.

"Does marijuana count? 'Cuz I don't mind a few joints after playing pool with the boys."

"Umm, I suppose it does count . . ." the biker said, and, thinking quickly on his feet, added, "Look, we're a gang for only the roughest, toughest men in town. Now, have you ever been picked up by the fuzz?"

"No," she replied, "but I've been swung around by the tits a few times."

•

Did you hear about the guy who had tried every diet in the world in an attempt to lose weight? He tried the Scarsdale diet, the navy diet, Weight Watchers, etc., and none worked. He was reading the paper one day when he noticed a small ad that read, "Lose weight $1.00 a pound," and simply listed a telephone number.

Having little to lose, the man called the number. A voice on the other end asked, "How much weight do you want to lose?"

To which the man responded, "Ten pounds."

The voice replied, "Very well, put your check in the mail and we'll have a representative over to your house in the morning."

About 9 A.M. the next morning, the man got a knock on the door. There stood a beautiful redheaded woman, completely naked except for a sign around her neck stating, IF YOU CATCH ME, YOU CAN SCREW ME.

Well, the overweight fellow chased her upstairs, downstairs, over sofas, through the kitchen, all around the house. Finally he did catch her, and when he was through enjoying himself, she said, "Quick, go into the bathroom and weigh yourself!" He did just that and was amazed to find that he had lost ten pounds, right to the ounce!

That evening, he called the number again. The voice on the other end asked, "How much weight do you want to lose?"

To which the man replied, "Twenty pounds."

"Very well," the voice on the phone told him, "put your check in the mail, and we'll have a representative over to your house in the morning."

At about 8 A.M. the next morning, the man received a knock on the door. When he opened the door, he saw a beautiful blonde dressed only in track shoes and a sign around her neck that said: IF YOU CATCH ME, YOU CAN SCREW ME.

The chase took a while longer this time, but the man finally did catch her. When he was through, she told him, "Quick, run into the bathroom and weigh yourself!" He ran to the bathroom and found he had lost another twenty pounds!

"This is fantastic!" he thought to himself. Later that evening he called the number again and the voice at the other end asked, "How much weight do you want to lose?"

"Fifty pounds!" the man exclaimed.

"Fifty pounds?" the voice asked. "That's an awful lot of weight to lose at one time."

The overweight man replied, "My check's already in the mail. You just have your representative over here in the morning," and he hung up the phone.

About 6 A.M. the next morning, the man got out of bed and got all fancied up, ready for the next representative. At about 7 A.M. he got a knock on the door. When he opened the door he saw this large gorilla with a sign around his neck stating, IF I CATCH YOU, I'M GOING TO SCREW YOU.

•

Husband and wife are waiting at the bus stop with their nine children. A blind man joins them after a few minutes. When the bus arrives, they find it overloaded and only the wife and the nine kids are able to fit onto the bus.

So the husband and the blind man decide to walk. After a while, the husband gets irritated by the ticking of the blind man's stick as he taps it on the sidewalk, and says to him, "Why don't you put a piece of rubber at the end of your stick? That ticking sound is driving me crazy."

The blind man replies, "If you would've put a rubber at the end of YOUR stick, we'd be riding the bus . . . so shut the hell up."

•

Bud and Jim were a couple of drinking buddies who worked as airplane mechanics in Atlanta. One day, the airport was fogged in and they were stuck in the hangar with nothing to do.

Bud said, "Man, I wish we had something to drink!"

Jim said, "Me, too. Y'know, I've heard you can drink jet fuel and get a buzz. You wanna try it?"

So they poured themselves a couple of glasses of high octane hooch and got completely smashed.

The next morning, Bud woke up and was surprised at how good he felt. In fact he felt *great*! *No* hangover! *No* bad side effects! Nothing! Then his phone rang and it was Jim.

Jim said, "Hey, how do you feel this morning?"

Bud said, "I feel great. How about you?"

Jim said, "I feel great, too. You don't have a hangover?"

Bud said, "No. That jet fuel is great stuff—no hangover, nothing. We ought to do this more often."

Jim said, "Yeah, well, there's just one thing."

Bud said, "What's that?"

Jim said, "Have you farted yet?"

Bud said, "No."

Jim said, "Well, *don't*, 'cause I'm in *Florida*!"

•

Have you ever spoken and wished that you could immediately take the words back . . . or that you could crawl into a hole? Here are the testimonials of a few people who did. . . .

## FIRST INCIDENT

I walked into a hair salon with my husband and three kids in tow and asked loudly, "How much do you charge for a shampoo and a blow job?" I turned around and walked back out and never went back. My husband didn't say a word . . . he knew better.

### SECOND INCIDENT

I was at the golf store comparing different kinds of golf balls. I was unhappy with the women's type I had been using. After browsing for several minutes, I was approached by one of the good-looking gentlemen who worked at the store. He asked if he could help me. Without thinking, I looked at him and said, "I think I like playing with men's balls."

### THIRD INCIDENT

My sister and I were at the mall and passed by a store that sold a variety of candy and nuts.

As we were looking at the display case, the boy behind the counter asked if we needed any help.

I replied, "No, I'm just looking at your nuts." My sister started to laugh hysterically. The boy grinned, and I turned beet red and walked away. To this day, my sister has never let me forget.

### FOURTH INCIDENT

While in line at the bank one afternoon, my toddler decided to release some pent-up energy and ran amok. I was finally able to grab hold of her after receiving looks of disgust and annoyance from other patrons. I told her that if she did not start behaving "right now" she would be punished. To my horror, she looked me in the eye and said in a voice just as threatening, "If you don't let me go right now, I will tell Grandma that I saw you kissing Daddy's pee-pee last night!"

### FIFTH INCIDENT

Have you ever asked your child a question too many times? My three-year-old son had a lot of problems with potty training and I was on him constantly. One day, we stopped at Taco Bell for a quick lunch in between errands. It was very busy, with a full dining room. While enjoying my taco, I smelled something funny, so of course I checked my seven-month-old daughter—she was clean. Then I realized that Danny had not asked to go potty in a while. I asked him if he needed to go, and he said, "No." I kept thinking, "Oh Lord, that child has had an accident, and I don't have any clothes with me." Then I said, "Danny, are you *sure* you didn't have an accident?" "No," he replied. I just *knew* that he must have had an accident, because the smell was getting worse. Sooooooo, I asked one more time, "Danny, did you have an accident?"

This time he jumped up, yanked down his pants, bent over, spread his cheeks, and yelled, "SEE, MOM, IT'S JUST FARTS!!"

## LAST BUT NOT LEAST INCIDENT

What happens when you predict snow but don't get any! We had a female news anchor who, the day after it was supposed to have snowed and didn't, turned to the weatherman and asked: "So Bob, where's that eight inches you promised me last night?"

•

An old lady dies and goes to heaven. She's chatting it up with Saint Peter at the pearly gates, when all of a sudden she hears the most awful bloodcurdling screams. "Don't worry about that," says Saint Peter, "it's only someone having the holes put into her shoulder blades for wings."

The old lady looks a little uncomfortable but carries on with the conversation. Ten minutes later, there are more bloodcurdling screams. "Oh, my God," says the old lady, "now what is happening?"

"Not to worry," says Saint Peter. "She's just having her head drilled to fit the halo."

"I can't do this," says the old lady. "I'm going to hell."

"You can't go there," says Saint Peter. "You'll be raped and sodomized."

"Maybe so," says the old lady, "but I've already got the holes for that!"